Animal
Adventures
IN
NORTH CAROLINA

 John F. Blair, Publisher
Winston-Salem, North Carolina

Animal Adventures
IN NORTH CAROLINA

Jennifer Bean Bower

JOHN F. BLAIR
PUBLISHER
1406 Plaza Drive
Winston-Salem, North Carolina 27103
www.blairpub.com

Manufactured in the United States of America

ALL PHOTOGRAPHS BY LARRY T. BOWER, JR., UNLESS OTHERWISE NOTED

COVER IMAGES
BACKGROUND:
A cria (baby llama) and its mother at Sunny Slopes Farm

TOP ROW LEFT TO RIGHT:
Monarch butterflies at all-a-flutter Butterfly Farm
Giraffe at Lazy 5 Ranch
Wolf at The Wolf Sanctum / Photograph by James Fisher, The James Fisher Gallery
Venomous eyelash viper at Cape Fear Serpentarium

BOTTOM ROW LEFT TO RIGHT:
Sand tiger shark at the North Carolina Aquarium at Pine Knoll Shores / Photograph by Craig Davies
Bald eagle at Carolina Raptor Center / Courtesy of Carolina Raptor Center
Ring-tailed lemurs at Santa's Land Fun Park & Zoo / Courtesy of Santa's Land Fun Park & Zoo
Tiger at Conservators' Center

BACKGROUND IMAGE ON BACK COVER:
Slow loris at Duke Lemur Center / Photograph by David Haring, Courtesy of Duke Lemur Center

IMAGES ON FRONTISPIECE AND TITLE PAGE
Ostrich at BirdBrain Ostrich Ranch
Kaela the tiger at Carolina Tiger Rescue / Courtesy of Carolina Tiger Rescue
Sand tiger shark at the North Carolina Aquarium at Pine Knoll Shores / Photograph by Craig Davies
Willow the barn owl at Carolina Raptor Center / Courtesy of Carolina Raptor Center

Library of Congress Cataloging-in-Publication Data

Bower, Jennifer Bean.
  Animal adventures in North Carolina / by Jennifer Bean Bower.
    p.   cm.
  Includes index.
  ISBN-13: 978-0-89587-382-8 (alk. paper)
  ISBN-10: 0-89587-382-6 (alk. paper)
  ISBN-13: 978-0-89587-510-5 (ebook)
  1. Zoos—North Carolina—Guidebooks. 2. Wildlife refuges—North Carolina—Guidebooks. 3. Nature centers—North Carolina—Guidebooks. 4. Farms--North Carolina—Guidebooks. 5. Parks—North Carolina—Guidebooks. 6. Animals—North Carolina--Miscellanea. 7. North Carolina—Guidebooks. I. Title.
  QL76.5.U6B69 2011
  591.756—dc22

Design by Debra Long Hampton

~~~~~~~~~~~~~~~~~~~~~~~~

For Larry, Addie, and Roxanne

Contents

Coast

Preface

Vacations, weekend outings, and day trips are always fun. Combine them with attractions that allow the viewing, touching, and feeding of animals and they suddenly becomes adventures. Most often, those who partake of such "adventures" are actually being educated about the natural world around them. In a society that thrives on technology, it is easy to become disconnected from the seemingly insignificant creatures so vital to our environment. Therefore, it is essential that someone, or someplace, remind us of their importance.

As a native and frequent traveler of North Carolina, I have spent an incredible amount of time searching out animal-related activities within the state. First and foremost, my reason for doing so is because I have a strong desire to learn about animals. Second, I enjoy being in their presence and find them inspiring.

During my visits to animal-related facilities, it became apparent through speaking with various people—particularly owners of farms and workers at rehabilitation centers—that children were becoming less and less aware of the natural world around them. To my surprise, I discovered many children were unable to make a connection between farm animals and food, while others could not name more than a few species of birds. One person asked me, "How will these children grow to care for or respect things they have no connection to?"

As I wondered about this, I began to think of the many amazing animal-related facilities in North Carolina that provide those connections on a daily basis. In fact, my thoughts took me to Carolina Raptor Center and how, many, many years ago, I was taught why people should not throw food on the roadside. The reason, which readers will discover in this guide, has never left my mind, as it taught a valuable lesson in how small acts can have major consequences.

Many people believe that, in order to effectively protect the environment, they must have considerable finances or travel to distant locations. The seventy facilities in *Animal Adventures in North Carolina* prove otherwise.

While they enjoy the animal-related facilities in this book, I hope visitors will listen to their tour guides, read the educational materials provided, and learn how they can make a difference in their communities and the world. I also hope readers will be encouraged to explore new destinations in North Carolina where they can experience animals in educational and fun-filled ways they never knew existed.

Key to Symbols

$ Admission fee

†∮† Restrooms

⊘ Food

⬤ Fishing

⊼ Picnic tables

⊡ Gift shop, merchandise for sale

⟨ Golfing

▦ Water or Drinks

V Vending machines

Introduction

Animal-related facilities successfully instill a responsibility for conservation in their visitors through a variety of exhibits and programs. A three-year nationwide study undertaken by the National Science Foundation in partnership with the Association of Zoos and Aquariums and the Institute of Learning Innovation found that "a visit to a zoo or aquarium in North America had a measurable impact on the conservation attitudes and understanding of adult visitors" and heightened "the public's appreciation for and commitment to animal conservation."

Because many people are not compelled to learn about, research, or protect something until they have examined it on a personal basis, there must be avenues for them to do so. Future stewards of the planet must be educated in ways that are personally tangible and relevant. In North Carolina, numerous facilities stand ready to provide that knowledge. In fact, Zoo and Aquarium Visitor, a website that delivers news from animal attractions around the world, ranked North Carolina seventh in its 2008 "Top 10 Animal Attraction States."

Animal Adventures in North Carolina will direct readers to aviaries, aquariums, farms, sanctuaries, wildlife rehabilitation centers, and zoos where they can discover new species of animals; observe how sick, injured, and orphaned animals are cared for; view animals' natural behaviors; learn where certain food products come from; grasp the importance of animals in the environment; enjoy activities in the company of animals; and be educated about how to champion the cause of animals.

Many readers will never have a chance to visit the lands where lions roam, barheaded geese fly, or polar bears swim, nor will they dive the depths of the ocean to view its abundant sea life. However, by visiting the animal-related facilities in this guide, they have an opportunity to explore species that dwell in faraway and inaccessible places. They will also have a chance to examine domestic animals and experience the lifestyles of those who care for them.

This guide is organized according to region: mountains, Piedmont, and coast. Although the information was accurate at the time of the writing, things such as hours of operation can and do change. In order to avoid disappointment, be sure to phone or visit the website of your intended location before making the trip. Also, because these facilities feature living creatures, be aware that certain animals could be off display due to weather conditions, illness, or death. If you plan on traveling to a location solely to see one particular species, confirm prior to your arrival that it will be on exhibit. Some facilities are not handicapped-accessible; if this is a concern, call before you go.

Most animal-related facilities do not allow pets, so keep this is in mind if you are considering bringing the family dog. Essential items for your adventures include good walking shoes, sunscreen, insect repellent, and hand sanitizer. Of course, the most essential item is a camera; don't leave home without it. Another item you should consider is cash, since several of the facilities in this guide do not accept credit or debit cards; again, call before you go.

Animals must always be respected. If you follow the rules of etiquette, both you and the animals will be ensured a safe and pleasant encounter. Never tease animals or throw objects at them. Foreign objects could be ingested, which might cause sickness, injury, or death. Never give food to animals unless it is provided by the facility, as most are on special diets. If visiting a facility where the animals are allowed to roam freely, try to keep a safe distance. Never run, grab, or chase the animals. Finally, always make sure you dispose of trash inside a container; otherwise, it could end up inside a habitat and cause an animal to become sick.

Numerous facilities offer memberships, sponsorships, or special activities in order to raise funds for the animals in their care. But you may not be aware that many facilities—particularly those that care for rescued, sick, injured, and orphaned animals—typically have a need for basic items such as paper towels and garbage bags. Before visiting, check the facility's website to see if it has a "wish list." If it does, take the opportunity to get involved by bringing a needed item when you visit. Should you decide to do so, contact the facility in advance to make sure the item is still needed and to alert it that a donation is coming.

The facilities in this guide will engage all of your senses. Yes, all of them! You should not expect to be a mere observer. Within these pages, you will find places to see animals you never knew existed, hear the eerie vocalizations of peculiar-looking birds, inhale the distinct smell of a binturong, touch the furry leg of a tarantula, and taste sweet, fresh goat's milk or a giant Malaysian freshwater prawn.

So what are you waiting for? Pick out a site, grab your camera, hit the road, and let the animal adventures begin. May you enjoy your travels and the animals—both native and nonnative—that call North Carolina home.

Mountains

Mountain Adventures

1. Hawkesdene House
2. Otter Creek Trout Farm
3. Santa's Land Fun Park & Zoo
4. English Mountain Llama Treks
5. Llamacaddy
6. Pisgah Center for Wildlife Education
7. Carl Sandburg Home National Historic Site
8. Western North Carolina Nature Center
9. Round Mountain Creamery
10. Full Moon Farm Wolfdog Rescue & Sanctuary
11. The Wolf Sanctum
12. Grandfather Mountain
13. Woolly Worm Festival
14. Genesis Wildlife Sanctuary
15. Tweetsie Railroad
16. Table Rock State Fish Hatchery

Trekkers ascend Hawkesnest Mountain to partake of splendid views and a three-course meal.
PHOTOGRAPH COURTESY OF HAWKESDENE HOUSE

Hawkesdene House

381 Phillips Creek Road
Andrews, N.C. 28901
Phone: 800-447-9549 or 828-321-6027
Website: www.hawkesdene.com
E-mail: innkeeper@hawkesdene.com

Hours: Lodging is available year-round. Llama treks are offered from mid-April through October; advance reservations are required.

Directions: From U.S. 19 Business West at Andrews in Cherokee County, turn left on Cherry Street, which becomes Bristol Avenue. Drive 3.3 miles to Phillips Creek Road, turn left, and watch for the sign after about 0.5 mile.

"Enjoy a mountain hiking and dining experience
with a woolly companion."
Hawkesdene House website

A luxurious retreat—Hawkesdene House—encompasses twenty-six acres of picturesque beauty in a scenic mountain valley at the town of Andrews. Roy and Daphne Sargent built Hawkesdene's main house and cottages in 1995. The two brought llamas to the estate and were the first to offer llama treks in western North Carolina. In 2002, Phil Rampy and Rob Scheiwiller purchased the Cherokee County

Scenic mountain valleys surround Hawkesdene House.
PHOTOGRAPH COURTESY OF HAWKESDENE HOUSE

property and added special-event facilities. However, one thing remained constant: the llama treks.

Llama treks are not limited to Hawkesdene House guests but are also enjoyed by the general public, although visitors who are not registered guests will likely want to spend several nights after viewing the estate. The nine-thousand-square-foot, three-level main house has seven bedrooms, seven and a half bathrooms, terraces, balconies, and an open-air pavilion. The one-, two-, and three-bedroom cottages offer indoor and outdoor dining areas and wood-burning fireplaces. The landscape exemplifies tranquility. Walking paths lead to herb and vegetable gardens, orchards, streams, and a private waterfall. No matter how small or large one's group, Hawkesdene House has the perfect amenities.

Llama treks typically last two to three hours. Accompanied by a guide and a team of sure-footed llamas—Hawke, Dene, Crazy Horse, and Scooter—guests traverse a rocky half-mile trail that ascends to the summit of Hawkesnest Mountain. In the words of Rob Scheiwiller, "The views are awesome, especially as you get closer to the top." The trek can be completed in about twenty to thirty minutes. Upon reaching the peak, guests will find a three-course meal—an appetizer, an entrée, dessert, and sparkling grape juice—waiting for them in the Hawkesdene Pavilion. After taking approximately an hour to savor the cuisine, the fresh air, and the scenery—perhaps even a sunset—guests will begin their trek back down the mountain.

A llama trek at Hawkesdene House is suitable for any individual who can walk a half-mile, although participants should be aware of the moderate incline. Since the llamas are outfitted, guests do not need gear, though some bring walking sticks. Participants need simply arrive, meet their llama companions, and embrace the hours spent at this beautiful Great Smoky Mountains retreat.

Tip

● Llama treks are extremely popular during the fall. The estate recommends making a reservation at least three days in advance. However, guests should probably call several *weeks* beforehand to guarantee a spot on a fall trek.

Otter Creek Trout Farm

1914 Otter Creek Road
Topton, N.C. 28781
Phone: 828-321-9810
Website: www.agr.state.nc.us/Ncproducts/ShowSite.asp?ID=2336
E-mail: ottercreektrout@yahoo.com

Hours: Open year-round. Advance reservations are required.

Directions: From U.S. 74 West north of the community of Topton, turn left on Wayah Road. Drive 5 miles and turn left on Otter Creek Road. The trout farm is on the right after about 1.5 miles.

> "You *Otter* Be Eating Our Trout!"
> **Otter Creek Trout Farm website**

Otter Creek Trout Farm is found by way of winding roads with awe-inspiring scenery. The journey to this remote area of Macon County takes travelers through Nantahala National Forest and alongside the white water of the Nantahala River. Pull-offs abound for tourists desiring stunning photographs, picnics, or the opportunity to catch trophy trout.

Alex and Nicole Denison were attracted to Macon County not as tourists but as trout farmers. Alex worked as a plumbing contractor for fifteen years but eventually got involved in biological-waste remediation and nonprofit education. His latter interests led him to aquaculture and eventually to a trout farm in Topton. Otter

Creek Trout Farm opened in 1985 as a part-time operation. In 2002, the Denisons purchased the nine-acre farm and developed it into a full-time enterprise. They accomplished this by increasing production, offering stocking options for private ponds and streams, providing opportunities for stream and pond fishing, and opening the farm for trout sales and aquaculture tours. Aquaculture, as defined by the North Carolina Department of Agriculture and Consumer Services, "is the business of farming aquatic plants and animals." According to the department, "North Carolina is one of the most aquaculture-friendly states in the U.S."

Tours of Otter Creek Trout Farm inform visitors about western North Carolina's aquaculture industry and trout in general. Two species of trout—rainbow and brown—are raised at the farm. They are received as fingerlings—as long as your finger—and grow to weights of one to over six pounds. It takes a fingerling approximately one year under perfect conditions to reach one pound. Reaching trophy size generally takes three years. As the trout grow, Alex separates them by size in concrete raceways. Based on their weight, he determines which ones will be supplied to restaurants, game lands, community fishing areas, and the general public. The Denisons sell around sixty thousand pounds of trout per year. According to the Rutherford County Center of North Carolina State University and North Carolina A&T State University Cooperative Extension, the Tar Heel State ranks second in the United States for trout production, generating nearly five million pounds a year.

Visitors will learn facts about rainbow and brown trout—neither of which is native to North Carolina—such as their life cycle, environmental requirements, and breeding practices. They will also become educated about trout-farming practices. Guests may be surprised to learn that Otter Creek primarily raises female trout. According to Alex, "Male trout are prone to fight with each other and tend to damage

Otter Creek's raceways provide an up-close look at trout.

Trout splash, circle, and churn the water while feeding.

the female during attempts at the mating process, so in order to ensure the quality of our trout, we focus on raising females."

The tour also addresses the challenges faced by North Carolina trout farmers. Two concerns are water quality and weather. Cool weather with sufficient rain is a necessity for a trout farm's survival. Parasite and viral illnesses can also be problems. Natural predators such as bears, herons, and kingfishers can be another cause for worry—unless, like Otter Creek Trout Farm, you are fortunate enough to have two Akita dogs faithfully guarding the property.

After learning about trout farming, visitors are treated to an entertaining display when Alex sparks a feeding frenzy by tossing several scoops of fish feed into the raceways. The trout splash, circle, and churn water in a chaotic race to eat their food. For tourists with high-speed film, this spectacle provides a unique photo opportunity.

At the end of the tour, guests can purchase trout or, for an extra fee, try their luck at fishing. Alex can provide inexperienced anglers with instruction and equipment—again, for an additional fee. Visitors who choose this option may fish from the raceway, ensuring a guaranteed catch, or try their luck in the Denisons' stream.

Whether guests choose to tour the farm, purchase trout, or go fishing, Alex and Nicole simply hope they will leave with a greater understanding and appreciation for this flourishing North Carolina industry.

Tips

- Be sure to schedule a tour in advance.

- Notice the stop sign at the top of the driveway and do not venture into the farm without checking in first; the Denisons' house is located across the street from the farm.

- Wear shoes appropriate for a wet environment, or at least ones you won't mind getting damp and muddy.

- If you would like to take home something other than trout, ask Nicole about her seasonal plants and organic homemade soaps. The Denisons also keep Russian hogs on their property and will let visitors view them if asked.

- A creek-side deck is available for picnics.

- Be sure to allow time to enjoy the Macon County scenery. Spectacular in any season, the region is most alluring in autumn, when it presents a vibrant sea of gold, red, and yellow.

Santa's Land Fun Park & Zoo

571 Wolfetown Road
Cherokee, N.C. 28719
Phone: 828-497-9191
Website: www.santaslandnc.com
E-mail: santa@santaslandnc.com

Hours: Open daily May through October, weather permitting. Hours are seasonal.

Directions: Santa's Land Fun Park & Zoo is on U.S. 19 (Wolfetown Road) a few miles east of the town of Cherokee in nearby Jackson County.

"...a Storybook Adventure in the Great Smokies..."
Santa's Land Fun Park & Zoo brochure

Barbados blackbelly sheep await visitors near a vending machine.

Stunning scenery, a variety of flora and fauna, Native American history, and an assortment of family-friendly amusements can all be found in and around the town of Cherokee. The Qualla Boundary is the tribal reservation of the Eastern Band of Cherokee Indians. Tourists come to experience the region's notable heritage and history. They find museums, galleries, shops, hiking trails, river adventures, and other sundry activities to fill their day. They may be surprised, however, to come across one of the largest zoos in the Smokies at an amusement park based on the magical world of Santa Claus.

Danny Lyons, owner of the park, and his father and brothers sought to create a one-of-a-kind attraction that would be unlike any amusement park in North Carolina. In 1966, the Christmas-loving family opened Santa's Land Fun Park & Zoo, which includes rides, exhibits, restaurants, shops, live entertainment, and a zoo.

The twenty-five-acre park is divided into three sections: Santa's Land, Fun Land, and Zoo Land.

Santa's Land features a charming cottage known as "Santa's House." There, children and the young at heart can meet Saint Nicholas—who by all standards appears to have come straight from the North Pole—have their photograph taken with him, and receive a "good conduct diploma." Visitors can also view Christmas-themed displays, take a ride on Santa's Express Train, or attend a magic show in the Jingle Bell Theatre. The star of the magic show is a white dove named Angel that wondrously appears the instant a colored balloon is popped. Guests of all ages are invited to meet and greet Angel at the end of each performance.

In Fun Land, visitors can peruse animated show houses, test their skills in the

Ring-tailed lemurs at Santa's Land Fun Park & Zoo
PHOTOGRAPH COURTESY OF
SANTA'S LAND FUN PARK & ZOO

game room, slide on "Big Rock Candy Mountain," observe exhibits related to mountain culture, have fun at the playground, or grab a seat on a kid-friendly amusement ride. The main feature of Fun Land, and the most popular attraction at Santa's Land, is the "Rudicoaster." Visitors may have ridden roller coasters before, but likely not one that is led by a red-nosed reindeer. Although Santa's Land does not exhibit any live reindeer, the Rudicoaster does make it possible for guests to "fly" with one.

Zoo Land is the place, according to the site's brochure, to get "face to face with some of the most beautiful, wild and exotic animals from around the world." Numerous animal exhibits were designed for tourists to feed—and in many instances pet— the inhabitants. Vending machines are located beside these particular enclosures. For the price of a quarter, guests can feed the animals through an opening in the pen or through a specially designed feeding trough. Some of the animals that can be fed are Barbados blackbelly sheep, miniature Sicilian donkeys, European fallow deer, American black bears, and pygmy goats. Miniature Sicilian donkeys, nearly extinct in their native region, have a distinguishing "cross" on their bodies. The cross consists of a dark stripe of hair that runs down the donkey's back and across its shoulders. Zoo Land's donkeys are talented actors that convince visitors to spend all of their quarters on them. Pygmy goats also entertain guests inside a cleverly built two-part enclosure connected by an overhead bridge. Visitors can persuade the goats to cross the bridge by placing food on the side where the goats are not currently residing.

Another nicely constructed exhibit takes the form of a gristmill. The mill's surrounding water is populated by rainbow trout—ones that greatly enjoy having food tossed to them. The trout are supplied to Santa's Land by the Eastern Band of Cherokee Indians and are eventually released into tribal waters. A sign by the millpond jokingly reads, "Feed them now—Catch them later."

Visitors who enjoy feeding fish will definitely want to ride a paddleboat on Whitebeard's Lake. Before leaving the dock, boaters should purchase a bag of food that contains treats for both fish *and* primates. Whitebeard's Lake not only offers an incredible display of fish and ducks but also provides refuge for several ring-tailed lemurs and capuchin monkeys. The water comes to life the instant one's boat leaves the dock, as countless Japanese koi come to the surface. The fish flock to the paddle-boats in anticipation of food. Boaters who do not throw food out far enough *will* get wet, as the koi uncontrollably splash while feeding. For some, the image may bring to mind a sea of piranhas devouring their prey. After depleting their fish food, boaters will want to pull alongside the ring-tailed lemur and capuchin monkey habitats to get an up-close look at these incredible primates. Boaters who paddle close enough can toss in monkey biscuits and peanuts.

Back on dry land, other animals await attention. Zoo Land houses a variety of birds including a blue-and-gold macaw, a golden pheasant, a peacock, and a domestic turkey. The brightly colored golden—or "Chinese"—pheasant is one of the most interesting specimens. According to the educational text panel, this bird is native to the mountains of western China, spends most of its time on the ground, and flies only in short, clumsy bursts.

Additional mammals located throughout the park include a dromedary camel, red kangaroos, llamas, a Russian hog, a serval, an African crested porcupine, a miniature zebu, and Patagonian cavies. Visitors who have never seen a Patagonian cavy may wonder just what type of animal they are looking at, as it has features of a rabbit, antelope, and kangaroo.

Although Zoo Land offers a vast array of animals to view, feed, and pet, visitors seem most excited by the American black bear cubs, Ruff and Buff. Their antics, sounds, and adorable faces capture the hearts of all who see them. Three times a day, Ruff and Buff are brought to an enclosed viewing area where the public can watch them feed and play. Their handlers present interesting facts related to American black bears and answer questions from the crowd.

Although Santa's Land is marketed to families with children, it is an entertaining place for all ages. Thanks to its variety of shops, eateries, entertainments, and animals, Santa's Land Fun Park & Zoo is a daylong excursion not soon to be forgotten.

Tips

- Bring *lots* of quarters or small bills for change, as the animals will beseech you to feed them more than one handful of food.

- Note that during the cool months, some animals may be off view.

Trekking in Panthertown Valley
PHOTOGRAPH BY BERT HENRY,
COURTESY OF ENGLISH MOUNTAIN LLAMA TREKS

English Mountain Llama Treks

767 Little Creek Road
Hot Springs, N.C. 28743
Phone: 828-622-9686
Website: www.hikinginthesmokies.com
E-mail: info@hikinginthesmokies.com

Hours: Open year-round. Advance reservations are required.

Directions: Hot Springs is located northwest of Asheville in Madison County near the Tennessee border. Participants meet at a specified location. Directions will be determined once a trek has been scheduled. Note that the Little Creek Road address is for contact purposes only and is not the physical location for the treks.

"Enjoy guided llama trekking through the Great Smoky Mountains
without carrying a backpack!"
English Mountain Llama Treks website

For many people, hiking in the mountains is a favorite activity. For others, the thought of toting water and other essentials on an uneven trail does not have much appeal. No matter. Lucy Lowe provides able hikers unforgettable adventures and nonhikers easy but extraordinary experiences.

Lowe began leading outdoor trips—hiking, canoeing, and back-country horse excursions—in the mid-1980s. She later operated a horseback riding business that put her on the same trails as English Mountain Llama Treks. Lowe became acquainted with the owners, and when they decided to retire in 2000, she and Laura Higgins purchased the company. Eventually, Lowe halted her horse trips and focused solely on llama treks. She became the sole proprietor after Higgins and her husband moved to Colorado.

Headquartered in Hot Springs in Madison County, English Mountain Llama Treks offers excursions ranging from two *hours* to three *days*. All ages are welcome. Participants are most likely to enjoy a trip if they are in at least moderate physical shape. Even so, the pace *is* adjusted to the slowest person in the group.

For those wishing to experience a trek but who are not up to a full day or overnight hike, Lowe offers her two-hour mini-treks. On private property just outside the Big Creek entrance to Great Smoky Mountains National Park, trekkers head out with lead ropes in hand and trusty llamas by their side. Lowe guides them along a trail that features a deserted cabin—with a 1950s Chevy outside—and a waterfall by an abandoned homestead. Upon arriving at the waterfall, participants enjoy a rest and a light snack before heading back.

Persons who wish to spend more time hiking in the company of llamas can choose a day or overnight trek. The majority of these take place at Max Patch, a high-elevation grassy bald in Pisgah National Forest. The Appalachian Trail crosses the

Moose and Calico waiting to be saddled
PHOTOGRAPH BY BERT HENRY,
COURTESY OF ENGLISH MOUNTAIN LLAMA TREKS

summit of Max Patch. During early spring, trekkers may have an opportunity to visit with Appalachian Trail hikers; Lowe even carries extra provisions to share with them. Max Patch is well known for its wildflowers and its breathtaking views. So spectacular are those views that many hikers equate standing on the crest of Max Patch to being on top of the world. Day treks at Max Patch average four and a half miles and last five to six hours. Lunch typically consists of fresh vegetables from Lowe's garden, deli meats, a selection of cheeses and breads, dip, chips, condiments, beverages (tea, lemonade, and water), and a homemade dessert (generally a Hershey bar or margarita pie). During the cold months, trekkers should expect a black bean or white chicken chili, condiments, beverages (hot apple cider, cocoa, and coffee), and an apple, pear, or rhubarb crisp dessert.

Participants in the overnight excursions will find trekking with llamas to be a real treat. The pack animals carry in all of the camping gear, as well as coolers filled with an incredible assortment of food for dinner and breakfast. "No one loses any weight on our treks," says Lowe. Dinner is usually chicken or steaks—cooked over a fire—with rice and vegetables. For dessert, trekkers are treated to either "grown-up" or regular s'mores—one uses dark chocolate, while the other uses Hershey bars. In the morning, they wake to homemade buttermilk pancakes with wild blueberries and real maple syrup. Again, beverages typically depend on the season.

During the trek, hikers will appreciate their llama companions. According to the English Mountain website, the animals "tend to notice wildlife and draw . . . attention to things you would normally not even see along the trail." Trekkers will also value Lowe, who is not only an outdoor enthusiast and guide but also a biologist and naturalist. Lowe has a special interest in wild edible and medicinal plants. When adventurous eaters are on the trek, she sometimes helps them forage part of the meal as they hike.

The two- and three-day llama treks are in Panthertown Valley, located in Nantahala National Forest. English Mountain is the only llama trekking business with a permit to hike and camp in the national forest. Panthertown Valley, according to Lowe, is nicknamed "the Yosemite of the East," due to its high granite domes and numerous waterfalls. Over the course of the long treks, Lowe keeps participants on track, well fed, and aptly entertained. Her family's roots are in western North Carolina, so she spent many a day listening to her grandmother's Appalachian tales. She now shares them along the trails and around her campfires.

Exploring the mountains of North Carolina in the company of llamas and Lucy Lowe—whether for a few hours or several days—is an adventure always to be remembered. The llamas allow participants to hike at ease, enjoy their surroundings, and not worry about necessities. These gentle companions enjoy being petted and give kisses for carrots.

Tips

- If you have never participated in a llama trek, or if hiking and camping are new to you, do not discount this wonderful activity. Simply call or e-mail Lucy, who will help you decide which trip is best suited to your wants and needs. Summer months and holiday weekends fill up fast, so try to reserve a spot early.

- Llamas are pack animals; they carry supplies, not people. Therefore, do not sign up for a trip expecting to ride a llama in the event you become tired.

Llamacaddy

Sherwood Forest Golf Course
U.S. 276 South
Brevard, N.C. 28712
Phone: 828-884-7825 (for llama reservations at the golf course) or 828-506-1017 (for information on trekking and other llama requests)
Website: www.llamacaddy.com
E-mail: Online form

Hours: Available year-round, weather permitting. Advance reservations are required.

Directions: Sherwood Forest Golf Course is located on U.S. 276 (Greenville Highway) several miles south of Brevard in Transylvania County.

"Simply put, llama caddies are one of the most memorable experiences you can have on the golf course."
Llamacaddy website

Eric English and Legend the llama at Sherwood Forest Golf Course
PHOTOGRAPH COURTESY OF LLAMACADDY

Mark English, owner of Llamacaddy, spent fifteen years learning about llamas, selecting ones with perfect dispositions, and training them to be golf caddies. Since llamas are pack animals, using them as caddies was a natural fit. In the spring of 2009, English and his llamas made their first appearance on Sherwood Forest Golf Course, located just outside Brevard. Not long thereafter, Llamacaddy gained the attention of the local, national, and international news media. More importantly, perhaps, the llamas acquired a local fan base and attracted many first-time golfers.

On the days the llamas are at the course, English sets up a corral where children—and adults—can pet and feed them. Local residents and tourists alike take pleasure in visiting with and learning about llamas. English says that by bringing the animals out to the golf course, he has created numerous llama lovers. The golfers are likely the llamas' biggest fans, despite the fact that the furry companions cannot give advice or retrieve balls. Nevertheless, the llamas bring a sense of tranquility to the fairways that keeps golfers relaxed in the event of bad swings or putts. As Llamacaddy says, these unique partners "have you smiling and having fun before you tee off."

English's llamas are also in the trekking business. Brevard is located in Transylvania County, best known for its 250 waterfalls. The area offers incredible hiking opportunities in Pisgah National Forest and DuPont State Forest. Travelers who would like to spend time in the company of llamas or in nature should contact English about his day and overnight treks. He makes sure guests enjoy their llama companions, the natural environment, and every aspect of their trip by adapting the treks to the ages and interest levels of participants. Lecture-based treks, in which a particular subject becomes the focus of the hike, can also be arranged. Themes can include flora and fauna, geology, history, and the night sky.

Llamacaddy clearly fulfills its mission, which is to offer "a fun and unique animal interaction experience that the entire family can enjoy." By making golf a sport for the whole family and offering treks for all ages, English has created a one-of-a-kind animal interaction. When traveling in or near Brevard, contact him to schedule a trek, to reserve a llama as your caddy, or just to learn what day the animals will be on the course. Even if you choose not to play golf, you can still pet and feed the llamas. Besides, llamas carrying golf clubs are not something you see every day and are definitely worth a photograph.

Tips

- Tuesdays and Saturdays are the best days to schedule Llamacaddy at Sherwood Forest Golf Course.

- English has taken his llamas to other courses and events. If you are interested in scheduling llamas at a course other than Sherwood Forest, do not hesitate to contact him.

Golfers with llama caddies at Maggie Valley Golf Club
Photograph courtesy of Llamacaddy

Brook trout are one of three species in the raceway.

Pisgah Center for Wildlife Education

1401 Fish Hatchery Road
Pisgah Forest, N.C. 28768
Phone: 828-877-4423
Website: www.ncwildlife.org
E-mail: lee.sherrill@ncwildlife.org

Hours: Open year-round Monday through Saturday from 8 A.M. to 4:45 P.M. Closed Easter weekend and most state holidays except Memorial Day, Independence Day, and Labor Day.

Directions: From the intersection of N.C. 280 and U.S. 276/U.S. 64 at the traffic light in the Transylvania County community of Pisgah Forest, follow U.S. 276 North for about 6 miles. Bear left on F.R. 475, travel 1.5 miles, and turn left at the sign for the center.

"Feed the trout at the Bobby N. Setzer State Fish Hatchery."
Pisgah Center for Wildlife Education brochure

Tourists exploring Pisgah National Forest are well aware of its natural beauty and vast recreational opportunities. Waterfalls beckon hikers and photographers. Sliding Rock thrills adventure seekers. Historic sites divulge the region's cultural heritage.

At the Pisgah Center for Wildlife Education in Pisgah Forest in Transylvania County, the main attraction is the innumerable trout that can be fed and viewed on an up-close basis. Visitors should begin their tour at the Bobby N. Setzer State Fish Hatchery and Raceway exhibit. Free to walk around the raceways—elongated concrete fish-rearing ponds that maintain a constant flow of fresh water—they will likely be amazed at the number of trout contained in them. A brochure explaining the hatchery and raceway operation is available at the entrance; guests should read it in order to have a clear understanding of the exhibit. A staff member is also on-site to answer questions and provide assistance.

Built in the late 1950s by the U.S. Fish & Wildlife Service, the facility served as a national fish hatchery for more than twenty years. Since 1983, the North Carolina Wildlife Resources Commission has operated it. According to the commission's website, the facility, North Carolina's largest trout hatchery, "consists of 16 indoor rearing tanks, where trout are kept until they are 'fingerlings' (about three inches long), and 54 outdoor raceways, where the fish are grown until they are 'catchable' size (at least 10 inches long)."

A cold-water facility, the Bobby N. Setzer State Fish Hatchery raises brook, rainbow, and brown trout for the commission's hatchery-supported trout waters program, thanks to which approximately eighty different streams and lakes in fifteen different counties are stocked with catchable hatchery-raised trout. Visitors can learn the process of breeding, feeding, and stocking trout by reading the educational text panels placed prominently around the raceways. Unfortunately, indoor rearing tanks are not part of the exhibit, but visitors can see the progression of trout from fingerlings to catchable size as they peer into the various raceways.

Adults may enjoy the site's informational brochure, *Raising Trout for North Carolina Waters*. Children, however, will most likely be attracted to the small red vending machines stationed around the raceways. A quarter is all that is needed to receive a handful of trout chow to feed to the fish. As the raceways contain different-sized trout, the chow creates varying amounts of splashing, depending on which raceway it is tossed into.

The exit leading out of the raceway exhibit takes visitors on a short, sometimes elevated trail through a hardwood forest. Along the trail, they will happen upon creative exhibits that address conservation and the work of the North Carolina Wildlife Resources Commission. While walking the trail, visitors should talk quietly, as there is always a chance they may spot native wildlife.

At the end of the trail—which completes the center's outdoor exhibits—visitors can stop and enjoy the smells and colors of a backyard wildlife garden. Depending on what's in bloom, they may have an opportunity to watch numerous pollinators—butterflies and bees—at work.

Past the garden, a door leads to the indoor exhibits. Entering the center, visitors may take a seat in the auditorium to view an award-winning documentary that examines the natural history of the mountains and the ways in which the North Carolina Wildlife Resources Commission works with the public to conserve wildlife. It offers a fascinating look at how the demand for natural resources has affected the environment of western North Carolina.

The Mountain Wildlife exhibit has been artfully designed to make visitors feel as though they are walking through a natural mountain environment. Guests will encounter numerous aquariums that highlight regional wildlife and aquatic habitats. As might be expected, the first aquarium features brook, brown, and rainbow trout. Beside the trout, visitors can view the small but unique-looking mottled sculpin, which is a food source for trout in the wild. They will also see the peculiar-looking hellbender, North America's largest salamander, as well as other mountain-dwelling fish including largemouth bass, bluegill sunfish, golden shiner, blacknose dace, river chub, central stoneroller (the males of this species create nests by "rolling" gravel with their noses, hence the name), and rock bass. They will also view a common snapping turtle, a common musk turtle, a garter snake, a red-spotted newt, and an American toad.

The Mountain Wildlife exhibit showcases regional fish, reptiles, and amphibians.

At the end of the Mountain Wildlife exhibit, visitors will step out into the North Carolina Wild Store, which offers a vast selection of educational materials related to the state's wildlife.

The Pisgah Center for Wildlife Education is a fun and enlightening attraction where visitors can discover the mountains' natural resources and learn about the work of the North Carolina Wildlife Resources Commission. The center's brochure proclaims, "We've got the fun and the fish, and it's free!" Indeed. What more could visitors ask for?

Tips

- Make sure you enter through the Bobby N. Setzer State Fish Hatchery and Raceway exhibit. There is no shade over the raceway, so be prepared for heat if you come in the summer. Also, don't forget to bring quarters for the fish food!

- The center offers exciting nature programs designed for all ages. Most programs are free, but preregistration is typically required. Check the center's online calendar to see if a program is available the day of your visit. If you don't, you may miss out on hiking to an active beaver pond, learning to fly-fish, or discovering how to raise trout.

- Since you are in the "Land of Waterfalls," make sure you visit a few!

- The state's other cold-water fish hatcheries—Armstrong State Fish Hatchery and Marion State Fish Hatchery, both in McDowell County—also welcome visitors, but they are not tailored for tourists like the Bobby N. Setzer facility is. Guests are permitted to view raceways containing trout ranging from fingerlings to catchable size. To learn more about the hatcheries, call or visit their websites. Armstrong State Fish Hatchery is located at 3336 Armstrong Creek Road in Marion; call 828-756-4179 or visit www.ncwildlife.org. Marion State Fish Hatchery is located at 645 Fish Hatchery Road in Marion; call 828-652-7802 or visit www.ncwildlife.org.

Carl Sandburg Home National Historic Site

81 Carl Sandburg Lane
Flat Rock, N.C. 28731-8635
Phone: 828-693-4178
Website: www.nps.gov/carl
E-mail: CARL_Administration@nps.gov

Hours: Open daily year-round from 9 A.M. to 5 P.M. Closed on Christmas.

Directions: From I-26 East near Hendersonville and Flat Rock, take Exit 53 and turn right on Upward Road. Travel approximately 2 miles, continue on North Highland Lake Road for 1 mile, and turn left on Greenville Highway (Route 225). Travel about 1 mile and turn right on Little River Road. Parking is on the left.

 (Admission is only charged to tour the house.)

>"... see the farm buildings, visit the goats, tour the dairy, and walk the trails."
>
>**National Park Service brochure for Carl Sandburg Home National Historic Site**

The extraordinary life and career of Carl Sandburg—American poet, minstrel, lecturer, biographer, and Pulitzer Prize–winning author—is imparted daily at Carl Sandburg Home National Historic Site in Flat Rock. The achievements of his wife, Lilian "Paula" Steichen Sandburg, an internationally renowned goat breeder, are also made known.

In 1945, Carl Sandburg and his family came to Flat Rock and purchased Connemara. Lilian found the property and knew it would be an ideal place to raise her milk goats and to provide a retreat where her husband could focus on his writing. The Sandburgs lived at Connemara for twenty-two years until 1967, when, at the age of eighty-nine, Carl passed away. In 1968, Congress authorized 264 acres to be recognized as Carl Sandburg Home National Historic Site. In 1974, the site opened to the public.

Today, visitors can tour the main house—which remains as the Sandburgs left

Goats at Connemara Farms are descended from Lilian Sandburg's original herd.

it—explore the grounds, walk the trails, meet the resident goats, tour the goat dairy, and participate in special-event programs. To reach the main house and goat dairy, tourists must traverse a short trail. Along the way, they will cross a bridge where they can stop and gaze across Front Lake. Although any time of year is nice for visiting, seeing the lake with autumn leaves reflected on the water is an awe-inspiring sight, and one that demands a photograph. Upon reaching the house, guests can browse the visitor center and gift shop—located under the porch—and purchase tickets for a tour of the home, should they be interested. Outside the main house, they can continue along the walking path leading to Connemara Farms Goat Dairy. Visiting the dairy is free.

At the dairy, guests will learn about Lilian Sandburg, a pioneer in the American goat industry. Lilian began raising goats in 1935, while the family was living in Michigan. To assist in the war effort, she had the idea of creating a Grade A goat dairy. She did not accomplish her goal until several years later, when the herd was brought to Connemara. Lilian's dairy operation reached its peak from 1946 to 1952, when the herd exceeded two hundred goats. Milk from the farm was sold to local dairies and individuals. But for Lilian, the sale of milk came second to her primary goal, which was the breeding and development of champion milk-producing goats. According to the site's informational handout, *A Place to Raise Goats*, Lilian's scientific breeding methods allowed her to produce "many champion animals and helped modernize the dairy goat industry, increasing its acceptance as a legitimate form of farming." In 1961, the dairy goat industry recognized Lilian for her leadership and for being an outstanding breeder.

As guests approach the goat dairy, the stunning red paint immediately attracts their attention. The red buildings with their rock elements, set atop a lush green pasture and surrounded by goats—some completely white in color—bring to mind the tranquility of a pastoral painting. Opening the gate to explore the dairy, guests are

Kids (baby goats) bring added enjoyment in April and May.

greeted by numerous goats—the descendants of Lilian's original herd. The three types of goats raised at Connemara are Nubian, Saanen, and Toggenburg. Nubian goats are easy to recognize, as they are large in size and have long, floppy ears and colorful markings. Saanen goats are medium to large in size, have erect ears, and are white in color. Toggenburg goats are medium in size, have erect ears, and are light fawn to dark chocolate in color.

The barn and pasture total approximately five acres. Visitors are allowed to join the goats inside the pasture to pet them and observe their behavior. In April and May, they get a special treat, as kids are born and bring a new level of entertainment. Guests will see much running, jumping, and butting of heads!

Park rangers and volunteers are on-site to answer questions about the goats and dairy, which was in operation from 1945 through 1967. The dairy section of the site has an interesting milk house exhibit, which offers educational text panels, a bottling machine, a milk cooler, milking equipment, and other essential objects. Various buildings such as the barn garage, storage sheds, and goat sheds are also on the site. Across from the goat dairy on the other side of a walking path, visitors can spend time admiring the vegetable garden or venture out on one of the many hiking trails to explore the surrounding woods and walk in the footsteps of the Sandburg family.

Carl Sandburg Home National Historic Site should be on the itinerary of every tourist who passes through Henderson County. The natural beauty of the property is unsurpassed, while the historical integrity of the site allows visitors to feel as though they have stepped back in time—back to when the Sandburgs called Connemara home.

Tips

- From the parking lot, you must walk a trail 0.3 mile long to reach the main house and goat dairy. Although a short hike, it does climb a hundred feet. If you are unable to walk the trail, you may use the phone in the parking lot or at the information station to call for assistance. Wear good walking or hiking shoes, and pay attention to where you step when exploring the areas around the goat barn.

● If you tour the site between August and early December, you might also want to visit Sky Top Orchard, located approximately five miles away at 1193 Pinnacle Mountain Road in Zirconia. The orchard features pick-your-own apples, peaches, pears, pumpkins, and grapes, as well as a barnyard area with sheep, goats, peacocks, chickens, and turkeys. Ducks and geese can also be seen in the orchard ponds. To learn more, call 828-692-7930 or visit www.skytoporchard.com. Do not use the physical address in a GPS; see the website for directions.

● If possible, make plans to visit Round Mountain Creamery near Black Mountain (see pages 29–33). This will allow you to compare the workings of a historic goat dairy farm with a modern one.

Western North Carolina Nature Center

75 Gashes Creek Road
Asheville, N.C. 28805
Phone: 828-298-5600
Website: www.wildwnc.org
E-mail: Staff directory online

Hours: Open daily year-round from 10 A.M. to 5 P.M.; admission ends at 4:30 P.M. Closed Thanksgiving and the day after, Christmas Eve, Christmas Day, New Year's, and Martin Luther King Jr. Day.

Directions: From I-40 West at Asheville, take Exit 53B and watch for signs for the center. Turn right on Fairview Road (U.S. 74 Alt.), travel about 0.5 mile, turn right on Swannanoa River Road (N.C. 81), proceed a mile, bear right on Azalea Road, and turn right on Gashes Creek Road. The center is on the right.

Eli Strull, education program specialist, handles non-releasable animals like Xena, a red-tailed hawk, in "Animal Moments" programs.
PHOTOGRAPH COURTESY OF
WESTERN NORTH CAROLINA NATURE CENTER

"Our dedicated and devoted staff will do everything to make your visit fun, educational, and memorable."
Western North Carolina Nature Center website

Western North Carolina is a nature lover's paradise. Outdoor recreation and spectacular scenery provide countless activities for tourists. Many visitors come in search of the area's native wildlife. Driving across Great Smoky Mountains National Park or along the Blue Ridge Parkway, travelers hope to catch a glimpse or a photograph of an animal other than what they can see in their own backyards. Sometimes they are lucky, other times not.

In Asheville, however, they are guaranteed to see and learn about the area's native animals. The Western North Carolina Nature Center, situated on forty-two acres in Buncombe County, is a living museum that exhibits plants and animals native to the southern Appalachians. The nature center's mission "is to increase public awareness and understanding of all aspects of the natural environment of Western North Carolina through hands-on and sensory experiences."

Visitors should first check in at the welcome center. Afterward, they can step outside, where a paved path leads through indoor and outdoor exhibits. The first stop along the path is Appalachian Station, an indoor exhibit that showcases reptiles, amphibians, and small mammals. Among the numerous turtles featured in the exhibit is a bog turtle—the smallest turtle in North America and an animal currently listed as a threatened species. Also exhibited are a variety of snakes including a timber rattlesnake, a rough green snake, a copperhead, a rat snake, and an Eastern hognose snake. The Eastern hognose snake has the unique defense of rolling on its back and playing dead when threatened. At certain times during the day, snakes—often including the rat snake—are brought out of their enclosures for a special hands-on discovery program. The program helps put aside misconceived notions about snakes. Tourists who suffer from arachnophobia may want to refrain from peering into two exhibits in the building, as one contains a black widow spider and the other a false black widow. Staff at the nature center feed the black widow two small crickets every two weeks and have had two spiders live to approximately one year of age. Amphibians—frogs, toads, and salamanders—fill many of the displays. Among the assortment of species are an American toad, a spring peeper, a gray treefrog, a wood frog, a pickerel frog, a hellbender, and a spotted salamander. A few small mammals may also be seen in the building, one of which is the least weasel, the smallest living carnivore.

Stepping out of Appalachian Station, guests should venture down to the Educational Farm, where kid-friendly animals await. Miniature Sicilian donkeys, Nigerian dwarf goats, and varieties of sheep provide hands-on encounters in the petting area. In and around the barn are several breeds of rabbits and chickens.

A special walk-through exhibit, "The Beauty of Butterflies," is shown adjacent to the farm each summer. Visitors who enter the display are surrounded by hundreds of free-flying native butterflies and moths. This is a wonderful opportunity to examine the colors and patterns of these winged creatures up close.

Beyond the butterfly exhibit is a large aviary that houses birds of prey such as the golden eagle, red-tailed hawk, and great horned owl.

Across from the raptors, a woodland area provides a natural habitat for two American black bears. By way of an elevated boardwalk, visitors walk above the habitat, where they can observe the bears at their daily routines. Continuing on the boardwalk, guests will also encounter a herd of white-tailed deer.

Returning to the paved walkway, visitors will soon arrive at the Appalachian Predators exhibit. Here, they will come face to face with bobcats, gray wolves, red wolves, and coyotes. In some instances, they are able to view animals from a distance of two feet. They also have an opportunity to see several animals no longer common in North Carolina. From reading the educational text panels around the gray wolf habitat, guests will learn how this animal once thrived in the state but, due to myths and misconceptions, was shot, trapped, and poisoned. According to the text, "The last known gray wolf in North Carolina was killed in the western part of the state in Haywood County in 1887." It is a stark reminder of what can happen when people are not educated about a particular animal and its value to the environment. The

Cody, a gray wolf, can be observed in the Appalachian Predators exhibit.
PHOTOGRAPH BY CHUCK WATSON, COURTESY OF WESTERN NORTH CAROLINA NATURE CENTER

same was true of the red wolf, which was nearly eliminated from the wild. Working in conjunction with the U.S. Fish & Wildlife Service, the Western North Carolina Nature Center participates in the Red Wolf Recovery Program by raising red wolves to ensure their survival. This is one of only forty red wolf breeding sites nationwide.

In the predator exhibit is the trailhead for the Trillium Nature Trail, an easy loop two-thirds of a mile long that provides an opportunity to explore the region's native plant life. After completing the nature trail, visitors will begin journeying back in the direction of the welcome center. Along the way, they will encounter more habitats, including ones for small mammals like raccoons and gray and red foxes. This area is a highlight for many, as the raccoons are quite entertaining. Near the small-mammal habitats, a sign educates visitors about the animals they have seen—or will see, depending on which direction they've taken along the path. Most of the animals at the nature center can no longer survive in the wild due to injuries or because they were kept illegally as pets and are now imprinted on humans, making them unfit to be released. Although they cannot live in the wild, each is an ambassador for its kind and has an important role in teaching humans why their species and the environment should be cared for and protected.

The final section of the nature center includes a songbird garden, a turtle pond, Otter Falls, and World Underground. Of all the animals at the nature center, the river otters of Otter Falls are without a doubt the most energetic. Visitors cannot seem to pull themselves away from the habitat as the playful otters swim, dive, stand, squat, roll around, and run back and forth across rocks in their enclosure. Sadly, river otters were almost lost to the region due to habitat destruction and trapping until reintroduction efforts began in the 1990s. Now, they are once again reestablishing themselves in western North Carolina. The last exhibit, World Underground, an indoor display, does not feature animals but illustrates processes such as how soil is formed.

Back at the welcome center, visitors can browse the gift shop and learn more about special programs like the "North Carolina Elk Experience," in which participants travel off-site to view elk in the Cataloochee Valley. The nature center also offers "Wolf Howl Evening Programs" and "Evening Photography Opportunities," which are presented on-site with resident animals. The most popular events of the year, however, are "Hey Day," a family farm festival; "Howl-O-Ween," a Halloween event geared toward families with young children; and the "Holiday Illumination Festival," which features outdoor lights shaped like animals.

One of nature center's goals, as stated on its website, "is to provide both children and adults with the opportunity to interact with and learn more about animals and plants . . . thereby increasing their appreciation and understanding of nature." It achieves this goal by presenting animals in natural settings that allow visitors to feel as if they are observing them in the wild. It also offers an "Animal Moments" program, which affords visitors the opportunity to have an up-close experience with an animal they would typically view from a distance. Through these interactions, visitors may see, touch, photograph, and hear native animals of the southern Appalachians. They will thereby acquire an appreciation for the region's unique environment and leave with a better understanding of how they can help protect each incredible species.

Tip

● The petting area closes at 4 P.M. and the predator habitat and nature trail at 4:30 P.M. Take this into consideration when determining your arrival time.

Round Mountain Creamery

2203 Old Fort Road
Black Mountain, N.C. 28711
Phone: 828-669-0718
Website: www.roundmountaincreamery.com
E-mail: pat@rmcreamery.com

Hours: Tours and cheese tastings are available by advance reservation only. The farm store is open Monday through Friday from 9 A.M. to 5 P.M. Call ahead to ensure that someone will be on-site.

Directions: From I-40 West near the McDowell County–Buncombe

County line, take Exit 73 toward Old Fort. Turn left on South Catawba Avenue and continue on Bat Cave Road for about 7 miles. Turn right at Old Fort Road. The creamery is on the left after approximately 4 miles.

~~~~~~~~~~~~~~~~~~~~~~

". . . come see first-hand how Round Mountain Creamery goat cheese is made from milking to finish."
Round Mountain Creamery website

The journey to Round Mountain Creamery leads travelers through the mountains and up a long and winding road. Located near Black Mountain about twenty-five miles from Asheville, the creamery encompasses twenty-eight acres of Buncombe County farmland. Opened in 2009, it is the first combined dairy goat farm and Grade A goat milk and goat cheese processing plant in North Carolina.

Drivers can easily spot Round Mountain Creamery from the road, as a large milk bottle—a design element of the creamery building—stands like a beacon on the hillside. Several Great Pyrenees dogs greet visitors as they enter the driveway and exit their vehicles. The likable dogs provide an important service to the creamery, as it is their job to protect the goats from predators like coyotes.

If no human farm hands are working outside, visitors should walk to the front of the farmhouse and knock on the door. There, creamery staff is on hand to greet guests and initiate the tour. Visitors will likely meet Linda Seligman, president of E.G.G. (Eggs, Goats, and Gardens) Farms, Inc., who readily shares information about her dairy goats as well as the business of producing sweet, fresh goat's milk in the creamery. Seligman, a veteran worker in the farming industry, knew from an early age she wanted to raise animals but couldn't decide which kind—until she met a goat. She fell in love with the animals' charming faces and gentle natures and started raising them. Visitors should take heed. There are lots of goats to be met at Round Mountain Creamery—over three hundred of them.

Tours begin outside the creamery building, where guests are shown how goats are prepared for milking. They are then taken inside the milking parlor and educated about the process. Visitors learn interesting facts related to milking, such as the schedule (the goats are milked twice a day, at seven in the morning and seven in the evening), what the goats are fed while being milked, the output (on average, one goat produces three quarts of milk a day), and the number of teats to the udder (four for a cow, two for a goat). Walking through the milking parlor to examine the machines is fascinating. If goats are being milked (this is not likely), guests will not be allowed to

The creamery's prominent milk bottle is visible from the road.

enter the milking parlor but instead can observe through a viewing window. Should a visitor or a group wish to see a goat being milked outside its regular schedule, Seligman is willing to arrange a demonstration if scheduled in advance.

The next stop is the pasteurization room. Visitors are not allowed inside but can watch the operation by way of a viewing window. Because Round Mountain Creamery is a Grade A processing plant, it is regulated by the North Carolina Department of Environment and Natural Resources, and its goat's milk is tested regularly under strict PMO (Pasteurized Milk Ordinance) guidelines. The pasteurization room is filled with sparkling stainless-steel equipment. Stainless-steel pipes from the raw-milk room in the milking parlor extend to the vat pasteurizer and exit into the cheese room. Graphs are on the wall. The room brings to mind a medical facility or research lab. During this part of the tour, visitors learn about the pasteurization process and the bottling process.

A favorite spot on the tour for many guests is the cheese room. Here, employees test the pH of the cheese in vats. At the right moment, the curd is hung up in order for the whey to further separate. Visitors can watch through a viewing window while learning about the process. Cheeses at Round Mountain Creamery are made from the goat's milk produced on the farm. The process is regulated by the Food and Drug Protection Division of the North Carolina Department of Agriculture and Consumer Services. Among the variety of cheeses produced are "Delicious Dill," "Goat with a Kick," "Very Nutty Blueberry," "Jazzed Goat," and "From the Garden."

After completing the inside tour, guests will venture outside to see the main attraction—the goats. Three species reside at the farm: Nubian, Alpine, and LaMancha. Each breed has a unique characteristic that allows it to be easily distinguished.

A tour of the creamery offers an up-close look at dairy goats.

Nubian goats have long, floppy ears, Alpine goats have erect ears, and LaMancha goats have such small ears that it appears they have none at all. Seligman says the La-Mancha goats "are the mischievous ones that make seeing the goats a fun experience. Their curiosity about visitors is as genuine as the visitors' curiosity about them."

Visitors who love baby animals will want to tour the creamery in the spring, when they will have the opportunity of seeing, petting, and perhaps cuddling an incredible number of newborn kids. While exploring the goat barns and pasture, it is possible guests will see such processes as does being hand-milked for their colostrum—a process that provides "first milk" for newborns—or goats having their hooves trimmed. The interaction with the goats is extremely up-close and personal. Because the tour is not rushed, visitors have ample time to pet the goats, watch their shenanigans, and simply enjoy being in their company.

At the conclusion of the tour, guests are brought to the farm store, where they are given a sample of goat's milk and cheese. The creamery staff seems to like this part of the tour best, as they revel in seeing expressions of delight come upon visitors' faces after tasting sweet, fresh goat's milk for the first time or trying one of their signature cheeses. Many people who cannot drink cow's milk are able to drink goat's milk, as the fat globules are easy to digest.

A tour of Round Mountain Creamery is quite the adventure. Seeing the step-by-step process by which food makes its way from animals to the table is an educational experience the public is not often privy to. Linda Seligman hopes children will leave her farm with an understanding that "milk comes from mother animals and not the grocery store" and that adults will "realize that a working farm can respect the animals and bring good, wholesome food to the table. Life is a cycle, and the farm experience can make that realization ring true."

The staff members at Round Mountain Creamery love their profession and want to share what they do with the public. Visitors will be fascinated to learn how raw goat's milk is turned into a safe and pasteurized product (Seligman stresses that the sale of raw goat's milk for human consumption is illegal in North Carolina), how cheese is made from the milk, and how various dehydrated herbs, spices, vegetables, fruits, and nuts are utilized to create a wide array of full flavors. Most of all, tourists will savor the time they spend walking a beautiful mountainside surrounded by hundreds of amiable goats that desire nothing more than to follow along, bleat their hellos, and wait for an occasional pat on the head.

Tips

- When walking outside with the goats, ask your guide about Linda Seligman's emus. Seligman wanted an emu ever since she saw one as a child. Now, she has several and is happy for visitors to view them in her upper pasture.

- Pack a blanket, some crackers, and a beverage. After purchasing some of Round Mountain Creamery's goat cheese and perhaps a bottle of goat's milk, head down to the Blue Ridge Parkway for an afternoon or evening picnic.

- When exploring other areas of the North Carolina mountains, plan to visit Connemara Farms Goat Dairy at Carl Sandburg Home National Historic Site in Flat Rock (see pages 22–25). This will allow you to compare the workings of a modern goat dairy farm with a historic one.

- Round Mountain Creamery is a sponsor of, and a participant in, the Spindale Dairy Goat Festival—held, of course, in Spindale, North Carolina. Every May, the festival offers a variety of activities and attractions including a youth dairy goat show, a goat parade, a men's goat beard contest, book readings, Heifer International presentations, a goat beauty pageant, food, music, arts and crafts, and goat-related products. To learn more, visit www.GoatFestival.com.

Full Moon Farm Wolfdog Rescue & Sanctuary

P.O. Box 1374
Black Mountain, N.C. 28711
Phone: 828-664-9818
Website: www.fullmoonfarm.org
E-mail: info@fullmoonfarm.org

Hours: Howl-Ins are held once a month from April to November. See the website for dates and hours. Otherwise, tours are by advance reservation only.

Directions: The sanctuary is not open to the general public. Full Moon Farm will e-mail directions to guests with reservations and those attending Howl-Ins.

"Without wolves, there would be no dogs."
Full Moon Farm Wolfdog Rescue & Sanctuary

Full Moon Farm, a rescue and sanctuary in Black Mountain, labors to protect wolfdogs in crisis and provide lifetime care for ones that cannot be placed in homes. Situated on seventeen acres in Buncombe County, the farm was founded in 2002 by Nancy Brown after she was contacted by the Federal Wolf Dog Rescue—now defunct—to assist with a rescue of animals from New Hampshire. Since that time, Brown has not ceased in her efforts to rescue and shelter wolfdogs that have been abused or neglected.

Full Moon Farm houses approximately seventy wolfdogs—all lifetime residents—that arrived as a result of other animal facilities ceasing operation, owner turn-ins, and animal-control pickups due to abuse, neglect, illegal ownership, running at large, etc. To break this cycle, Brown spends a great deal of time educating the public about wolfdogs and dispelling myths that surround them. Eventually, she would like to have an on-site educational facility complete with a veterinary clinic, intern lodging, and meeting facilities so accredited continuing-education programs could be provided for animal-control officers, shelter workers, veterinarians, and vet technicians; the programs would address such subjects as phenotyping—observ-

*Maid Marion is a mid-content wolfdog rescued out of
McDowell County, North Carolina.*
PHOTOGRAPH USED WITH PERMISSION OF FULL MOON FARM WOLFDOG
RESCUE & SANCTUARY

able physical characteristics or behavioral traits—body language, and myth busting in regard to wolfdogs. Until that time, and likely afterward, Brown and her team of loyal volunteers will continue to educate the public about wolfdogs through public presentations. They also open the sanctuary for Howl-Ins, during which visitors can meet wolfdogs face to face, hear their howls, and learn facts regarding the animals.

Full Moon Farm welcomes visitors by advance reservation and during its monthly Howl-Ins, offered from April to November. Tourists interested in attending a Howl-In should e-mail or phone the sanctuary for directions. Howl-Ins typically begin at 3 P.M. and continue until 5 P.M., when a potluck supper is served. Visitors arriving for a Howl-In should check in at the welcome hut—a Full Moon Farm banner is clearly visible—where they will sign a photography waiver and wait for their tour to begin. The welcome hut also offers a selection of souvenirs.

When the tour begins, guests are escorted around the grounds to meet several resident wolfdogs and be educated about these oft-misunderstood animals. Perhaps one of the greatest myths about wolfdogs is that they are 50 percent wolf and 50 percent dog. According to Brown, "Eighty-five percent of the wolfdogs in America are wolfdog-to-wolfdog bred and three to five generations removed from the pure wolf. Wild wolves are *never* used as breeding stock." Most wolfdogs are mixed with dogs that resemble wolves, like German shepherds, Alaskan malamutes, and Siberian huskies. According to Full Moon Farm's informational handout, *What Is a Wolfdog?* the animals do have a pure wolf ancestor within the last five generations. Depending upon where that ancestor lies, a wolfdog is referred to as low, mid-, or high content in regard to its wolf percentage and ranked according to F (filial) generations—the number of generations removed from the pure wolf. For example, an F1 ranking

Mani, a high-content wolfdog, was cast in the movie, Mandie and the Secret Tunnel.
PHOTOGRAPH USED WITH PERMISSION OF FULL MOON FARM WOLFDOG RESCUE & SANCTUARY

would mean that one of a wolfdog's parents was a pure wolf. An F3 ranking would denote that a great-grandparent was a pure wolf. An animal ranked F5 has had its wolf genes "bred out."

Led from one enclosure to another, Howl-In attendees view wolfdogs spanning the scale and learn about their differences. They also discover the circumstances under which the animals came to live at the sanctuary. Visitors will be pleased to meet wolfdogs like Maid Marion, a mid-content wolfdog captured in McDowell County. An abandoned pet, Maid Marion roamed the county frightening residents, who mistook her for a wolf. Blamed for killing chickens and a neighborhood dog, she was soon held in an animal shelter. When Brown retrieved Maid Marion, she found her in need of medical attention; Maid Marion's eye was deflated and infected and had to be removed. Nevertheless, according to Maid Marion's biography, "her eye, a testament to her former hard life, does nothing to dim her beauty."

Other animals on the tour include Banjo, a high-content wolfdog with lineage from a 1920s fur farm; Noshoba, a low-content wolfdog that is peculiar looking, as he was mixed with a Great Pyrenees; Mani, a high-content wolfdog that was cast in the movie *Mandie and the Secret Tunnel*; and Pandora, a mid-content wolfdog that came to the sanctuary after a court case in West Virginia. Although diagnosed with cancer, Pandora eats well and enjoys running and playing with other wolfdogs in her enclosure.

Despite the fact that the residents of Full Moon Farm are not pure wolves, visitors may think twice when they hear the mountain come to life in a chorus of howls. However, wolfdogs are not wild. Rather, they are domestic animals with special needs. No matter how much they resemble or sound like wolves, they could *not* survive in the wild.

Upon completing the tour, visitors are welcome to walk around the sanctuary, to take photographs, to ask questions, to view the animals, and to stay for a concluding potluck meal. Full Moon Farm provides a main entrée and drink. Howl-In attendees are asked to bring a side item. A small donation is requested for the meal.

As stated in the farm's informational handout, wolfdogs were "created by humans" and "depend on humans for food . . . protection, and often for companionship." Make a date to visit during one of the Howl-Ins, which provide a fun educational experience the entire family will howl about.

Tips

- Don't forget a side item for the potluck. Visitors often bring vegetable trays or Kentucky Fried Chicken side items.

- The farm is just a hop, skip, and jump from Round Mountain Creamery (see pages 29–33). As the Howl-Ins take place in late afternoon, schedule a tour at the creamery earlier in the day, pick up some cheese for the potluck, and experience two animal adventures in one day.

The Wolf Sanctum

131 Wolf Crossing
Bakersville, N.C. 28705
Phone: 828-688-9005
Website: www.wolfsanctum.org
E-mail: director@wolfsanctum.org

Hours: From May through October, The Wolf Sanctum holds an open house every Saturday, weather permitting, from noon to 6 P.M. Otherwise, tours are by advance reservation only.

Directions: From U.S. 226 North at Bakersville in Mitchell County, turn right on Maple Avenue. At the end of Maple Avenue, turn right on Cane Creek Road. In 3.5 miles, you will see a large white sign for The Wolf Sanctum. Turn left and follow the gravel drive uphill, then turn right to enter the wolf compound.

"... an educational opportunity whereby individuals can
observe wolves and participate in guided tours of
The Wolf Sanctum's facilities."

The Wolf Sanctum website

Home to the Museum of North Carolina Minerals, the North Carolina Mineral and Gem Festival, and Spruce Pine, the noted "gem mining capital of the United States," Mitchell County is an alluring destination. Other treasures also await discovery. The Wolf Sanctum, located in the small town of Bakersville, is a place of refuge where captive-born wolves and wolfdogs rescued from abusive or inappropriate environments receive permanent sanctuary. Founded in 2001 by Elizabeth "Liz" Mahaffey, The Wolf Sanctum houses pure wolves and high-content wolfdogs in its thirty-seven-acre facility. Resident animals have been spayed or neutered, are not available for adoption, and will remain for life. As the facility is a sanctuary and not a zoological park, Mahaffey provides tours once a week for limited hours during certain months of the year.

Upon exiting their cars, visitors are immediately greeted by the sound of Celtic music, the stares of curious wolves and wolfdogs, and a lively hello from Mahaffey. Her love of wolves and wolfdogs began in 1990, when she accepted two wolfdogs from a friend who was trying to find them homes. At the time, Mahaffey was living in Georgia and working as a law-enforcement officer. After retiring in 2001, she moved to Bakersville and realized her dream of creating a wolf educational facility and sanctuary.

The art of howling is demonstrated at The Wolf Sanctum.
PHOTOGRAPH BY JAMES FISHER,
THE JAMES FISHER GALLERY

The Wolf Sanctum Visitor Center
PHOTOGRAPH COURTESY OF
THE WOLF SANCTUM

Mahaffey's "rescues," now numbering eighteen, are radiant creatures with intriguing and ofttimes heartbreaking stories. Cherokee White Rose, an Arctic wolf, was rescued from a home where she was abused by her male caretaker, which caused her to develop an animosity toward the male population. Her years at the sanctuary, however, have turned negative views into positive ones. Cherokee White Rose is a star attraction of The Wolf Sanctum. Visitors have the opportunity to touch this white beauty, albeit through the fence of her enclosure. Other residents of the sanctuary were removed from roadside zoos and backyard breeders. One was found wandering in a residential neighborhood. Another was discovered when only a few weeks old on a game farm in an extremely sick condition. Their stories are the driving force behind Mahaffey's dedication to providing them a safe and nurturing habitat.

Visitors not only get an up-close look at the resident animals and hear their heart-stirring howls but also leave with a greater understanding of wolves and wolf-dogs. Wolves at the facility represent several subspecies of the gray wolf. Mahaffey feels strongly that the public should be educated about this top predator's crucial and necessary role in the environment. She discusses wolf facts versus fiction, wolf behavior, and current conservation efforts. She also encourages visitors to read about and support foundations that are involved in researching, reintroducing, and preserving wolves; published and research materials are accessible on-site.

Environmental groups, school groups, Cub Scouts, and other interested parties are offered the opportunity to participate in Mahaffey's "Wolf Trek" program. Program attendees are given an educational overview of the wolf, a tour of the sanctuary, a video presentation entitled *A Baby Timber Wolf Grows Up*, and various educational handouts. The free "Wolf Trek" program is available to groups of no more than twelve.

At the end of the tour, visitors are encouraged to browse the gift shop, which offers handcrafted artwork and professional photographs of each resident animal.

Mahaffey is an artist member of the Toe River Arts Council. Her artwork—some of which creatively incorporates wolf hair into the design—can be seen and purchased in the gift shop.

Tips

* Mahaffey warns against trusting GPS units to locate the facility; use the directions provided on the website. Before traveling to the facility, call to confirm it will be open.

* If you want to experience another unique Mitchell County attraction, plan your visit to coincide with Bakersville's Annual Rhododendron Festival, held in June. To learn more about the festival, visit www. bakersville.com.

Grandfather Mountain

2050 Blowing Rock Highway
Linville, N.C. 28646
Phone: 828-733-4337 (entrance)
  or 828-733-1059 (nature museum)
Website: www.grandfather.com
E-mail: nature@grandfather.com

Hours: Open daily year-round except Thanksgiving, Christmas, and bad-weather winter days. Ticket sales end one hour prior to closing. Spring and fall hours are 8 A.M. to 6 P.M. Summer hours are 8 A.M. to 7 P.M. Winter hours are 9 A.M. to 5 P.M.

Directions: Grandfather Mountain is located off U.S. 221 about 2 miles north of Linville in Avery County. It is 1 mile south of Milepost 305 on the Blue Ridge Parkway.

An American black bear is one of several animals in Grandfather Mountain's wildlife habitats.

> "You'll be enchanted by graceful deer . . . laugh at entertaining black bears . . . hear the cry of mountain lions and watch otters dive and spin under water."
>
> **Grandfather Mountain brochure**

First-time visitors to Grandfather Mountain cannot fully imagine the amazing journey they are about to embark upon. But soon after entering the mountain's admission gate and beginning the trek to the summit, it will become apparent they are in an extraordinary place. Grandfather Mountain encompasses nearly 3,200 acres in Avery County. Almost three-quarters of that acreage is designated as a North Carolina state park, while the remainder is a scenic, fun-filled travel attraction. Grandfather Mountain has an elevation of 5,946 feet and was created nearly 730 million years ago; however, in 1962, the United States Geological Survey found that some local rock formations date back 1.1 billion years. The Cherokees called the mountain Tanawha, meaning, "fabulous hawk or eagle," but pioneers saw a face on the mountain that to them resembled an old man. Today, one of the most popular activities for visitors is finding his face—a profile—amid the cliffs.

Throughout its long history, Grandfather Mountain has felt the footsteps of explorers and witnessed the arrival of tourists—first on horseback, then by automobile. The mountain has also heard the construction of roads, buildings, and the bridge that made it famous. For years, the Linville Improvement Company operated Grandfather Mountain. When it dissolved in 1952, Hugh MacRae Morton became the mountain's sole owner. Under his proprietorship, the road up the mountain was widened to two lanes and finally reached the summit. There, he built the noted "Mile

High Swinging Bridge." In 1968, Morton purchased two bears, a male and a female, with the intention of setting them loose. The female, Mildred, would not go. An enclosure was built for Mildred, who became a permanent and popular resident of Grandfather Mountain. Eventually, other animal habitats—ones that featured animals native to the mountain—were created as well.

Morton diligently worked to make the mountain accessible to the public and to preserve and protect its natural environment. In 1992, the United Nations Educational, Scientific and Cultural Organization (UNESCO) selected Grandfather Mountain for recognition as a member of the international network of Biosphere Reserves. Grandfather Mountain is not only a travel attraction, wildlife sanctuary, and nature preserve but also a habitat for seventy-three rare species of plants and animals, thirty-two of which are globally impaired. Hugh Morton died in 2008, but his mission continues. Ownership of the 720-acre travel attraction was transferred to the Grandfather Mountain Stewardship Foundation, whose objective "is to steward the property in a way that protects the natural wonder of the geographic land *and* offer the general public access to its fantastic scenery."

Mountain tourists will indeed behold stunning views on the trek to the summit, which is an adventure in itself. Hairpin curves lead past overlooks, trailheads, rock formations, and picnic areas. Halfway to the summit, visitors will arrive at the Grandfather Mountain Nature Museum, where exhibits showcase the mountain's history and diverse wildlife and plant species. The museum also contains an auditorium, a restaurant, and a gift shop. Guests enjoy eating at the restaurant, where a large window looks out onto numerous bird feeders that provide impromptu entertainment.

Outside the nature museum are a picnic shelter, a butterfly garden, a fudge and ice-cream shop, and a walkway leading to the mountain's environmental habitats. The habitats, which comprise nearly four acres around the museum, allow visitors to view animals in their natural settings. The most popular is the American black bear habitat. Unfortunately, guests can no longer see Mildred, as she passed away in

A sizable habitat allows white-tailed deer to be observed within their natural environment.

1993. For decades, visitors could purchase and toss peanuts to the resident bears, but the Grandfather Mountain Stewardship Foundation did away with the practice on June 1, 2010, in order to create a more natural environment for both the bears and the public. Visitors still enjoy observing the bears' behavior, which is often quite entertaining.

Guests will also encounter golden eagles, river otters, white-tailed deer, and cougars. The cougars—also referred to as mountain lions, panthers, and pumas—are favorites. These large, muscular cats are not likely to be seen in the wild—at least not in North Carolina. According to an educational text panel beside the habitat, the Eastern cougar is thought to be extinct in the wild. Although a small population of Florida panthers exists, these are considered the most endangered land mammals on the North American continent. Likewise, Western cougars are threatened by hunting and loss of habitat. Morely, a golden eagle, is greatly admired by tourists. He came to the mountain in 1984 after being rehabilitated from a gunshot wound. Morely is missing a third of his wing and can no longer take flight.

After viewing the environmental habitats, visitors can continue their climb to the top of the mountain. At the summit, they can explore the visitor center and cross the Mile High Swinging Bridge, the highest swinging footbridge in America. The views from the bridge—and atop the mountain peaks on the other side—cannot adequately be described. John Muir, founder of the Sierra Club, visited the summit in 1898. In an article for the *American Museum Journal,* he expressed his emotions after seeing those views: "I couldn't hold it in, and began to jump about and sing and glory in it all."

Those who visit Grandfather Mountain have access to an incredible nature preserve and a family-friendly travel attraction that provides unforgettable scenery, native mountain wildlife, interactive programs, a famous bridge, and an opportunity to be overwhelmed—like John Muir—by the splendor of nature.

Tips

- Be sure to check out the daily and special-event Naturalist Programs, as some include interactive animal presentations.

- Be prepared for cool weather. Temperatures are typically ten degrees colder than in the foothills.

- Bring a picnic lunch and take advantage of the *hundreds* of picnic tables—particularly the one at Cliffside, where the view is incredible.

● Due to the extremely sharp curves, bicycles, vehicles pulling trailers or other vehicles, and motor homes longer than twenty-eight feet are not permitted on the summit road.

● You may want to spend a night or two in the area to enjoy other animal-related facilities such as Tweetsie Railroad's Deer Park (see pages 52–55) and Genesis Wildlife Sanctuary (see pages 48–52). If you visit during the third weekend of October, be sure to check out the Woolly Worm Festival (see pages 44–47).

Woolly Worm Festival

Avery County Chamber of Commerce
4501 Tynecastle Highway, Unit #2
Banner Elk, N.C. 28604
Phone: 800-972-2183 or 828-898-5605
Websites: www.averycounty.com or www.woollyworm.com
E-mail: events@averycounty.com

Hours: The festival is held annually on the third weekend of October. See the website for exact dates and hours.

Directions: Banner Elk is located at the junction of N.C. 184 and N.C. 194 in northeastern Avery County. Look for the signs for parking on Main Street (N.C. 194). Note that the Tynecastle Highway address above is for contact purposes and does not lead to the festival.

> "Don't miss this one of a kind festival where racing
> woolly worms is a highlight."
> **Woolly Worm Festival website**

Stock-car racing is without a doubt one of North Carolina's most popular sports. On weekends during race season, dedicated fans flock to racetracks to cheer for their favorite drivers. But some people may not be familiar with another form of racing in

Woolly worm race contestants take their place on stage.

the state. In these particular races, observers also shout for their preferred contenders. However, the participants do not race for cash but for the privilege of foretelling winter weather.

Each year on the third weekend of October, the Woolly Worm Festival is held on the grounds of Banner Elk Elementary School in downtown Banner Elk. The festival is cosponsored by the Avery County Chamber of Commerce and the Kiwanis Club of Banner Elk. These two agencies, with the help of event proceeds, support community programs and children's charities. The main feature of the festival, and the one that draws spectators from all parts of the country, is the comical, you-have-to-see-them-to-believe-them woolly worm races.

Jim Morton founded the Woolly Worm Festival in 1978 as a way of locating an "official worm" that could predict the upcoming winter weather. Morton was aware of mountain folklore regarding worms' ability to foretell the weather but discovered that different worms gave contrary forecasts. Therefore, according to Scott Nicholson in "Crawling Down Memory Lane" in the 2009 *Woolly Worm Gazette*, Morton "was immediately struck by the need to have a process for selecting which woolly worm to believe." The races proved to be the perfect solution, as the final winner would be selected as the official winter weather forecaster.

What exactly *is* a woolly worm? According to the same issue of the gazette, a woolly worm is actually a woolly bear caterpillar, the larva of an Isabella tiger moth. Sometimes black and sometimes brown, the worms often feature burnt-orange midsections with black bands on each end of the body. It is the woolly worms' coloration that "forecasters" view to make their weather predictions. If a winning woolly worm exhibits more brown than black on its body, a mild winter will be forecasted. However, if more black can be seen, then cold and snowy days lie ahead. Nevertheless, severe winter predictions do not worry woolly worms, as they can survive temperatures as low as −90 degrees!

A woolly worm is actually a woolly bear caterpillar.
PHOTOGRAPH COURTESY OF THE AVERY COUNTY CHAMBER OF COMMERCE

Visitors to the festival will have numerous opportunities to purchase their own racing woolly worms. Vendors of the would-be racers are located on the streets surrounding the event, as well as at the gate entrance where admission tickets are sold. After purchasing a ticket and a woolly worm, it is essential to get in line, pay your worm's entry fee, and register for a heat race. Festival attendees are allowed to bring their own woolly worms; however, in the event it is not a *true* woolly worm, it will be disqualified. Woolly worms must be named before they can enter a race. If you plan on competing, try to think of a name ahead of time. Previous racers have borne such names as Cletus Worm, Pokey, Speedy Gonzales, Davy Crockett, Valentino, Smokey, Woolly Bo Billy, Fuzzy, and Moe Joe.

The number of contestants and the weather conditions determine the number of heats held on Saturday. Once scheduled for a heat, participants must wait for their race number to be called. Excitement builds as contestants take the stage, which is the back of a flatbed truck, and stand in front of a decorated board that holds twenty-five three-foot-long vertical strings. Judges next instruct competitors to place their woolly worms on the strings but to make sure they stay behind a certain marked point; judges do watch for false starts. Finally, at the command "*Go!*" a truly amazing spectacle occurs. Hilarious antics unfold as participants try to encourage their woolly worms to quickly move up the strings. An interesting catch to the race is that competitors are not permitted to touch their worms, the strings, or the race board. Clever contestants—especially ones who have raced before—use unique methods for getting their worms to advance up the strings and cross the finish line first. Some whistle at their racers. Many clap feverishly. Several blow heavily at the worms from underneath, a few with the help of a straw. All can be heard yelling their woolly worms' names.

At the end of each heat, a winner is declared and a small cash prize is awarded. Heat winners enter a semifinal in which the champion receives a larger cash prize. At the end of the day, when the last race is over, the winner will, as stated in the 2009 *Woolly Worm Gazette,* "gain the reputation, honor and prestige of having one heck of a fast woolly worm, one fast enough to win you one thousand big ones and the gratitude of thousands of people waiting on your worm to determine their winter weather."

The festival and the races continue on Sunday. However, the second-day competitions are for fun and small prizes only. Although the event began with a few vendors and several hundred attendees, it now draws thousands of attendees and hundreds of merchants. It offers crafts, musical entertainment, photographic opportunities—a life-sized woolly worm named Merryweather roams the premises—and food vendors. Visitors will be glad they chose to partake of this standout fun-filled extravaganza. The Woolly Worm Festival elicits smiles, laughter, frivolity, and community fellowship from all who attend. Nothing can be compared to standing behind a tiny woolly worm and coaching it to climb a string as fast as it can. When your worm stops halfway up the string, turns around, and stares you dead in the face with a you-must-be-joking look, it is a scene that will make you smile each time you remember it.

Tips

- If you arrive before 11 A.M., you will *likely* avoid traffic congestion and find a free parking space—yes, free parking is available. If you cannot find a free parking space or don't see a sign, ask one of the police officers directing traffic. If you are going with the sole intent of racing a woolly worm, it is imperative that you arrive *and* register your worm early in the day; I always arrive before noon. Heat races fill up fast, and everyone is not guaranteed a spot. It would be most disappointing to drive to the festival, buy your worm, and discover all the races are full.

- After racing your worm, you can either keep it or turn it in to the festival. If you take it home, you can care for it over the winter; instructions can be found online. Then, come spring, you can watch your worm create a cocoon and later see it emerge in the form of a beautiful Isabella tiger moth.

- Genesis Wildlife Sanctuary (see pages 48–52) is just a stone's throw from the festival; if your worm doesn't make it to the finals—meaning you don't have to stay all day—you may want to visit the sanctuary the same day.

A sedated bobcat receives care from Leslie Hayhurst, founder of Genesis Wildlife Sanctuary.
PHOTOGRAPH COURTESY OF
GENESIS WILDLIFE SANCTUARY

Genesis Wildlife Sanctuary

210 Grassy Gap Creek Road
Beech Mountain, N.C. 28604
Phone: 828-387-2979
Website: www.genesis-wildlife.org
E-mail: genewild@skybest.com

Hours: Open daily year-round from 9 A.M. to 5 P.M.

Directions: From U.S. 321 North at the town of Beech Mountain, make a sharp left turn on Buckeye Road. Travel about a mile and turn right on Russell Norris Road. After about 2 miles, bear left on Spring Branch. Drive approximately 0.5 mile, turn right on Coy Harris Road, then bear right on Buckeye Road. In less than 0.5 mile, turn left on Buckeye Creek Road. Travel about 2.5 miles and bear left on Grassy Gap Creek Road. The entrance is on the left after another 0.5 mile.

". . . a haven for injured, orphaned and abused animals . . ."
Genesis Wildlife Sanctuary website

Beech Mountain, North Carolina—"Eastern America's Highest Town"—is a popular vacation destination. During winter, travelers flock to the area for cold-weather activities such as skiing, tubing, snowboarding, ice skating, and sledding. In summer, tourists come for the mild climate. Colorful leaves and the one-of-a-kind Autumn at Oz Party—a weekend celebration at the former Land of Oz theme park—bring excursionists in the fall. But another opportunity—one that can be enjoyed no matter the season—is less known among Watauga County tourists.

Genesis Wildlife Sanctuary, founded in 1993 by Leslie Hayhurst, is "dedicated to rescue, rehabilitation, release and education." Hayhurst began the sanctuary in her home until the increasing number of animals in need made it apparent she needed a larger facility. However, a bigger house was still unable to accommodate the multitude of wildlife requiring care. Eventually, she raised the funds to construct a conservation center at a one-acre site on Beech Mountain.

The sanctuary rescues and rehabilitates native wildlife and exotic animals. Its goal for native wildlife is to successfully release each animal back into the wild, while the desire for exotics is to find them "forever" homes. The sanctuary provides permanent care for animals that cannot be released or adopted. The number of animals tended to by Hayhurst and her team is quite impressive—five to six hundred indigenous birds, reptiles, and mammals annually, the majority of which are released back into the wild. The sanctuary typically arranges adoptions for 80 percent of exotics and maintains the remaining 20 percent.

Genesis Wildlife Sanctuary is one of only a few rehabilitation centers in North Carolina able to provide on-site intensive care and surgery. It is also one of the few centers that functions as a nature center for the public. Tours of the sanctuary are self-guided. However, if visitors would like a guided tour, they can call and schedule one in advance or knock on the door of the center to see if a staff member is available. Guests who arrive without prearranged tours are permitted to walk the property and view a variety of the sanctuary's permanent residents in their outdoor habitats.

One of the first habitats to be seen—or perhaps heard—is a songbird aviary that showcases an array of colorful creatures. Among the many birds on the grounds are a vulture, a broad-winged hawk, red-tailed hawks, barred owls, great horned owls, and screech owls. These raptors are permanent residents due to problems such as broken wings, gunshot wounds, blindness, brain injuries, and other afflictions that prevent them from flying or surviving in the wild.

The mammals at Genesis Wildlife Sanctuary include bobcats, groundhogs, and wolves. Although each mammal has a compelling story, one resident is guaranteed to leave a lasting impression in the hearts of everyone he meets. When Wobbles the groundhog emerged from hibernation one year, he was brutally attacked by dogs. As a result, he suffers from shaken baby syndrome and has permanent brain damage. Although he is unable to stand upright and staggers when he walks, Wobbles seems to greatly enjoy his habitat as well as his daily diet of fresh dark greens, cooked sweet potatoes, fruit, and vegetables. Speaking of food, every bird, mammal, and reptile at

Wobbles the groundhog suffers from shaken baby syndrome as a result of being attacked by dogs.
PHOTOGRAPH COURTESY OF
GENESIS WILDLIFE SANCTUARY

the sanctuary is prepared a special platter each day. Depending on the animal, the meal might consist of fresh fruits, vegetables, or meats. Local grocery stores donate the produce, as well as a large quantity of meat.

Harley is another groundhog visitors should not miss, as he is something of a celebrity. For the past seven years, one of the sanctuary's groundhogs has traveled to Raleigh to officially predict the weather on Groundhog Day. Harley has been the star weather forecaster in recent years. According to the sanctuary, Harley, whose stage name is Sir Walter Wally, "loves the attention."

Visitors who schedule a tour may be able to see some of the exotic rescues, which include parrots, rabbits, guinea pigs, and other adoptable animals. Many parrots are surrendered to the sanctuary, as owners often report they can no longer care for their pets or that the birds have loud or destructive behaviors. Seventy-five parrots were brought to the sanctuary in 2007 and forty-five in 2008. Those who may be considering a pet should visit the sanctuary's website prior to visiting, as animals available for adoption can be viewed online.

Upon completing the tour, visitors can drive a short distance to the sanctuary's satellite location to see even more animals. The Dan and Arlene Schmidt Animal Habitat is the sanctuary's new three-acre home. More than two hundred people attended the grand opening on May 23, 2009. The habitat is located at the base of The Lodges at Eagles Nest. The animal enclosures, tucked within a forested area, feature distinct wooden elements and designs that blend naturally into the environment. Animals currently residing at this location include several species of raptors, peacocks, guineafowl, peafowl, and rabbits. Mammals such as bobcats will be added in the future. Like the original sanctuary, this location is open daily from 9 A.M. to 5 P.M. for self-guided tours.

Genesis Wildlife Sanctuary not only provides treatment, rehabilitation, and permanent care to animals but also offers a variety of programs that encourage children and adults to learn about the natural world and ways they can protect it. The sanctuary states, "We believe that our only hope for the survival of the wildlife is the teaching of its importance to those who will be their protectors. It is in this spirit that we offer our experiences to groups of all ages, but, in particular, the children."

In the future, the sanctuary would like to expand by relocating to a larger location on Beech Mountain. The original facility would remain but function only as a rehabilitation center. Other goals include raising funds to construct a permanent outdoor habitat for two resident wolves, Isis and her daughter, Sabriel, who came to the sanctuary after being rescued from a private owner. An outdoor habitat would allow the wolves to roam and be viewed by the public.

When asked about the highlight of her work at Genesis Wildlife Sanctuary, Hayhurst said, "Every time we adopt out or release something, it's hard work with a beautiful ending." She further stated, "The volunteers and board members of Genesis feel extraordinarily blessed to have the opportunity to work with our wildlife. It is more of a privilege to have this opportunity than work."

Whatever season visitors find themselves in Watauga County is the perfect time to visit Genesis Wildlife Sanctuary. The animals and staff have both sad and inspiring stories to share, stories that are sure to educate guests about the important role of wildlife and the daily steps that can be taken to protect it.

Tips

- Schedule a tour in advance. Learning about the animals and the reasons they came to and still reside at the sanctuary is most educational. The animal habitats are outdoors, so dress for the weather.

- Should you visit the satellite center at Eagles Nest, you will have to pass through a secured gate, as the habitats are located on the grounds of a private community. Tell the security guard you are there to view the wildlife habitats. He will make a copy of your driver's license and give you a temporary pass. The habitats at Eagles Nest may not be open in winter, so check with the sanctuary before driving out.

● Located close to Genesis Wildlife Sanctuary is Falls Trail, a moderate 1.6-mile loop that follows a creek and ends with a view of a waterfall. Buckeye Lake and Buckeye Recreation Center, also close by, offer a variety of recreational activities as well as restrooms, picnic tables, and vending machines. The trailhead, lake, and recreation center are all visible from the sanctuary.

● If you have time, consider visiting other High Country attractions such as Tweetsie Railroad (see pages 52–55) and Grandfather Mountain (see pages 40–44). Should you visit on the third weekend of October, make sure you grab a caterpillar and attend the Woolly Worm Festival (see pages 44–47) in Banner Elk.

Tweetsie Railroad

300 Tweetsie Railroad Lane
Blowing Rock, N.C. 28605
Phone: 800-526-5740 or 828-264-9061
Website: www.tweetsie.com
E-mail: info@tweetsie.com

Hours: The schedule is seasonal. Phone or visit the website for exact dates and hours.

Directions: Tweetsie Railroad is on U.S. 321 between Blowing Rock and Boone in Watauga County.

"... check out the friendly animals at the Deer Park ..."
Tweetsie Railroad website

The sound of Tweetsie Railroad's Number 12 steam locomotive—listed on the National Register of Historic Places—has been attracting crowds to Blowing Rock since 1957. Tweetsie began as an excursion railroad but progressed into a Wild West town complete with amusement rides, live shows, eateries, shops, the Deer Park,

Animal feed is available for purchase at the Deer Park entrance.

and other entertainment venues. Situated on two hundred acres in Watauga County, Tweetsie Railroad is North Carolina's first theme park and one of the state's best-known attractions.

Upon their arrival, visitors enter through a ticket office and exit onto Main Street, a lively place where train smoke fills the air, conductors shout "All aboard," cowboys and can-can girls socialize with guests, and a row of Western-themed shops and eateries awaits patronage. It is also a place where photographic opportunities abound. For most tourists, a stroll on Main Street is not complete without having their images captured inside the Tweetsie Jail, atop a fake horse, or beside one of the many cowboys or can-can girls.

In Tweetsie Junction—the first section of the park beyond Main Street—the Feed and Seed Restaurant offers a variety of food choices, as well as a cool place on a summer day to relax and refuel. The famous Tweetsie Palace Saloon is also in this section of the park. At certain times of day, it offers guests a glimpse of an 1800s saloon show. Alcoholic beverages are not served, but patrons can purchase ice cream, soft drinks, pretzels, nachos, and other tasty snacks.

At the Country Fair area of the park, visitors can enjoy amusement rides, test their skills in the arcade, or try their luck at other carnival-type games. Between Tweetsie Junction and the Country Fair, guests can board a chairlift to the top of Miner's Mountain. The chairlift provides a wonderful opportunity to catch a cool mountain breeze, a few minutes of silence, or a glimpse of bright-colored leaves, for those who visit in the fall. Visitors wary of riding the chairlift can take the bus that boards at Tweetsie Junction or the walking trail that begins in the Country Fair.

On Miner's Mountain, visitors will discover additional places to eat, another large gift shop, amusement rides—including the beloved Mouse Mine Train Ride—gem mining, gold panning, a playground, live entertainment, and the Deer Park. When opened to the public in 1962, the Deer Park contained only a small number of

European fallow deer, pygmy goats, and fowl. Over the years, however, it has grown to include more than ninety animals.

Before entering the Deer Park, guests have the option of buying inexpensive cones of food. All animals in the park can be fed; some can be hand-fed, while others must be fed by way of a trough. Therefore, the park is divided into two sections. In the hand-feeding section are European fallow deer, pygmy goats, Nubian goats, and pot-bellied pigs. The European fallow deer are smaller than native white-tailed deer and have three common coats: chocolate, white, and spotted. Beautiful in every respect, they are clearly the highlight of the park.

Guests can feed and pet European fallow deer in the Deer Park.

Although the animals in the hand-feeding section are behind wooden fences, guests have ample opportunities to pet them when they approach to feed. Visitors who do not choose to feed or pet will enjoy watching the animals—especially the pygmy goats, who like to perform by climbing and jumping upon the various bridges, steps, and boulders placed throughout their enclosure.

The other section of the Deer Park is home to emus, llamas, miniature horses, and donkeys. Here, visitors are asked to refrain from hand-feeding. Instead, they pour food into troughs. These particular animals are actually easier to pet than those in the other section, especially when they are eating.

Visitors to the Deer Park will greatly appreciate the facility's cleanliness. The park's paved walkways are constantly being swept by Tweetsie employees. Guests needn't worry about messing up their shoes. At the exit, a hand-washing station is available for those who petted or fed the animals.

Throughout the year, Tweetsie offers special events such as the "Fourth of July Fireworks Extravaganza," the "Riders in the Sky Concert," and the "Ghost Train Halloween Festival." Animal lovers might be interested in planning their visit when the "K-9s in Flight Frisbee® Dogs" show is offered. The show is noteworthy not only because it is highly entertaining but also because its performers are dogs that have been rescued or adopted from animal shelters. These amazing dogs have been featured on numerous television programs and in magazines and newspapers. The dogs and their trainer are strong advocates for pet adoptions and use the show to educate attendees about shelter animals. Guests who attend have the special opportunity to meet the trainer and his "K-9 stars" at the conclusion of the show.

A fun way to spend a day in the Blue Ridge Mountains, Tweetsie Railroad offers a variety of entertainments suitable for all ages. For those who want to combine animal-related experiences with theme-park excitement, it is a perfect choice.

Tips

● Don't forget to browse Tweetsie Railroad's calendar and plan your visit for a day when the "K-9s in Flight Frisbee® Dogs" will be on-site.

● Tweetsie is not a great value for those visiting *solely* for the Deer Park, as tickets are priced to include all of the park's offerings. Should you purchase a cone of food to take in the Deer Park, do not stick the whole cone over the fence. If you do, one animal will snatch the entire cone from your hand and you will immediately lose all of the food. Instead, break the cone apart or pour a small amount of food in your hand. Your food will last longer, and more than one animal can partake of the tasty treat.

● Speaking of food, if you've worked up a hearty appetite after a long day at Tweetsie, you may want to head north approximately five miles to the Dan'l Boone Inn, where incredible family-style meals are served daily. Be aware, however, that you will likely have to stand in line to get in. The inn is located at 130 Hardin Street in Boone. To learn more, call 828-264-8657 or visit www.danlbooneinn.com.

Table Rock State Fish Hatchery

3419 Fish Hatchery Avenue
Morganton, N.C. 28655
Phone: 828-437-3977
Website: www.ncwildlife.org
E-mail: gene.wilson@ncwildlife.org

Hours: Open year-round Monday through Friday from 8 A.M. to 4 P.M.

Directions: The hatchery is in Burke County about 10 miles north of Morganton. From I-40 West, take Exit 103 (the Morganton/Rutherfordton exit). Turn right on Burkemont Avenue (U.S. 64), drive approximately 1 mile, and turn left on West Fleming Drive (U.S. 70). West Fleming Drive turns into Sanford Drive (U.S. 64 Bypass). After about a mile, turn left on North Green Street (N.C. 181). Travel approximately 8 miles, turn left on Fish Hatchery Road, go a little over 3 miles, and turn right on Fish Hatchery Avenue. The road dead-ends at the hatchery.

"The public is welcome to tour the hatchery . . .
or use the picnic grounds . . ."
**North Carolina Wildlife Resources
Commission website**

Table Rock State Fish Hatchery, located near Morganton, is North Carolina's only cool-water hatchery. Water temperatures at Table Rock do not drop as low in the winter as at the state's three cold-water hatcheries (also located in the mountains), thus the "cool water" classification. The North Carolina Wildlife Resources Commission constructed the hatchery in 1946. According to the commission's website, "Up to 60,000 brook, brown and rainbow trout are held at Table Rock during the winter for final grow-out before stocking in public trout water in early March. Trout stocking at the Table Rock hatchery is completed by May, when water temperatures become too warm to sustain trout."

The scenery at Table Rock State Fish Hatchery is an added attraction.

Interior of Table Rock State Fish Hatchery

During summer, the hatchery stocks channel catfish for the Community Fishing Program. Over forty lakes and one stream have been designated CFP sites. As stated on the commission's website, these locations "are intensely managed bodies of water receiving monthly stockings of catchable-sized channel catfish from April–September."

The cool-water hatchery is also where walleye, smallmouth bass, and muskellunge are raised for release into public waters. From late March until June, these fish spawn and grow, first in the hatchery and then in the ponds. It is during the spring months that the hatchery may be of special interest to visitors.

As guests drive through the gates, they are immediately in awe of the scenery before them. Seventeen square ponds stretch across the expanse—one after another—while a flume of flowing water runs beside them. In the distance, Table Rock Mountain forms a majestic backdrop.

Guests park next to the hatchery building, which will likely be the first stop on their self-guided tour. Those who visit in April, May, or June should have the opportunity to see *thousands* of fry (newly hatched fish), which, no matter the species, resemble tiny needles swimming in the water. It is an amazing sight to behold.

After the fish have grown, they are transferred to the on-site ponds. Visitors are not permitted to drive to the pond area but are allowed to walk there. Informational signs on the hatchery building direct guests to the ponds and note the type of fish contained in each one. Visitors will not see fish in the ponds unless they are being fed or come to the surface—which is not often. Interestingly, however, they *will* see frogs and tadpoles—hundreds of them—as well as a few toads. Frogs and toads are typically seen the same months fish are hatched. The most numerous frogs on the hatchery grounds are pickerel frogs. In the flume, visitors will see frogs, toads, and a variety of fish of varying sizes. As the water is clear and shallow, they can examine the fish in great detail.

Learning about the work of the North Carolina Wildlife Resources Commission and discovering how fish are raised to stock public waters is intriguing. Although not typical tourist destinations, the state's hatcheries offer the public a chance to view different stages in the life cycles of fish. The Table Rock facility is a peaceful retreat, a Burke County treasure, and a special place to spend a morning or afternoon.

Tips

- The fish hatcheries are generally closed to guests on state holidays. Before visiting any of them, call to inquire whether or not staff is available for tours or if newly hatched fish can be seen. April seems to be the best month to visit Table Rock State Fish Hatchery—but again, call first. When speaking with a staff member, ask what time fish are fed to ensure you see that activity as well. If you visit the hatchery when no fish are being hatched and arrive after the fish have been fed, you will have nothing to view but the scenery.

- Pack a lunch and enjoy the facility's picnic area.

- In case you are thinking about purchasing fish during your visit, you should note that state-operated hatcheries stock public waters and do not sell fish for private lakes or ponds.

- To learn more about the North Carolina Wildlife Resources Commission's Community Fishing Program and Fishing Tackle Loaner Program, visit www.ncwildlife.org.

Piedmont

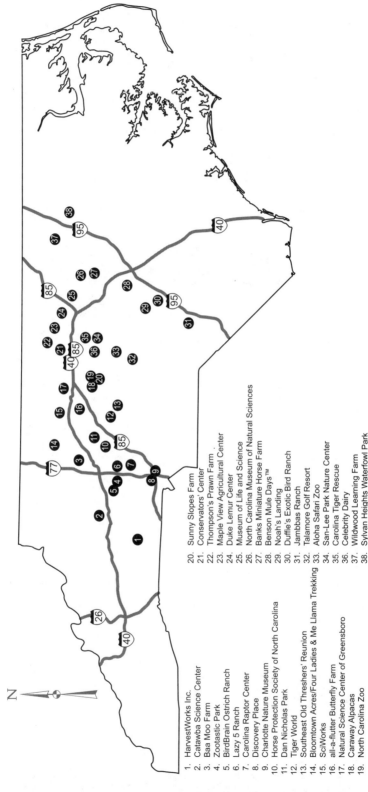

Piedmont Adventures

1. HarvestWorks Inc.
2. Catawba Science Center
3. Baa Moo Farm
4. Zootastic Park
5. BirdBrain Ostrich Ranch
6. Lazy 5 Ranch
7. Carolina Raptor Center
8. Discovery Place
9. Charlotte Nature Museum
10. Horse Protection Society of North Carolina
11. Dan Nicholas Park
12. Tiger World
13. Southeast Old Threshers' Reunion
14. Bloomtown Acres/Four Ladies & Me Llama Trekking
15. SciWorks
16. all-a-flutter Butterfly Farm
17. Natural Science Center of Greensboro
18. Caraway Alpacas
19. North Carolina Zoo
20. Sunny Slopes Farm
21. Conservators' Center
22. Thompson's Prawn Farm
23. Maple View Agricultural Center
24. Duke Lemur Center
25. Museum of Life and Science
26. North Carolina Museum of Natural Sciences
27. Banks Miniature Horse Farm
28. Benson Mule Days™
29. Noah's Landing
30. Duffie's Exotic Bird Ranch
31. Jambbas Ranch
32. Talamore Golf Resort
33. Aloha Safari Zoo
34. San-Lee Park Nature Center
35. Carolina Tiger Rescue
36. Celebrity Dairy
37. Wildwood Learning Farm
38. Sylvan Heights Waterfowl Park

Q-tip and Fuzzy are HarvestWorks' resident alpacas.

HarvestWorks Inc.

891 North Post Road
Shelby, N.C. 28150
Phone: 704-487-7777
Website: www.HarvestWorksInc.org
E-mail: Tours@HarvestWorksInc.org

Hours: Open year-round Monday through Friday from 8 A.M. to 4 P.M. Weekend hours are seasonal; the facility typically operates from 10 A.M. to 4 P.M. on weekends from April through September. Phone or visit the website for dates, hours, and special-event listings.

Directions: From U.S. 74 West at Shelby in Cleveland County, bear right on East Marion Street (U.S. 74 Business), drive 1.5 miles, bear right on North Post Road (N.C. 180), and continue approximately 2 miles. HarvestWorks is on the left.

"... meet and feed the awesome miniature animals!"
HarvestWorks Inc. brochure

HarvestWorks' turkey may be the most handsome in the state.

Travelers who find themselves in Shelby should make plans to visit Harvest-Works Inc. A partner company to Cleveland Vocational Industries, HarvestWorks serves children and adults with developmental disabilities. Under the supervision of trained professionals, its clients participate in educational and recreational projects designed to enhance their social skills, develop their creativity, and help them attain personal goals. Many of their assignments in the unique agricultural environment of HarvestWorks involve farm-related activities like working in greenhouses and car-ing for animals. One of the largest human-service providers in Cleveland County, HarvestWorks has the mission of enriching "the lifestyles of individuals with disa-bilities by integrating the community into their daily lives." When members of the public visit HarvestWorks, clients are able to "socialize, meet new people, have fun, work, learn, love, and be a part of the community." Attracting people to Harvest-Works, which opened to the public in 2009, is likely not a difficult task, as its rural atmosphere and varied activities make the twenty-plus-acre facility—soon to double in size—a pleasurable outing for anyone.

Upon arriving, visitors should check in at the main building. There, staff mem-bers will provide information regarding available activities and take payment for certain attractions. The restaurant inside the building serves lunch Monday through Friday and when the facility is open on weekends. Also located in the building is the gift shop, where crafts made by HarvestWorks' clients are available for purchase. The gift shop is open year-round and can be visited during regular hours, seasonal week-ends, and special events.

Outside, visitors can explore the grounds and enjoy various attractions and activities including gem mining, a tractor-and-wagon ride, greenhouses, a "Moon Bounce" inflatable, a playground, walking trails, and a petting zoo. At the gem mine, colorful stones and mineral specimens abound. The tractor-and-wagon ride offers a relaxing jaunt to points of interest around the farm. The greenhouses should not be overlooked, as visitors can view organic vegetables as well as bluegill sunfish and tilapia during certain months of the year. The fish are utilized in HarvestWorks' restaurant and are also sold to the public. At the greenhouses, guests might also have a chance to see the many worms grown on the farm. Worm castings are used by HarvestWorks to create Wiggly Grow™, a natural liquid fertilizer that is sold in recycled containers.

HarvestWorks' main attraction is its petting zoo. The animals there are some of the most gentle in the state. The residents include Donkey-Donkey, a miniature donkey that politely begs visitors to rub his neck by laying his head sideways over the gate to his enclosure; Peanut Butter, a miniature horse that competes with Donkey-Donkey for attention; El Toro and Isabella, a pair of miniature zebus; Thorn, a miniature ram; Dandelion and Amber, two miniature sheep; Sugar, a miniature goat; Q-tip and Fuzzy, a pair of alpacas; Charlotte and Wilbur, two miniature pot-bellied pigs; Franklin, an African spur thigh tortoise; several rabbits; chickens; and a pair of magnificent turkeys. If a handler is on-site, visitors can feed the animals and be educated about them. For those who pet or feed the animals, a hand-washing station is available.

In addition to daily and seasonal activities, HarvestWorks offers various special events throughout the year. During the "Spring Farm Tour," held annually in May, visitors can partake of HarvestWorks' regular attractions, learn about upcoming events, hear live musical performances, and perhaps watch a puppet show. Other yearly programs include the patriotic "Flag Day Ceremony," the popular "Kid-Friendly Halloween Trail Ride," and the fun, family-oriented "Christmas on the Farm" celebration.

HarvestWorks diligently serves the community by assisting those in need and providing a venue for the enjoyment of inexpensive, educational, and safe recreation. In an effort to expand its programs, HarvestWorks is working to construct a handicapped-accessible playground and water park, to augment the gem-mine operation with an on-site lapidary, and to increase the number of animals in the petting zoo.

Tourists passing through Shelby are encouraged to stop at HarvestWorks, where they can meet the folks who make this organization a success, greet the clients, enjoy activities, and visit with adorable miniature animals that are guaranteed to put a smile in anyone's heart.

Tips

- The number of animals at HarvestWorks is small, so you may want to visit during a special-event program, particularly the "Spring Farm Tour."

- Most attractions including the petting zoo are free; should you see a two-dollar fee posted on the HarvestWorks website, this information is incorrect. Fees are charged for gem mining, food, gift-shop items, and to attend special-event programs.

● Activities listed as being available at HarvestWorks are generally offered on weekends and during special events; not all activities may be available during the week. The petting zoo, however, is available for visits whenever HarvestWorks is open.

● If you are especially interested in seeing the fish or worms, call ahead to learn what months they will be on view in the greenhouse.

● If you plan to eat at the restaurant, especially on a weekend or during a special-event program, call and confirm its hours of operation.

Catawba Science Center

243 Third Avenue NE
Hickory, N.C. 28601
Phone: 828-322-8169
Website: www.catawbascience.org
E-mail: info@catawbascience.org

Hours: Open year-round Tuesday through Friday from 10 A.M. to 5 P.M., Saturday from 10 A.M. to 4 P.M., and Sunday from 1 P.M. to 4 P.M. Closed on Mondays except for Martin Luther King Jr. Day, Easter Monday, Memorial Day, and Labor Day.

Directions: From I-40 West in Catawba County, take Exit 125 (the Hickory exit) and turn right on Lenoir Rhyne Boulevard. Travel approximately 1.5 miles and turn left on First Avenue SE. In less than 0.5 mile, turn right on Fifth Street SE, then bear right on Highland Avenue SE. Turn left on Sixth Street SE, which becomes Third Avenue NE. The center is on the right.

"Get an up-close look at different species of sharks and stingrays in CSC's marine touch pool . . ."
Catawba Science Center website

In 1997, *Reader's Digest* magazine named Hickory, North Carolina, the tenth-best place to live and raise a family in the United States. Hickory has also been declared an "All-America City" on three separate occasions. According to the Hickory Metro Convention and Visitors Bureau website, the area has "small town charm and big city amenities, including one of the best convention centers in North Carolina."

Located in the rolling foothills of the Blue Ridge Mountains, Hickory offers visitors a variety of recreational parks and outdoor activities. It also provides an impressive array of cultural attractions, one being Catawba Science Center, named after the county in which it resides. Founded in 1975, the center was originally housed in a four-thousand-square-foot Victorian structure. During the 1980s, it became evident a new facility was needed to support the growing attendance. By 1986, the community identified the former Hickory High School as an appropriate facility to house both Catawba Science Center and other area cultural organizations. After $3 million was raised and renovations were completed, the center moved into its new space in April 1986.

Since that time, Catawba Science Center has continued to expand its facility, exhibits, programs, and activities. The focus of its exhibits is on physical, natural, and earth sciences. For example, hands-on displays in an area called Energy Avenue encourage visitors to explore light, electricity, and sound. EarthWatch Center features an impressive exhibit in which guests can sit at a table, push a button, and experience what an earthquake feels like. Visitors who wish to learn about the stars and planets can tour the Hall of Astronomy or attend one of the daily shows in the state-of-the-art Milholland Planetarium.

An Amazon leaf fish illustrates how camouflage is used to catch prey.

Guests can examine a horn shark in the marine touch pool.
PHOTOGRAPH COURTESY OF CATAWBA SCIENCE CENTER

For animal enthusiasts, the Naturalist Center houses an impressive collection of reptiles, amphibians, insects, and arachnids. Visitors may encounter a juvenile American alligator, an African spur thigh tortoise, a desert tortoise, a tokay gecko, a Sudan plated lizard, a tomato frog, Madagascar hissing cockroaches, emperor scorpions, and a rose-haired tarantula. One of the most interesting specimens is the tomato frog. A native of Madagascar, it is red in color and resembles a ripe tomato. When threatened or taken as prey, it secretes a glue-like substance that forces its captor to release it.

On weekends, public demonstrations allow visitors to meet residents of the Naturalist Center on an up-close and personal basis. Among the programs are "Meet the Gator," "Amazing Arthropods," "Learning About Lizards," "Meet the Skink," and "Slithering Snakes."

Besides living specimens, the Naturalist Center exhibits preserved examples of North Carolina wildlife. Those displays and others of fossils, shells, rocks, and minerals provide continuous hands-on learning opportunities for visitors of all ages.

For many, the highlight of the center is the Saltwater Aquarium Gallery. The gallery features a marine touch pool showcasing live sharks and stingrays. Catawba Science Center was the first facility in North Carolina to exhibit sharks in this manner. At the pool, visitors have the incredible opportunity to touch horn sharks and white-spotted and brown-banded bamboo sharks. Native to the Pacific Ocean, these docile sharks average three to three and a half feet in length at maturity. The other sea life in the marine touch pool includes lookdown fish and Southern and cownose stingrays, all of which reside in the Atlantic Ocean and frequent the waters off North Carolina. To further visitors' experiences at the pool, live shark feedings—informative, engaging, and highly popular events—are presented daily.

The Saltwater Aquarium Gallery also features a coastal Carolina marine touch pool. This pool contains sea life such as reef fish, hermit crabs, horseshoe crabs, conchs, sea urchins, and sea stars. Visitors can touch the marine life but are reminded to keep animals underwater at all times. Aquariums in this exhibit house a nice selection of vibrant fish like blue tang, flame angel, clownfish, raccoon butterfly, firefish, and others.

Exiting the saltwater exhibits, visitors will next enter the Freshwater Aquarium Gallery. Here, they will find themselves in a creatively designed exhibit called Expedition Amazon. The display visitors will immediately notice is Amazon Basin, which showcases several varieties of turtles; fish, including ocellated river stingrays; a Brazilian rainbow boa; an Amazon tree boa; a barred parakeet; a skeleton tarantula; and poison dart frogs.

Another exhibit in this area is a series of biotope aquariums featuring fish species native to the whitewater, brackish, and blackwater streams of South America. Visitors will enjoy seeing an assortment of predator, camouflaged, and endangered species up close. The camouflaged species aquarium, which houses fish with descriptive names like twig catfish, Amazon leaf fish, and South American bumblebee catfish, contains the most interesting and unique-looking specimens in the exhibit.

The Amazon Oxbow, another exhibit in Expedition Amazon, contains fish found within an Amazon oxbow lake. Oxbows are crescent-shaped lakes in lowland Amazonia that form when a river changes course. These lakes are typically warmer and more acidic than the Amazon. This aquarium, which is larger than the others in the exhibit, includes redtail catfish, tiger shovelnose catfish, silver arowana fish, and peacock bass.

The most memorable aquarium in Expedition Amazon is the electric eel habitat. This exhibit features an LED display that is wired to probes in the eel's tank. Visitors can therefore see lights and hear sounds produced by the eel's electrical discharges. Members of the knifefish family, electric eels can grow up to six feet in length and have the ability to generate powerful electrical shocks for hunting and self-defense. The electric eel at Catawba Science Center does not have to worry about hunting, however, as she is fed shrimp and worms every other day.

In addition to its permanent displays, the center hosts a variety of traveling exhibits. One such exhibit is the Flutter-By Butterfly Habitat, which is offered to the public every two or three years. This display allows visitors the chance to interact with hundreds of native and semitropical butterflies and moths in an outdoor flower garden.

Catawba Science Center is a place of wonderment and education for guests of all ages. Tourists in the Hickory area should indeed make plans to visit.

Tips

● If you are visiting without children, make sure you do not overlook the Naturalist Center. It is not in the same building as the aquariums and the planetarium.

● If the day is nice, you may also want to visit Bakers Mountain Park. Located approximately twelve miles from the center, Bakers Mountain is the highest point (1,780 feet) in Catawba County. Six miles of trails allow visitors to explore a variety of wildlife and plants, while an observation point near the top provides a spectacular view of the area. The park is located at 6680 Bakers Mountain Road in Hickory. To learn more, call 828-324-8461 or visit www.co.catawba.nc.us/depts/parks/Bakrmain.asp.

Baa Moo Farm

2529 Jennings Road
Olin, N.C. 28660
Phone: 704-876-1732
E-mail: baamoo@bellsouth.net

Hours: Open from 9 A.M. to 2 P.M. twice a year on the second Saturdays of May and October. Advance reservations are required at other times.

Directions: From I-77 North in Iredell County north of Statesville, take Exit 59, turn left on Tomlin Mill Road, travel approximately 1 mile, turn right on Jennings Road, and drive about 4.5 miles. The farm is on the left.

$ 🚻 🥤 🎪 🏛

"Experience the feeling of open country and the freedom of farm life!"
Baa Moo Farm brochure

Entrance to Baa Moo Farm

Baa Moo and a bottle of milk! It's a farmer's life indeed! For anyone who has ever longed to partake of life on an old-fashioned farm, a trip to Olin is a necessity. Baa Moo Farm, situated on sixty-five acres in Iredell County, allows tourists—city slickers included—to participate in a variety of hands-on farm-related activities.

Owned and operated by Calvin and Judy Sell, Baa Moo Farm opened for tours in September 1994. Calvin was raised on a tobacco and dairy farm in Walkertown, North Carolina, and attended North Carolina State University. In 1979, he and Judy purchased a farm and began raising sheep and cattle. To support the farm financially, Calvin undertook another line of work, but the strain of two occupations did not help him achieve his goal for Baa Moo. Therefore, the couple began researching ideas that would allow the farm to sustain itself. They soon realized agricultural tourism, or agritourism, would be "the perfect solution."

Prior to opening for agricultural tours, the Sells met with elementary-school officials to plan farm-related activities that would complement the curriculum for kindergarten and first-grade students. Judy wanted to show children where food comes from and how it is produced. This was important to her, she says, because "many children have never thought of food coming from anywhere but the grocery store." In developing educational tours and expanding them to attract the general public, the Sells wanted to create an experience that would allow each guest to have an opportunity "to be a part of every facet of the farm without feeling rushed or crowded," Judy says.

During the tour, Calvin makes a point of explaining how agricultural tourists are the farm's main "crop." Although the farm has other sources of revenue (among them selling cattle and sheep for food, leasing Texas longhorn calves and sheep for junior rodeos, selling wool from sheep, and producing grain and hay), admission fees provide the largest percentage of income. Tours of the farm are available by advance

Guests can bottle-feed calves at Baa Moo Farm.

reservation from April to November. However, on the second Saturdays of May and October, Baa Moo Farm opens its doors to the general public. Referred to as "Family Days," these are events in which visitors can observe, participate in, and become educated about farm life and animals.

Visitors to the Family Day events should check in at the Barnyard General Store, where admission is collected, souvenirs and drinks are sold, and staff is on hand to explain the day's events. Upon leaving the general store, guests will immediately hear a chorus of welcoming moos. The sounds originate from a white building with red doors where triangular cutouts allow the occupants—adorable black-and-white and sometimes brown calves—to stick their heads out. The calves eagerly await tourists, who, with the help of staff, are given bottles of milk to feed them. Visitors may be surprised to learn that bottle-feeding a calf is not as easy as it looks. Children love being face to face with these precious yearlings; even adults can't get enough of their cute countenances. All in all, the calves can easily be declared the stars of the farm.

Guests can walk the farm at their leisure to peruse, and in some instances pet, the resident pigs, donkeys, goats, horses, ducks, and peacocks. At the sheep pen, staff members dispense food that guests can hand-feed to the appreciative flock. Next to the sheep pen is a large coop where visitors, with assistance from staff, can gather eggs and feed chickens. Upon entering the large barn, guests will meet Baa Moo Farm's milk cow. On tour days, the gentle bovine is brought in from pasture to demonstrate the ancient art of milking. Tourists with an adventurous spirit can try their hand at milking, while others can simply view the process.

After walking the grounds, visitors may want to rest their feet by taking a wagon ride through the farm's woods, fields, and streams. During the excursion, Calvin Sell, who operates the wagon, stops by his herd of Texas longhorn cattle to discuss the breed and indulge guests with an up-close view. These grand animals seem to know exactly where the wagon will stop and appear to enjoy displaying their impressive horns to flashing cameras.

Visitors should not leave without taking advantage of the staged photo opportunities. For example, they can climb aboard a John Deere tractor, sit behind the wheel, and appear as though they are real-life farmers. It makes a wonderful souvenir of an enjoyable day. However, even without a photograph, guests will long remember the sights and sounds of Baa Moo Farm.

Tips

- To really enjoy your visit, wear clothes you don't mind getting dirty, and arrive before noon to participate in everything the farm has to offer. For a fun farm experience, let the chickens peck the corn from your hand—it doesn't hurt—instead of throwing it on the ground.

- Call or verify directions on the farm's website, as GPS units and MapQuest have been known to lead visitors astray.

Zootastic Park

448 Pilch Road
Troutman, N.C. 28166
Phone: 888-966-0069 or 704-245-6446
Website: www.zootasticpark.com
E-mail: info@zootasticpark.com

Hours: Open Monday through Saturday from 9 A.M. to 5 P.M. and Sunday from 1 P.M. to 5 P.M. The park is closed during winter but opens for special holiday events.

Directions: From I-77 South in Iredell County, take Exit 42 (the Troutman exit). Turn left off the exit onto U.S. 21, travel approximately 1 mile, turn right on Ostwalt-Amity Road, drive about 1.5 miles, and turn left on Pilch Road. The park is on the left after 0.5 mile.

"Fantastic Fun for All Ages!"
Zootastic Park brochure

Zootastic Park is North Carolina's newest animal attraction. Scottie Brown, the founder and owner, created the park to share his love and knowledge of animals and to provide a fun and educational attraction for families. In March 2010, Brown, along with son Jerod, daughter Sarah, and son-in-law Shawn, opened the park to the public.

Zootastic Park is not your average animal attraction. It was constructed to look and feel like an old-time Western town. As soon as visitors enter the driveway, they begin to see rustic buildings, wagons, and other Western-themed items.

Upon stepping inside the main entrance, which resembles a large barn, guests have the option of a guided or self-guided tour. The better choice—and the one preferred by Zootastic staff—is the guided tour, as guests will learn about and interact with the animals instead of just looking at them. Guided tours begin every thirty minutes. The interest level of participants determine how long they last.

Visitors commence their tour inside the Sheriff's Office, where several wild creatures—a serval, a Patagonian cavy, and a skunk—are held in the town's jail. Flower the skunk is brought out for visitors to examine and pet. The opportunity to touch an animal with such a "stinky" reputation is a highlight of the tour.

The next stop is the Assayer's Office, which houses several Gunnison's prairie dogs. One of the prairie dogs is typically removed from its habitat so visitors can observe and pet it.

The Post Office contains enclosures, but they are not for mail. Instead, they hold a variety of reptiles including a ball python, a corn snake, a bearded dragon, a green iguana, and a fat tail gecko. The tour guide will likely bring out a number of reptiles for visitors to touch; encounters are usually with the corn snake, the bearded dragon—a reptile made famous in the movie *Holes*—and the fat tail gecko. Visitors

A serval in the park's re-created "jail"

Visitors get an up-close view of a fat tail gecko.

will also see a ferret and a juvenile African crested porcupine. The ferret might also be brought out for petting.

All towns require a Barber Shop, but no haircuts are given in Zootastic Park's salon. Visitors are entertained by the squawks, chirps, and whistles of the birds that call the shop home. They especially enjoy meeting Marley, a Moluccan cockatoo, and Rainbow the macaw.

Beyond the Barber Shop are the General Store, which houses a gift shop, and the Saloon, where snacks are available.

After completing the indoor tour, visitors are taken outside, where a multitude of animals awaits discovery. These include African spur thigh tortoises, a raccoon, a coati, chinchillas, a North American porcupine, pheasants, and guineafowl. The North American porcupine is a treat, as it is a species not often seen at North Carolina animal parks.

On the Safari Trail, visitors accompany their guide on a covered walkway to view and learn about blackbuck antelopes, goats, pot-bellied pigs, donkeys, Barbary sheep, American bison, an alpaca, a llama, Texas longhorns, a zebra, rheas, ostriches, and emus. Guests are allowed to pet some of these animals—the tour guide tells which can be petted and which cannot—if they approach the fence.

The last stop is an extremely large barn. Inside, visitors will meet a variety of animals, some typical of a barnyard and others not expected there. Animals visitors would expect to see include a pony, sheep, goats, rabbits, horses, cows, chickens, and turkeys. Others not so common are a kangaroo, a camel, an African crested porcupine, and a yellow-knobbed curassow. Several pig-tailed macaques are directly outside the barn.

Upon completing their tour, guests are at their leisure to stroll the grounds, browse the general store, or watch one of Zootastic Park's comical Wild West shows.

As the park is still in development, visitors will discover new attractions each time they return. Brown is working on the second half of the Western town and plans to add more animals—perhaps a giraffe barn where visitors can walk on an elevated platform and view the animals at eye level. He also hopes to offer a tram ride along the Safari Trail and create new programs and events. Currently, Zootastic Park offers several holiday events. Two of them—"Bootastic" and "Christmas Wonderland of Lights"—are not to be missed. "Bootastic" is a Halloween event and includes a haunted house, a haunted trail ride, a not-so-scary "bootastic" show, and a family night full of special activities. During "Christmas Wonderland of Lights," visitors can view more than one million lights over the course of a two-mile drive. At the end, they will enjoy a light show set to music in the Western town. Christmas revelers can meet Santa Claus, ride ponies around Christmas trees, visit the petting zoo, and roast marshmallows.

Everyone who visits this Western-themed animal attraction will have a fun and educational experience. Zootastic Park is definitely a one-of-a-kind Iredell County attraction.

Tip

- Be sure to choose a guided tour when given the option.

~~~~~~

BirdBrain Ostrich Ranch

6691 Little Mountain Road
Sherrills Ford, N.C. 28673
Phone: 704-483-1620
Website: www.birdbrainranch.com
E-mail: info@birdbrainranch.com

Hours: The ranch is typically open to the public year-round on weekends after 1 P.M.; however, the staff prefers advance reservations. Group tours are by advance reservation only.

Directions: The ranch is west of Sherrills Ford in Catawba County. From I-77 South, take Exit 36 (the Mooresville/Lincolnton exit) and turn right on N.C. 150. Travel approximately 9 miles, turn right on Little Mountain Road, and drive about 2 miles. The ranch is on the left.

> "BirdBrain Ostrich Ranch will not only amaze the kids . . . it's guaranteed to be an experience for all ages!!"
> BirdBrain Ostrich Ranch postcard

Most people would jump at the chance to board a time machine and return to the age of dinosaurs. Although that opportunity does not exist, visitors can drive a car to Sherrills Ford and experience an up-close encounter with what may be *Tyrannosaurus rex*'s nearest relative.

Pat Roberts and Mike Todd, the owners of BirdBrain Ostrich Ranch, begin farming ostriches in 1993. They purchased their seventeen-acre Catawba County farm in 1996 with the goal of raising wholesome meat for the local market. Roberts and Todd opened their farm to the public because they wanted to share facts about this prehistoric bird with visitors. For example, one of the "Fun Facts" presented on the ranch's educational handout is that "ostrich[es] have more in common with dinosaurs than other types of animals or birds."

The most important factor in Roberts and Todd's decision to offer tours was a desire to inform consumers about food quality. For example, the ostriches raised at BirdBrain are nourished without the use of chemicals, steroids, or growth hormones. The owners talk a great deal about why this is important, as well as how diet, fresh water, and clean water containers play a major role in determining the taste and overall condition of the meat produced.

When guests arrive at the ranch, they are greeted by a multitude of curious ostrich eyes with long eyelashes—actually tiny feathers—staring at them from behind a fence. After Roberts or Todd offers a greeting, the tour begins inside a small building. Guests are given a brief history of the ostrich industry. They learn that ostriches

The ostrich may be the nearest relative of a Tyrannosaurus rex.

Bart is one of many ostriches at the ranch.

are the largest of all birds, are native to Africa, were first imported to the United States in the late 1800s, were first sought for their plumage, and were hunted for their hides and meat. These facts are illustrated through antique postcards, catalogs, engravings, and stock certificates. The discussion progresses to the present and examines the types of goods made from ostriches today. Visitors are shown examples of items such as boots, wallets, upholstery, feathers, carved eggs, and soaps.

Upon exiting the building, guests can get up-close views of approximately fifty ostriches in enclosures. One of the highlights of the tour is the discussion of the breeding season. During that time, males—called roosters—make loud, booming-type sounds and perform elaborate dance-like displays with their wings. As the level of testosterone increases in their bodies, their legs and beaks turn pink to red in color. It is quite something to behold for those who visit during breeding season. Roosters, according to the ranch's "Fun Facts," are "black and white and produce the best plume feathers."

Female ostriches, or hens, have dull gray feathers. But what they don't have in plumage they make up for in eggs. An ostrich hen can lay one egg every forty-eight hours. An ostrich egg—which is the largest egg in the world—can weigh three to five pounds. Visitors often ask if ostrich eggs are edible, and the answer is yes. According to Todd, some people with allergies to chicken eggs can actually consume ostrich eggs without a problem. For those who have never viewed an ostrich egg, plenty can be seen at the ranch.

Roberts and Todd clearly have a personal relationship with their ostriches and enjoy sharing their knowledge with the public. That connection is best seen when they proudly introduce guests to Bart, who was hatched in 1993 and is the ranch's original rooster.

Visitors to BirdBrain Ostrich Ranch will depart with knowledge about ostriches and a greater awareness of food quality and production. But beyond the information they glean, they will find it amazing to stand in proximity to birds, some over ten feet tall, with such large eyes, giant beaks, and massive reptilian-looking legs and toes. It is when scrutinizing those legs and toes that they may get a sense of the birds' prehistoric ancestors and imagine, just for a moment, that they are in the presence of living dinosaurs.

Tips

- It is best to call ahead to ensure someone will be on the property to give a tour. Chicks hatch from spring through fall, so if you would like a special treat, call ahead and ask when baby ostriches can be seen.

- Ostrich meat is sold on-site, so bring a cooler if you plan to make a purchase. If you do not want to buy meat but would like to sample it, travel a few miles down the road to the Landing Restaurant at Lake Norman Motel, where BirdBrain ostrich burgers are sold. The restaurant is located at 4491 Slanting Bridge Road in Sherrills Ford. To learn more, call 828-478-5944 or visit www.lakenormanmotel.net.

- If you have time, consider planning your tour of Lazy 5 Ranch (see pages 77–81) for the same day, as it is approximately twenty-one miles away.

Lazy 5 Ranch

15100 Mooresville Road
Mooresville, N.C. 28115
Phone: 704-663-5100
Website: www.lazy5ranch.com
E-mail: Lazy5Ranch@aol.com

Hours: Open year-round Monday through Saturday from 9 A.M. until one hour before sunset and Sunday from 1 P.M. until one hour before sunset.

Lazy 5 Ranch allows visitors to go on safari without purchasing a passport.

Directions: From I-77 in southern Iredell County, take Exit 36 at Mooresville and follow N.C. 150 East for 10 miles. The ranch is on the left.

~~~~~~

"Come feed animals from around the world!"
Lazy 5 Ranch brochure

Henry Hampton—a man well known from his thirty-five years of raising exotic animals—had a desire to create a park where children and adults could learn about and enjoy his unique collection. He established a plan to create a park in Mooresville. Hampton's son suggested the name Lazy 5 Ranch, as the family, according to the park's website, "consisted of 5 'lazy' people." In 1993, the state's only drive-through animal park opened to the public. As stated in Lazy 5 Ranch's exhibit catalog, the ranch's purpose is to not only educate and entertain but also to help in "the recovery of several endangered species including the Grevy's zebra, scimitar horned oryx and ring-tailed lemur." The scimitar horned oryx, native to Africa, is a highly endangered species. According to the ranch's exhibit catalog, the myth of the unicorn was derived from this animal, due to the fact that, when viewed from the side, its face resembles that of a horse and appears to have a single, curved horn.

Visitors to Lazy 5 Ranch will embark on a three-and-a-half-mile adventure that features over 750 animals from six continents. All but a few can be observed freely roaming the property. When guests stop at the entrance gate, they will be asked if

A giraffe awaits the stop of a horse-drawn wagon at Lazy 5 Ranch.

they have reservations for a wagon ride (those without reservations may luck out and find extra seats available) or if they will be driving through the park. If entering in a car, visitors purchase buckets of food at the gate and then proceed to the safari trail. Those riding on a wagon will park and walk to the loading area. A bucket of food is included in the price of the wagon ride and will be waiting on board. No matter what their mode of transportation, however, visitors should first visit the Trading Post and purchase a Lazy 5 Ranch exhibit catalog. The catalog's listings of animals and pertinent facts about them make the journey more enjoyable *and* educational.

As the safari trail is best experienced from a seat on a wagon, the description below is given from that point of view. Draft horses pull the wagons. As soon as they take their first step, the adventure begins. The sound of horses' hooves, the clanking of their gear, and the jostling of the wagon create an environment that removes guests from present-day concerns. As the wagon makes its way onto the trail, animals approach from all different directions and proceed to follow beside and behind it. Anxious and excited visitors begin oohing, aahing, and pointing. At several spots along the trail, the driver will stop so guests can pet and feed the animals. The driver will also talk about the animals and present interesting facts about particular species. Animals that often follow the wagons or wait near the entrance of the trail include ostriches, emus, rheas, llamas, Vietnamese pot-bellied pigs, European fallow deer, nilgais, and elands. The elands make a big impression. Native to Africa, they are the largest and perhaps most beautiful of the antelope species.

At one stop, the driver leads the wagon into a large, open field. Here, visitors are literally at face level with a diverse collection of animals. As soon as the wagon stops, animals that were grazing or lying in the field take notice and begin to slowly approach. Visitors—with buckets in hand—excitedly await their arrival. They may see wildebeests, water buffalo, American bison, Scottish Highland cattle, Brahma bulls, and yaks, as well as the smaller animals that continually follow the wagon.

The wildebeests, native to Africa, are the most captivating animals on the safari trail, as it is not often that people can see them on an up-close basis. Sitting on a wagon surrounded by a great number of large animals is truly an amazing and memorable experience. This stop also offers an opportunity for some impressive photographs.

On the way to the next stop, the wagon will likely pass a large herd of Watusi cattle, the largest horned cattle in the world. Because of the animals' long horns, the wagon does not stop; visitors are not permitted to feed or pet the cattle. Beyond the cattle is a Southern white rhinoceros that is kept in its own habitat and does not roam freely. Native to Africa, the rhinoceros is a critically endangered species. Just past the rhinoceros habitat is the giraffe barn. Visitors standing on the wagon are at the perfect height to feed the giraffes. For many, the giraffe barn is a highlight of the trip.

Heading toward the exit, visitors will continue to see a large number of animals, and the driver will stop several times to allow additional feeding and petting. Upon disembarking the wagon, visitors can explore Lazy 5 Ranch's exhibit and petting areas. In these areas, certain animals can be fed and petted, while others can only be observed. Animals encountered here may include kangaroos, dromedary camels, miniature Sicilian donkeys, llamas, black-tailed prairie dogs, ring-tailed lemurs, Flemish giant rabbits, and various species of goats. Lazy 5 Ranch displays a large number of birds, including varieties of pigeons, pheasants, chickens, and an East African crowned crane. It also has a beautiful walk-through aviary that includes doves, ducks, and other species.

After viewing the animals, visitors can enjoy the playground, pick up a souvenir at the Trading Post, or grab a bite to eat at the snack shop. Lazy 5 endeavors to provide a "constantly changing environment by adding new exhibits as well as increasing the variety of animals seen in the drive through safari areas," according to the ranch's website. Guests will likely encounter a new species no matter how many times they visit. Besides, where else can they go on safari without packing a suitcase, purchasing a passport, or boarding a plane?

Tips

- It cannot be stressed enough that a wagon ride is the best way to experience Lazy 5 Ranch, as the animals are most accessible. To ensure a seat on a wagon, reserve a spot ahead of time. Should you choose to drive through in your car, be aware that animals—particularly the small ones—may stand on your car door to reach the food. That will depend on how you hold your food bucket. Also, you may have food pellets strewn throughout your car if you make the mistake of holding your bucket in your lap and letting the animals reach in through the window.

The best tip for feeding from a car is to hold the food bucket firmly at arm's-length outside the car window. If driving through Lazy 5 Ranch, try to arrive early to beat the crowd. That way, you won't feel rushed to move on after stopping to feed the animals. Also, be sure to read the ranch's rules if driving through in your car. The rules will be given to you before entering; they list a few animals that should not be petted or fed.

● Note that Lazy 5 Ranch does not accept debit or credit cards.

● After touring Lazy 5 Ranch, you may want to head to BirdBrain Ostrich Ranch (see pages 74–77), which is about twenty-one miles away.

Carolina Raptor Center

6000 Sample Road
Huntersville, N.C. 28078
Phone: 704-875-6521
Website: www.carolinaraptorcenter.org
E-mail: Staff directory available online

Hours: From April to October, the center is open Monday through Saturday from 10 A.M. to 5 P.M. and Sunday from noon to 5 P.M. From November to March, it is open Wednesday through Saturday from 10 A.M. to 5 P.M. and Sunday from noon to 5 p.m. It is closed Thanksgiving, Christmas, and New Year's.

Directions: From I-77 South in Mecklenburg County north of Charlotte, take Exit 23 (the Gilead Road exit) and turn right. Travel approximately 1 mile, turn left on McCoy Road, drive about 2 miles, and turn right on Hambright Road. After approximately 1.5 miles, turn left on Beatties Ford Road, drive about 1 mile, and turn right on Sample Road. The center is on the left.

"Come Visit, Come Learn, Come Be Amazed!"
Carolina Raptor Center Trail Guide

Willow, a barn owl, can be seen in the "Backyard Tails Free Flight Program."
PHOTOGRAPH COURTESY OF
CAROLINA RAPTOR CENTER

Located on fifty-seven-acres in Latta Plantation Nature Preserve, the Carolina Raptor Center offers a chance to observe an outstanding collection of birds of prey. More importantly, the center educates visitors about their role in conserving these amazing creatures.

The facility, which began as a rehabilitation center at the University of North Carolina at Charlotte, is dedicated to rehabilitating injured and orphaned raptors. Its goal is to release the birds back into the wild. Each year, it cares for approximately seven hundred injured or orphaned raptors, the majority of which are released. Some, however, are unable to be released and become permanent residents. It is these raptors that deliver a strong message about environmental stewardship to visitors walking the self-guided education trail.

When visitors arrive at the center, they are given a trail map that denotes the types of raptors to be seen and the rules to be followed. They should also pick up a listing of the day's programs before proceeding outside. Exiting the center, guests follow a dirt trail through a partially wooded area past numerous aviaries. As they stop at each enclosure, they will likely be captivated by the awesome beauty of the birds yet grieved by the injuries and circumstances that brought them to the Carolina Raptor Center.

Among the large variety of raptors at the center are American kestrels, bald eagles, golden eagles, barn owls, barred owls, short-eared owls, long-eared owls, Eastern screech owls, great horned owls, broad-winged hawks, Cooper's hawks, Harris hawks, red-shouldered hawks, red-tailed hawks, rough-legged hawks, sharp-shinned hawks, merlins, Mississippi kites, Northern harriers, peregrine falcons, black vultures, and turkey vultures. These include a host of remarkable personalities. Visitors may have a chance to view Cinnamon, an American kestrel, and Willow, a barn owl, both of which were illegally raised by humans. At the eagle aviary, they will learn the story of Derek and Savannah, two resident bald eagles whose eaglets were the first to be hatched in captivity in North Carolina. The eaglets were eventually released into the wild.

Near the beginning of the trail is the weathering area. Here, typically on weekends, Carolina Raptor Center staff bring out four or five birds for a fascinating and educational program. They talk about raptors in general, discuss why those particular birds reside at the center, and educate attendees on how they can actively engage in conservation and protection of raptors. Attendees are asked what they think is the most frequent cause of injuries to raptors. Many guess gunshot wounds, others say animal attacks, and some reply crashing into windows. They are astonished when the staff member reveals that colliding with cars is the number-one cause. The disheartening fact is that everyone in attendance has likely been guilty of an act that can cause such a disaster. Everyone is aware that littering is illegal. But many people think nothing of throwing apple cores, banana peels, or other food items on the roadside. The act may perhaps be justified because it will feed a hungry animal. Indeed, the food lures rabbits and small rodents like mice—raptors' prey—to the roadside. And once a raptor locks onto that prey and does not see approaching vehicles, a collision may ensue. It is incredible how such a small act most people don't even think about can have a detrimental effect on the environment. It is messages like this that the Carolina Raptor Center shares with the community. Staff members discuss other issues that cause raptors to reside at the center as well.

Other programs offered at certain times each week, month, or season include a "Vulture Feeding," the "Behind the Scenes Tour," "Meet the Keeper," "Trail Trivia Tours," and the "Backyard Tails Free Flight Program." During the Behind the Scenes

Adler, a bald eagle, is a permanent resident of Carolina Raptor Center.
PHOTOGRAPH COURTESY OF
CAROLINA RAPTOR CENTER

Tour, visitors explore the education trail, visit the raptor hospital, and see sights not generally available to the public.

Special-event programs are also offered throughout the year. Two of the most popular are "PhotoWild" and "Halloween Hoot-n-Howl." "PhotoWild," typically offered twice a year—in spring and fall—allows photographers a four-hour shoot with resident raptors. "Halloween Hoot-n-Howl" features activities such as book readings, costume contests, hayrides, and raptor presentations.

No matter what type of program or event is offered at the Carolina Raptor Center, the goals are always to educate visitors about raptors and ignite a spark that inspires them to want to learn more. At no other facility in North Carolina do visitors have an opportunity to see such a diverse and large collection of raptors. It should not be missed by anyone traveling through Mecklenburg County. Visitors will gain a new appreciation for raptors and their important role in the environment. They will also learn how they can make small changes to ensure the survival of these *and* other species.

Tips

- The self-guided trail is not paved, so wear shoes that are comfortable and suited for uneven terrain and that you won't mind getting dirty.

- Located on the same road as the Carolina Raptor Center are several other facilities of interest within Latta Plantation Nature Preserve. One is the Latta Plantation Nature Center, where visitors can view several species of frogs, turtles, lizards, and snakes and enjoy hiking trails, fishing opportunities, and even Segway tours. The Latta Plantation Equestrian Center offers guided trail rides, pony rides, hayrides, and riding lessons. At Historic Latta Plantation, visitors can tour a nineteenth-century backcountry cotton plantation and see several types of farm animals. To learn more about these attractions, visit the Latta Plantation Nature Preserve website at www.charmeck.org. Click on "Recreation and Culture," then "Park and Rec Facilities," then "Nature Centers," and finally "Latta Plantation."

A White's treefrog can control the amount of water evaporated through its skin.

Discovery Place

301 North Tryon Street
Charlotte, N.C. 28202
Phone: 704-372-6261
Website: www.discoveryplace.org
E-mail: Online form

Hours: Open year-round Monday through Friday from 9 A.M. to 4 P.M., Saturday from 10 A.M. to 6 P.M., and Sunday from noon to 5 P.M. Closed Easter, Thanksgiving, Christmas Eve, and Christmas Day.

Directions: From I-77 South at Charlotte, take Exit 11 onto I-277 South toward Brookshire Freeway East. Travel approximately 1.5 miles, take Exit 3B (the Church Street/Tryon Street exit), go straight on West Eleventh Street, and turn right on North Tryon Street. Discovery Place is on the right within 0.5 mile.

"Celebrate biodiversity and Earth's amazing, colorful and quirky species . . ."
Discovery Place Magazine, summer 2010

Since 1981, Discovery Place has fascinated, educated, and entertained audiences of all ages. Originally a 72,000-square-foot hands-on science and technology center, the museum has expanded into a 160,000-plus-square-foot complex that includes interactive hands-on exhibits; educational, meeting, and support spaces; the Discovery 3D Theatre; the IMAX® Dome Theatre; and a parking complex. In fulfilling its mission "to ignite wonder as a preeminent science education center providing extraordinary experiences that engage people in the active exploration of science and nature," Discovery Place never ceases its efforts to bring state-of-the-art exhibits and programs to the public.

The recent completion of a $31.6 million renovation introduced "a new, reimagined and contemporary Discovery Place to the community," according to the museum's website. Two major highlights of the renovation are the new World Alive and Fantastic Frogs exhibitions.

World Alive, the largest of the museum's displays, celebrates earth's biodiversity. As guests walk down the hallway toward the exhibit, located on level one, they first see a massive interactive fiberoptic globe. Surrounding the globe are more than three hundred photographs—World Alive's biodiversity gallery—showcasing life from a variety of different regions, cultures, and ecosystems.

Across from the biodiversity gallery are World Alive's two interactive learning labs, Explore More Life and Explore More Collections. In Explore More Life, guests can get acquainted with sea urchins, starfish, and horseshoe crabs in a marine touch tank; see a variety of fish in small aquariums; examine various one-celled organisms and other objects through a microscope; and view invertebrates such as shrimp, mantises, walking sticks, and sponges.

The Explore More Collections lab challenges visitors to think about how objects in the natural world are related and to learn what constitutes a collection. Here, they will see and examine a variety of displays including mounted wildlife exhibits, skulls, tree cuttings, gemstones, and North Carolina state symbols.

World Alive's most appealing exhibit is the Rainforest Habitat. Guests enter through what appears to be a researcher's hut. The interior has educational text panels and a video regarding rainforest research projects. Visitors then open a door into a steamy rainforest. Lanterns, cargo boxes, trails extending into the habitat, long, hanging roots of native plants, and an assortment of animals give the exhibit a realistic feel. Guests have an enjoyable time trying to locate the animals, which include birds such as the crested wood partridge, the Mandarin duck, the red-faced parrot finch, the jambu fruit-dove, and the Brazilian cardinal; tortoises; a Madagascar giant day gecko; a freshwater stingray; silver arowana fish; and several species of poison dart frogs. The Rainforest Habitat overlook, located on level two of the museum, has a small "swinging bridge" that is highly popular with children and provides a nice setting for photographs. The special programs held daily at the Rainforest Theatre and

World Alive features an interactive fiberoptic globe surrounded by hundreds of photographs that showcase the earth's diversity.

inside the researcher's hut are designed to give visitors an up-close experience with one of the museum's animal residents. Upon arriving at the museum, check the daily visitor guide to see what programs are offered, as well as times and locations.

The last section of the World Alive exhibition showcases underwater ecological communities, courtesy of fifteen tanks of aquatic habitats containing twenty-four thousand gallons of seawater. The display holds an incredible array of marine life. Interestingly, the most beautiful of the aquatic habitats does not contain fish at all but instead holds a variety of colorful and oddly shaped sponges. Among the good number of fish to be seen, visitors may discover a few species they have not encountered before, such as the mummichog (said to have been the first fish in space when carried on Skylab 3 in 1973), the oyster blenny, the engineer goby, the fairy wrasse, and the peacock mantis shrimp.

Other attractions on level one of the museum include KidScience and the Discovery 3D Theatre.

Level two contains Explore More Stuff, and five large exhibition areas: Project Build, Cool Stuff, Fantastic Frogs, THEM, and Think It Up.

Although a small exhibition, Fantastic Frogs by itself makes a trip to Discovery Place worthwhile. The exhibition takes a graphic-novel approach; information is conveyed in comic-book form. This unique presentation emphasizes the "superpowers" of individual frog species and how they use those "powers"—camouflage, poisonous secretions, feigning death, adapting to harsh living conditions, etc.—to survive. Visitors will be amazed to see bizarre frog species and uncover their secret techniques for survival. They will likely come across amphibians they never knew existed, such as the pacman frog, a native of South America that is able to puff itself up and appear "too big to be swallowed"; the tomato frog; the Oriental fire-bellied toad; the Vietnamese mossy frog, which, as its name implies, looks like a "clump of moss or a convincing cluster of lichen"; the Solomon Island leaf frog; the Chinese gliding frog; the White's treefrog; the wood frog; the American bullfrog; the marine toad; and several species of poison dart frogs, including the golden poison dart frog, "thought to be the world's most poisonous frog." Although measuring an average of one to two inches and weighing less than an ounce, this frog has enough venom to kill ten men. A native of South America, the golden poison dart frog lives in a small area of rainforest on the Pacific coast of Colombia. It is on the endangered species list. After viewing the exhibit, visitors are left with the question of whether or not frogs will be able to survive the present threat they face—environmental change accelerated by human behavior. Fantastic Frogs is an outstanding exhibition that showcases an extraordinary collection of amphibians and helps the public comprehend the important role they play in ensuring the survival of each species alive in the world today.

After completing the tour of Fantastic Frogs, guests can explore other level-two exhibitions such as THEM and Think It Up. THEM might have visitors washing their hands an extra time or two, as it explores bacteria, microbes, and parasites that live in and on the human body.

Before leaving Discovery Place, guests should check out the Science Buzz kiosks, multimedia interactive science experiences located throughout the museum; browse Shop Science on level two; and grab a bite to eat at the Community Café on level one. Lastly, guests cannot visit Discovery Place and forgo the IMAX® Dome Theatre, the largest screen in the Carolinas. The presentations, especially the ones related to animal life, are always memorable.

Visitors should not bypass this attraction even if they do not have children. Discovery Place makes learning about "Earth's amazing, colorful and quirky species" fun no matter what one's age.

Tips

- If you plan to visit on a weekday without children, make sure school is in session. If it is not, the museum will likely be crowded.

- The on-site Community Café offers a varied selection of healthy and fresh foods—and some of the best-tasting cupcakes around! Should you decide to eat there, be aware that the kitchen closes one hour earlier than the museum.

● Be sure to park in Discovery Place's parking deck, located at the corner of Sixth and Church streets. To enter Discovery Place, go to level three and cross the walkway leading directly into the museum. If you bring your parking stub into the museum, you can prepay for it when you purchase your admission ticket; otherwise, remember to keep at least ten dollars on hand to pay for parking.

● The Charlotte Nature Museum (see pages 89–93) is only about four miles away. If you have time, visit both attractions in one day.

Charlotte Nature Museum

1658 Sterling Road
Charlotte, N.C. 28209
Phone: 704-372-6261
Website: www.charlottenaturemuseum.org
E-mail: Online form

Hours: Open year-round Tuesday through Friday from 9 A.M. to 5 P.M., Saturday from 10 A.M. to 5 P.M., and Sunday from noon to 5 P.M. Closed New Year's, Easter, the Fourth of July, Thanksgiving, Christmas Eve, and Christmas Day.

Directions: From I-77 South at Charlotte, take Exit 9 onto I-277 North toward John Belk Freeway for a little over 2 miles. Take Exit 2A and turn right on Kenilworth Avenue. Travel about 0.5 mile, turn left on East More-head Street, drive another 0.5 mile, and bear right on South Kings Drive. In about 1 mile, this road changes to West Queens Road. Proceed almost 0.5 mile, turn right on Wellesley Avenue, and turn left on Sterling Road. The nature museum is on the right after less than 0.5 mile.

~~~~~~~~~~~~~~~~~~~

**"With indoor and outdoor exhibits any time of year is a
wild time to visit Charlotte Nature Museum."**
Charlotte Nature Museum website

The Charlotte Nature Museum opened in 1951, becoming one of the first facilities in the Southeast to focus on bringing families and nature together. Although
designed for children ages three to seven, it offers a variety of programs and exhibits
appropriate for all ages.

Upon entering the museum, visitors step inside the Great Hall, where the first
exhibit—Beginnings—and several corridors await. Beginnings is an exhibit in which
live animals and interactive displays document life cycles. Children learn the reasons
why some animals (chicks) hatch from eggs while others (mice) do not. They then
witness live examples of both. Beginnings also showcases tadpoles in various stages
of metamorphosis.

Down the corridor from Beginnings, visitors can explore other exhibits including Peetie's Place, Our Big Backyard, Insect Alley, the Butterfly Pavilion, Creature
Cavern, and the Paw Paw Nature Trail.

Peetie's Place is a nature-based activity room where children can read books, create puppet shows, and play with a variety of fun and educational toys.

Our Big Backyard encourages youngsters to explore the movement of water and
to discover the world beneath their feet, including the creatures that live there.

Insect Alley offers an opportunity to examine various live insects such as walking

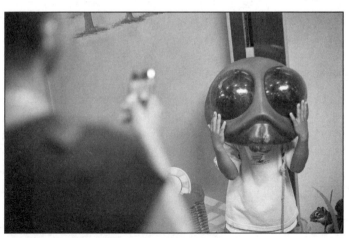

Visitors have an opportunity to examine the world from a fly's point of view.
PHOTOGRAPH COURTESY OF DISCOVERY PLACE INC.
(CHARLOTTE NATURE MUSEUM)

Queen Charlotte, the resident groundhog, predicts the weather on Groundhog Day. Photograph courtesy of Discovery Place Inc. (Charlotte Nature Museum)

sticks. Walking sticks, whose bodies mimic twigs, are intriguing creatures. The same camouflage that makes them difficult to see in the wild can make them hard to distinguish even in a display habitat. For those who would like to examine the world from a fly's point of view, the museum has created an oversized head that allows guests to see their surroundings through the insect's compound eyes. And for those who have always wanted to know what they would look like with the body of a bug, they can position themselves behind what appears to be the underside of a beetle. The caption above the insect body reads, "The Cutest Bug at The Charlotte Nature Museum."

Inside the Butterfly Pavilion, visitors can enjoy a peaceful walk among free-flying butterflies in a kaleidoscope of colors. A chrysalis house inside the pavilion documents the life cycle of these delicate winged insects and makes it possible for guests to watch them grow.

Creature Cavern features the most live animals and is likely the most popular of the museum's displays. Here, visitors will see animals native to the Carolinas that have been deemed nonreleasable, as they are unable to survive in the wild. One of the residents is a barred owl named Nelly. In pursuing a rodent that was eating food tossed from a car on a roadside one evening, Nelly was struck by a vehicle. She sustained major injuries that caused blindness and brain damage and left her with three breaks in one wing. Nelly's story allows the museum to make a connection between humans and the impact of their actions on local wildlife. Guests will also encounter other animals including Queen Charlotte (the museum's resident groundhog), owls, birds, a mink, opossums, skunks, a flying squirrel, snakes, turtles, and a skink. Each animal is an ambassador for its species, and all have special stories to share.

If the weather is pleasant, visitors will enjoy exploring the Paw Paw Nature Trail, an easy loop on an elevated boardwalk into a hundred-year-old forest full of native wildlife and plants.

Back inside the museum, guests can browse the Trail's End Store or participate in one of the museum's educational programs. "Creatures of the Night"—a presentation by Grandpa Tree around a "nighttime campfire"—discusses nocturnal animals. Nature-based puppet shows are delivered by the Charlotte Nature Museum's professional Puppet Theatre. "Chat with a Naturalist" offers an up-close experience with a resident animal or a special tour of one of the museum's exhibits. Guests should check the daily visitor guide to see which programs are offered and to confirm times and locations.

Special-event programs held throughout the year include "Creature Feature," which is offered one Saturday during most months. "Creature Feature" provides the public a close encounter with an animal and a presentation by a local expert in the field. The program is typically accompanied by puppet shows, story time, crafts, body painting, and snacks. One of the most popular event programs takes place on Groundhog Day, when the public flocks to the museum to watch Queen Charlotte make the upcoming winter weather forecast—six more weeks of winter if she sees her shadow, an early spring if not.

The Charlotte Nature Museum provides exceptional exhibits and educational experiences that will inspire visitors, particularly children, to learn more about, and develop a greater appreciation for, the natural world around them. Those who visit this Mecklenburg County attraction are guaranteed to spend an afternoon uncovering, in the words of the museum, "fun surprises around every corner."

Tips

* Those without children should not be deterred from visiting. Should you visit on a weekday without children, however, make sure it is when school is in session, as the museum may be crowded otherwise.

* Though the museum does not offer food or drinks, it encourages picnicking on its back deck, which you may want to consider on a favorable day.

* After touring the museum, spend some time in Freedom Park. This ninety-eight-acre park located behind the museum features a concession stand, walking trails, a "Naturescape" trail that allows visitors to watch birds and butterflies from ten different stations, and a seven-acre lake; Freedom Park participates in the North Carolina Wildlife Resources Commission's Community Fishing Program. The park is located at 1900 East Boulevard. To learn more, call 704-432-4280 or visit www. charmeck.org. Or you might drive to Discovery Place, located approxi-

mately four miles away, and explore its engaging World Alive and Fantastic Frogs exhibitions. To learn about Discovery Place, see pages 85–89.

Horse Protection Society of North Carolina

2135 Miller Road
China Grove, N.C. 28023
Phone: 704-855-2978
Website: www.horseprotection.org
E-mail: hps@horseprotection.org

Hours: Open Saturday from 10 A.M. to 4 P.M.

Directions: From I-85 South at China Grove in southern Rowan County, take Exit 68, follow U.S. 29 Bypass South for approximately 1.5 miles, and turn right on East Church Street. After less than 0.5 mile, bear left on West Church Street (N.C. 152). Drive 0.5 mile, turn right on Miller Road, and continue a little over 2 miles. The Horse Protection Society is on the right.

"Hearts, Hands, Helping Horses"
Horse Protection Society of North Carolina

For abused, neglected, and unwanted equines, the Horse Protection Society of North Carolina provides a hospitable and healing refuge. It is a last-chance resort or a permanent place of rest for many a weary horse. The Rowan County facility has a mission "to make the world a better place for horses through education, rescue, and rehabilitation."

Founded by Joanie Benson in 1991, the society was incorporated as a nonprofit in 1999. That year was also memorable because the organization found itself caring for thirty-four American saddlebred horses that had been deserted and left to starve in an extreme example of animal abuse. The Horse Protection Society brought the case—the first felony animal cruelty case in the state—before the North Carolina Superior Court and won. Since that time, the society has trained inspectors to perform ongoing abuse and neglect investigations with the goal of educating owners

*Fancy, a twenty-year-old thoroughbred mare, arrived at the sanctuary
emaciated and sick but is now in recovery.*

on how to better care for their horses. If an owner does not wish to be trained, the
society will offer to take the animal; abuse cases are prosecuted only when necessary.

Horses taken in by the society generally arrive in sick, frail, or emaciated condition. As Joanie Benson states, "We take in the horses no one else will take." Some
horses require around-the-clock care. With only a volunteer staff, the society feeds,
cleans, medicates, and administers all necessary care. The goal is to successfully rehabilitate and find each horse a suitable home.

Horses that live at the facility are classified into four groups: saddle pals, pasture pals, equines in recovery, and permanent residents. Saddle pals are horses whose
health has returned; they are able to carry riders and can be adopted. Pasture pals
are in good health; they are able to be adopted but have issues that prevent them
from being ridden. Equines in recovery are horses that are undergoing rehabilitation. Until they have fully recovered, it is not known into which category they will be
placed. Permanent residents are horses that require long-term health treatment, are
age thirty or older, or are not suitable for adoption. The Horse Protection Society is
their permanent home.

During visiting hours, a volunteer or perhaps Joanie Benson will give a tour of
the facility, introduce the horses, and explain the volunteer, membership, and spon-
sorship opportunities available. As guests begin their tour, they may behold a recent
addition, which in all probability may resemble what can only be described as a skeleton draped in fur. Benson stresses that most horses arrive in this condition, and that
they are the reason the society exists. At present, the society cares for approximately
fifty horses. However, that number could rise, as calls consistently come in from
animal-control agencies and people who can no longer maintain their horses.

Horses in various stages of recovery enjoy large pastures and an abundance of hay.

Strolling the grounds among free-roaming horses in pastures, barns, and stalls, visitors have an opportunity to meet and greet the likes of Diego, Midnight Sun, Noble, Firelight, Jelly Bean, and Navajo.

Diego, a saddle pal, came to the society after financial hardship prevented his owners from properly feeding him. Fortunately, he gained his weight back and is strengthening his muscles.

Midnight Sun, a pasture pal, arrived extremely thin and so frightened that she did not want to venture from the barn. Although she still bears emotional scars, she loves being in the company of humans.

Noble, a stately black Tennessee walking horse, is an equine in recovery. Diagnosed with recurrent airway obstruction, Noble showed up slightly dehydrated and one hundred pounds underweight. Thanks to constant care, Noble has improved.

Firelight, another equine in recovery, was near death when he was signed over to the society. So starved he could barely stand, he had extreme diarrhea, and his muscles were being reabsorbed by his body. After being cared for by dedicated volunteers, Firelight has gained over a hundred pounds and is recuperating.

Jelly Bean, a permanent resident, has a truly touching story. According to his biography on the society's website, the miniature horse "stood alone in a grassy field sleeping on the freezing ground in the winter and baking in the sun in the summer. . . . He foundered several times and his hooves grew to 7–8 inches long. Eventually his owner . . . called a vet to put him to sleep. Jelly Bean was only seven years old. The vet refused . . . and called a client in N.C. . . . When the woman came to pick up Jelly Bean the next day, she discovered that his hooves had been hacked back and he was in such pain that he could barely stand let alone walk. Carefully, he was lifted into a trailer and taken to safety and medical care." Today, Jelly Bean is recovering nicely and has acquired many friends—both humans and horses. His horse friends are said to find Jelly Bean "very charming," as he greets them with "little kisses and nips."

Navajo, another permanent resident, will stay in the mind of many a visitor. An incredibly handsome Arabian, Navajo is forty-five years old and in relatively good health despite being blind in one eye.

Considering the circumstances the above-listed horses and others at the facility have endured, one might assume they would be skittish or even aggressive around people. However, just the opposite is true. Visitors will find these horses amiable, gentle in spirit, and almost humble in attitude. Benson believes horses can understand what humans are saying and feeling, and that the horses that reside at the society respond to emotions, particularly laughter. If this is true, the horses may realize their caretakers and weekend visitors genuinely respect and care for them. The society welcomes new members and volunteers who make a connection with a particular horse or the horses in general. Becoming a member or volunteer allows a person the chance to visit more often, to participate in activities such as feeding, and to be notified when help is needed. Volunteers and members are not required to have experience working with horses, as the society trains new participants.

The Horse Protection Society of North Carolina vows not to cease its efforts to prevent the abuse and neglect of horses. In an effort to reduce the number of unwanted equine births and end overbreeding, the organization began funding the Stallion to Gelding Support Program, which offers free gelding services. As the society looks toward the future, its goal is to eventually acquire a larger facility. For now, it will continue to educate people—particularly horse owners—about the proper care of equines. It will also provide each horse in its care with food, shelter, daily essentials, veterinary care, and an abundance of love.

Tips

- Upon your arrival, you may not see anyone. Just walk around and you will eventually find someone working in the barn or behind the house. However, do not open any gates or venture behind fences.

- You will be walking through pastures and horse stalls, so wear shoes you do not mind getting dirty.

- Visiting the Horse Protection Society is not the same as touring a zoo. You face a good possibility of seeing a horse, or horses, in extreme physical conditions that can be emotionally overwhelming. On the other hand, it is intensely rewarding to meet horses that have survived, and are currently being rehabilitated from, the effects of neglect and abuse. Take a look at the society's website before your visit to read the biographies of the resident horses. You will be amazed to learn what they have been through and how far they have come. This will also allow you to pick out a special horse you may want to meet that day.

• If you are interested in adopting a horse, call ahead. You may be able to come early (around 9 A.M.) and watch the horses under saddle.

• If you happen to visit the society on the third Saturday of July, you may also want to attend the annual China Grove Farmers Day, held in downtown China Grove. The Main Street event offers a variety of vendors, musical entertainment, fresh produce, displays of antique farm equipment, and much more. To learn more, visit www.chinagrovenc.gov.

Dan Nicholas Park

6800 Bringle Ferry Road
Salisbury, N.C. 28146
Phone: 866-767-2757 or 704-216-7803
Website: www.dannicholas.net
E-mail: bringlde@co.rowan.nc.us

Hours: Open daily year-round except for Christmas, Thanksgiving, and New Year's. Hours are seasonal. Attractions do not operate on the same schedule as the park, so call or visit the website for hours.

Directions: From I-85 South in Rowan County, take Exit 79, turn left on Old Union Church Road, and drive 3 miles. Turn right on Goodman Lake Road, continue for less than 0.5 mile, turn left on Bringle Ferry Road, and travel 3 miles. The park is on the left.

Ruff, an American black bear, appears to be waving at his admirers.
PHOTOGRAPH BY CINDY BERNHARDT, COURTESY OF ROWAN COUNTY PARKS AND RECREATION

~~~~~~~~~~~~~~~~~~~~~~~~~~~~~~~~~~

"Come and learn about the wild plants and animals
of Rowan County and see living creatures eye to eye."
Dan Nicholas Park website

Entering Dan Nicholas Park, visitors immediately see a sign that proclaims this unique attraction to be "Your Greatest Entertainment Bargain." They will be amazed to find that the sign rings true, as the admission for most attractions is one dollar or less.

The Rowan County Parks and Recreation Department operates Dan Nicholas Park, named for the man who donated 335 acres of land to the county in 1968. Since that time, the park has expanded to its present 425 acres, which include a 10-acre lake. Recreational activities abound. Most are typical of county parks. Visitors will find picnic shelters, hiking trails, volleyball courts, tennis courts, horseshoe pits, sports fields, a playground, fishing opportunities, paddleboats, a large campground with sites for tents and recreational vehicles, and rental cabins.

The central area, however, offers a variety of attractions not so common at city or county parks. Visitors can test their skill at two eighteen-hole miniature golf courses, take a spin on Haden's Carousel, cool off at the Hurley Water Plaza, enjoy a leisurely ride on a miniature train, or search for treasure at the Miner Moose Gem Mine. The mine is quite popular. Once tourists finish panning, they can proceed to the gem-mine shack, where an experienced rock hound will identify their findings. They can also turn their found gems into custom pieces of jewelry.

The most crowd-pleasing attractions are the ones that involve wildlife. Dan Nicholas Park has three separate facilities for visitors to tour.

The park's Nature Center was built in 1975; a new reptile exhibit and an aquarium opened in 2006. Inside, visitors will see a variety of snakes, lizards, turtles, and even alligators. The Nature Center was creatively designed to give visitors the sense that they have happened upon a shack in the middle of the woods. Creatures that might reside in those woods surround the shack. Staff members are on hand, particularly during weekends, to answer questions. On occasion, they bring out small animals for guests to touch and examine on an up-close basis. The Nature Center houses the Cheerwine Aquarium, which showcases several species of fish. Tourists will be pleased to know that no fee is charged for this attraction.

Next to the Nature Center is the T. M. Stanback Petting Barn, where a nominal entrance fee is charged. The original barnyard was constructed in 1986 but was destroyed by fire in 2006. The following year, the barn was rebuilt and reopened. Guests will meet a friendly collection of animals here. In fact, they may want to visit the petting barn last because one particular animal is hard to leave behind. Penny the pot-

Penny the pig enjoys playing with her favorite purple ball and receiving endless belly rubs.

bellied pig loves people, her purple ball, and having her belly rubbed. When tourists stop at her pen, she rolls her ball to gain their attention. Penny then approaches the fence, where she lies on her side to ask for a belly rub. When visitors oblige her request, she closes her eyes and proceeds to oink and grunt. When guests finally pull themselves away from Penny, they can meet other animals such as a miniature donkey, Jacob sheep, goats, and a belted Galloway cow. Various species of birds are on display at the barn, but visitors are not allowed to touch them. Nonetheless, they can get an up-close look at the birds, which include a bronze turkey, a red golden pheasant, guineafowl, a dove, a golden pheasant, and a peacock. The barnyard area also has a nice exhibit of farming tools and equipment. When visitors depart, a hand-washing station is available for those who petted the animals.

The largest and favorite animal attraction is Rowan Wildlife Adventures. Visitors will be surprised to discover such a diverse collection of animals and high-quality exhibits in a place where only a minimal entrance fee is charged. The large habitats inside Rowan Wildlife Adventures are designed to represent the animals' natural settings. Visitors are led to each habitat by way of a paved trail. They will first encounter a pair of bald eagles. Next, a platform allows tourists to observe turtles in a bog. A few more steps and guests can sit and watch butterflies as they feed in the butterfly garden. However, the habitat up ahead will likely keep them moving along. The American black bear habitat is a highlight, especially on warm weekends. Park staff offer public programs that include feeding the two bears and learning about their natural history. An interesting fact presented on the educational text panel outside the bear habitat tells how North Carolina holds the record for the heaviest black bear officially weighed in the United States and Canada. The bear—from Craven County—weighed 880 pounds.

Other animals along the path include a red-tailed hawk, a broad-winged hawk, a black vulture, a turkey vulture, an owl, a wild turkey, bobcats, a raccoon (visitors can peer into a tree and see it sleeping), an albino raccoon, a groundhog, white-tailed deer, a red fox, and red wolves. One of the most captivating animals is Alfred the albino raccoon. According to Bob Pendergrass, the Nature Center supervisor, Alfred became trapped in a farmer's cornfield when he was young. Because Alfred could not be relocated, he came to live at Rowan Wildlife Adventures. Alfred has white fur and pink eyes, which make him an easy target for prey. In the wild, his lifespan would be much shorter than that of other raccoons; therefore, he is considered a rare specimen. The red wolves are also fascinating, as they are one of the most endangered species in the world. Rowan Wildlife Adventures participates in the Red Wolf Species Survival Plan and breed its wolves as needed. Pendergrass says that the facility's red wolf pair was allowed to breed in 2007 and produced five female pups. Three were introduced into the wild by fostering them into two separate dens in eastern North Carolina.

Visitors greatly enjoy Dan Nicholas Park, as the entire facility is beautifully landscaped and remarkably free of litter and debris. Even the petting barn is amazingly clean. Interestingly, gold was discovered and mined near the site of the park during the nineteenth century. Today, visitors do not have to search to locate treasure; they have only to visit Dan Nicholas Park.

Tips

- Make sure you arrive early enough in the day to enjoy all the park's offerings.

- Be sure to visit the concession stand located beside Lake Murtis, as that is where cones of feed for the ducks are available for purchase.

- If you have time before or after your visit, head to Eagle Point Nature Preserve or Dunn's Mountain Park, where hiking trails provide an opportunity to see native flora and fauna. Both facilities are operated by the Rowan County Parks and Recreation Department and are located within six miles of Dan Nicholas Park. To learn more, visit www.co.rowan.nc.us. Click on the drop-down box labeled "Departments," then on "Parks & Recreation."

Lil Wayne the liger with his friend Miracle, the tiger.
PHOTOGRAPH COURTESY OF TIGER WORLD

Tiger World

4400 Cook Road
Rockwell, N.C. 28138
Phone: 704-279-6363
Website: www.tigerworld.us
E-mail: tigerworldsc@aol.com

Hours: Open year-round Thursday through Tuesday from 9 A.M. to 5 P.M. for self-guided tours. Closed Thanksgiving and Christmas. Advance reservations are required for educational and special-event tours.

Directions: From I-85 in southern Rowan County, take Exit 68, travel approximately 5 miles on N.C. 152 East, and turn right on Cook Road, which dead-ends at Tiger World.

> "A Fun and Educational Place to Experience
> Endangered Species Up Close and Personal"
> **Tiger World brochure**

The small town of Rockwell in eastern Rowan County accommodates several sizable residents. These grand inhabitants with sharp teeth and brilliant coats await visitors daily at a facility appropriately called Tiger World. Tourists searching for this conservation and educational center may think they have made a navigational error when turning onto Cook Road, as the residential area seems an unlikely setting for meat-eating animals. Near the end of the road, however, they will see the silhouettes of majestic creatures in the distance and be assured they have taken the right track.

Tiger World occupies the property that was formerly the Metrolina Wildlife Park, which closed in 2007. Many of Tiger World's residents were already on-site when Lea Jaunakais assumed ownership. Jaunakais, the president and founder of Tiger World, opened the new facility—which comprises thirty-one acres—in 2008. According to Charles D. Perry in "Home sweet den" in the January 5, 2008, edition of *The Herald* of Rock Hill, South Carolina, Jaunakais developed a concern for tigers at the age of three while watching a National Geographic program about the destruction of tiger populations by humans. She cultivated that passion through years of study, training, work, and research and eventually fulfilled her dream of creating a facility that not only safeguards threatened and endangered species but also educates the public about their plight.

Within a year of its opening, Tiger World rescued over ten tigers, lions, servals, and leopards. One of those rescues, a leopard named Begara, suffered a broken hind leg. She was immediately transported to a veterinary specialist, who found it necessary to amputate the limb. The procedure saved Begara's life. After several months of healing, she was able to run and jump again. Other rescues involved two tigers brought to the facility after the death of their owner. The tigers had been kept in a private home, where they were confined to small enclosures void of key components necessary for their health and well-being. The female tiger required surgery, as her claws were overgrown and penetrating the pads of her feet. Both tigers now run, play, swim, eat, and interact with their handlers.

Tourists can view Begara and other animals at the park on an up-close and personal basis. As a matter of fact, in some instances, they can stand within five feet of a

Lilly the tiger and Fozzy the lion
PHOTOGRAPH COURTESY OF
TIGER WORLD

tiger—a true highlight of the facility. Tiger World is home to several types of tigers including white Bengals, Bengals, and Siberians. It also houses the remarkable liger. For many visitors, this may be their first time seeing a liger, as this species is not commonly exhibited at North Carolina facilities. A liger, which is a hybrid cross between a female tiger and a male lion, exhibits characteristics of both animals. Ligers have diffuse stripes and vocalize like both tigers and lions. They typically grow bigger than either of their parents, making them the largest of all cat species. Two ligers, Radar and Lil Wayne, are exhibited at Tiger World. Radar was brought to the facility when he required a new home, and Lil Wayne was born shortly after Jaunakais purchased the property. A tubal ligation was performed on Lil Wayne's mother, Lilly, to prevent further pregnancies. Only on occasion does Tiger World permit its tigers to reproduce. If contacted by another licensed zoo for a tiger, the staff will determine if any of its available tigers fulfills the park's need. If not, then breeding may be scheduled. When cubs are born at the facility, the public is allowed by advance reservation to meet and interact with them. Tiger World does not provide this special treat on a regular or annual basis.

In addition to tigers, visitors may observe baboons, monkeys, lions, jaguars, panthers, Syrian bears, lemurs, a lynx, emus and various other birds, tortoises, crocodiles, lizards, snakes, and many other animals. Bags of food for non-meat-eating residents are available for purchase at the ticket booth.

Tiger World offers educational tours in addition to the self-guided tours. These reservations-only tours allow guests the opportunity to walk the grounds in the company of a licensed animal handler, who provides detailed information about each animal, as well as educational coloring books to young participants. A "Carnivore Feeding Safari Tour" is offered on Thursday evenings and also requires advance reservations. Participants who opt for this unique tour will witness the primal feeding behaviors of carnivores. Staff members feed their big cats eighteen hundred pounds of butchered chicken, beef, and pork per week.

Text panels on display throughout Tiger World educate visitors taking the self-guided tour, which is available without reservations during regular hours. The panels cover such subjects as the declining number of animal populations in the world, how that number is due to human interference, and steps that can be taken to ensure animals' survival.

By allowing guests to examine animals—particularly tigers—up close, Tiger World hopes to inspire people to learn more about, and help protect, endangered and threatened species. It also hopes to instill a realization that one person's actions can make an impact in the world. As Tiger World's brochure states, it provides "a unique experience for young and old alike—an intimate backstage pass to the world of exotic animals."

Tips

● The healthy population of Canada geese at Tiger World will beg for your food. Keep in mind that if you feed them at the beginning of your tour, you will not have any food left for the rest of the animals. Also, unless you *do* plan to feed the geese, one bag of food per person is sufficient, as you will be allowed to feed certain animals only.

● Pay attention when being told the layout of the facility or you could miss seeing the white Bengal tigers.

Southeast Old Threshers' Reunion

Denton FarmPark
1072 Cranford Road
Denton, N.C. 27239
Phone: 336-859-2755
Website: www.threshers.com
E-mail: manager@threshers.com

Hours: The reunion is held for five days surrounding July 4. The gates open daily at 8 A.M., shows begin at 9 A.M., and trams are in operation from 9 A.M. to 5 P.M. Phone or visit the website for exact dates.

Directions: From N.C. 109 South in southeastern Davidson County, turn left at the second stoplight in Denton and follow the signs to the parking areas.

"The greatest steam, gas, & antique farm machine show
in the Southeastern US"

Southeast Old Threshers' Reunion brochure

Spectators watch a demonstration of the horse-powered cotton gin.

For many, the Southeast Old Threshers' Reunion is a must-attend Fourth of July event. Held at Denton FarmPark, the five-day festival has, as proclaimed in its brochure, "something for everyone." Organized in 1970 through the partnership of Brown Loflin and Howard Latham, the reunion has evolved into an event that attracts nearly fifty thousand visitors each year. Taking place on more than one hundred acres in Davidson County, the reunion offers a variety of activities—most of which relate to the history of farm machinery—for visitors of all ages.

Upon arriving, guests immediately hear the sounds of, and see the smoke from, steam- and gas-powered engines. Thousands of operational engines, tractors, and antique pieces of equipment—including a steam shovel, a sawmill, a shingle mill, a veneer mill, a steam crane, a rock crusher, a wood splitter, a gold-ore stamping machine, a 1901 printing press, and an 1898 cotton compress—are displayed at the festival. Daily demonstrations of such operations as threshing, baling, and plowing let the public see the historical progression from steam- to gas-powered machinery.

Visitors may be surprised to see demonstrations of an even earlier power source—horsepower! At the Southeast Old Threshers' Reunion, presenters explain how draft horses more quickly and efficiently completed labor-intensive agricultural work originally done by hand. For example, workers originally separated cotton from the seeds by hand, a tedious process. But when Eli Whitney invented the cotton gin, he greatly improved productivity. Whitney created a small gin that could be hand-cranked and a large gin that could be harnessed to a horse. In a letter to his father that can be read on the website of the National Archives under "Teaching With Documents," Whitney stated, "One man and a horse will do more than fifty men

Horse pulling competitions demonstrate the strength of draft horses.

with the old machine." A late-model cotton gin powered by two horses walking on a treadmill can be seen in action at the reunion. The horses keep a steady pace as a worker and one lucky volunteer feed cotton into the gin. After the separated cotton is collected, visitors are welcome to take a few pieces with them as souvenirs of the demonstration.

Other demonstrations showcase horses threshing with their hooves in the tramping barn, shelling corn, and baling hay. In the shelling and baling demonstrations, large Belgian draft horses power the machinery by walking at a set pace in a circle. Visitors can sit on bleachers to watch or stand beside the corral and get an up-close view. Although the demonstrations are presented only a few times per day, they are indeed crowd pleasers.

The most memorable event of the reunion is the horse pulling competition, presented only one day during the festival. It is a most incredible sport to watch, as the raw power of the draft horses is made clear. Horses that compete in the pulls are massive animals. Most weigh over a ton and make the largest of their human handlers appear small. As the horses are paraded to the pulling area, people scurry out of the way while making excited remarks about the impressive animals and even the size of their hooves, which wear shoes that appear to have spikes. Those "spikes" are actually heel caulks—extra pieces of metal—that help the horses dig into the ground and gain better traction as they pull. The horse pulling competition offers much excitement; however, the crowd is asked not to cheer until *after* the pull is completed, as the horses could mistake the noise for a command. The competition has lightweight and heavyweight divisions. Of course, the team from each division that pulls the heaviest load wins.

The Southeast Old Threshers' Reunion has ample other activities to keep visitors returning for several days throughout the event. Entertainers—particularly country, bluegrass, and gospel singers—provide daily performances in the music hall; vendors sell arts and crafts and other items, as well as an assortment of food (the smell of which creates a fair-like atmosphere); animals bring smiles to all who enter the barnyard petting zoo; an auction is held; antique tractor pulls are presented; a lawn mower pull and adult and kiddie pedal pulls are held; a sheep-herding demonstration is given; and the Handy Dandy Railroad offers steam train rides throughout the day.

Visitors also have the opportunity to tour the many restored buildings on the grounds of Denton FarmPark, including a country store and post office, a nineteenth-century tramping barn, a granary, a blacksmith shop, a smokehouse, a plantation house, the two-story George E. Sperling Grist Mill (where stone-ground cornmeal is available for purchase daily), the Old Jackson Hill Church (where services are held on Sunday at 9 A.M.), a log cabin, the Elliott Brothers Service Station, a shoe shop, and a machine shop. Guests can also browse the collections inside the radio and doll museums.

A visit to the Southeast Old Threshers' Reunion is a great way to learn something new or perhaps reminisce about the past. Seeing the progression from horse-powered to gas-powered machinery will no doubt make visitors appreciate their modern conveniences. It will also help them realize the essential role draft animals played in building, tilling, plowing, and powering our nation. Visitors will be glad they made the event part of their Fourth of July festivities.

Tips

- Be prepared for heat—a hat and sunscreen are essential—and a considerable amount of walking. You may want to bring an umbrella or a hand-held fan, as shade is hard to come by during the events, particularly at the horse pulling area.

- Horse demonstrations are offered once a day at various times. If you do not want to miss a certain demonstration, call in advance for the schedule.

- Camping is available on the grounds; see the website for the fee schedule and other information.

Silvertip the llama greets trekkers by sniffing their hair.

Bloomtown Acres/
Four Ladies & Me Llama Trekking

4179 Divine Llama Lane
East Bend, N.C. 27018
Phone: 336-972-3986
Website: www.bloomtownacres.com or www.fourladiesandme.com
E-mail: bloomtownacres@yahoo.com

Hours: Open year-round except during midsummer. Advance reservations are required.

Directions: From U.S. 52 North near the Forsyth County–Stokes County line, take Exit 123 (the King/Tobaccoville exit) and turn left on South Main Street. In about 0.5 mile, South Main Street becomes Doral Drive. Travel approximately 1.5 miles and turn right on Tobaccoville Road. After about a mile, bear right on Ridge Road. Drive 3 miles, turn right on Reynolda Road (N.C. 67), go about 4 miles, turn right on Macedonia Road, and continue about 1 mile. Divine Llama Vineyards is on the left.

〜〜〜〜〜〜〜〜〜

"Enjoy hiking with llamas in Yadkin Valley Wine Country..."
Bloomtown Acres/Four Ladies & Me Llama Trekking brochure

The Yadkin Valley is widely known for its vineyards, wineries, and wine-related events. According to the website of the Division of Tourism, Film and Sports Development of the North Carolina Department of Commerce, "The Yadkin Valley is North Carolina's first federally recognized American Viticultural Area." It boasts "nearly 30 wineries and 400 acres devoted to vineyards." The region attracts a multitude of tourists, who come to sample wine, bask in the relaxing landscape of the vineyards, and enjoy a gourmet meal at one of the many vineyard restaurants. They may not be aware, however, that one vineyard offers those experiences in the company of cuddly and friendly llamas.

Michael and Patricia West, the owners of Four Ladies & Me Llamas, joined with Thomas and Julia Hughes to open Divine Llama Vineyards in May 2009. Located in East Bend, the seventy-seven-acre vineyard contains one of the largest llama farms in the state. Over forty llamas—along with miniature horses, a miniature donkey, waterfowl, exotic chickens, and, of course, crias (baby llamas), which can be seen in the spring and fall—populate this Yadkin County vineyard.

Shortly after opening Divine Llama Vineyards, the Wests partnered with Mark and Sharon Berry, the owners of Bloomtown Acres—another llama farm in East Bend—to create a unique activity that would involve both wine and llamas. They began accepting reservations for llama trekking and picnics on the vineyard property during the fall of 2009.

Visitors are given a menu prior to the trip to make their food and wine selections; one bottle of Divine Llama Vineyards wine per couple is included in the cost of the trek. On the day of the trek, participants meet at a particular location on the vineyard property, where their energetic hosts, Mark and Sharon Berry, introduce them to their llama trekking companions. In most instances, guests will have the pleasure of trekking with Silvertip and Fiddlesticks, two charming male llamas that like to greet newcomers by sniffing their hair. These sure-footed animals have been trained to carry lunch and other necessities on the trail. They can also tote jackets and rain gear, should guests wish to bring them.

Before starting a trek, participants are shown how to properly lead their llamas. Once they are comfortable doing so, the trek commences. Walking toward the trail entrance, trekkers can absorb the vineyard's outstanding scenery. The view of Pilot Mountain is exceptional, and the architecture of buildings and barns set amidst ripening vines and rolling fields is captivating. Colorfully coated llamas fill the surrounding pastures. Many of them follow the trekkers along the fence rail until the walk progresses into the woods.

Harvesting grapes at Divine Llama Vineyards
Photograph courtesy of
Divine Llama Vineyards
and Farm

Entering the forest, participants traverse hilly terrain that follows and crosses wide streams; at several places, they must choose to jump or walk across. Halfway through the hike, Mark and Sharon lead trekkers to a remote creek-side area. There, they prepare a picnic lunch while hikers and llamas have a chance to relax. Participants are treated to a candlelit feast accompanied by the soothing sounds of nature—bubbling water from the stream, rustling leaves, and hums from curious llamas.

After guests have had ample time to digest their meals, the llamas are repacked and the trek continues. Out of the woods and off the trail, trekkers can return to the barn by way of a pasture or a gravel driveway. Those who choose the pasture can visit with the miniature horses and Bucky the miniature donkey.

Before departing, guests are invited to the tasting room (a modest additional fee is charged) for a sampling of seven Divine Llama wines. Among the favorites are "Red Rita" and "In a Heartbeat"—blends of wine named for llamas that reside at the vineyard.

Divine Llama Vineyards also welcomes the public during harvest season. Grapes are typically harvested during the last week of August and the first three weeks of September. During the harvest, grape-picking volunteers and their bucket-carrying llama companions gather the fruit together. Afterward, volunteers and staff enjoy a meal, wine, and festive talk of llamas.

Trekking with llamas and partaking of a picnic on the grounds of Divine Llama Vineyards combine to make a memorable experience. The friendly hosts and owners will do all they can to accommodate guests' needs and make the excursion a gratifying event. Whatever the occasion—whether family outing or romantic rendezvous—an afternoon spent trekking with llamas is an out-of-the-ordinary occurrence that participants will long remember.

Tips

● Note that trips are payable by cash only.

● Remember, trekkers only lead llamas; they do not ride them. The trek is approximately two miles long and typically lasts about three hours. The terrain is a bit steep in places, so consider your physical condition before scheduling an excursion. Mark and Sharon Berry offer shorter distances, so feel free to discuss other options with them.

● Make sure you wear good walking—or preferably hiking—shoes, keeping in mind they may get muddy or wet. Bathrooms are not available on the trail, so visit the facilities prior to heading out on your trip.

● Keep in mind that you have to continue your hike after lunch. Therefore, you may want to order something on the light side.

● If you are interested in volunteering for the grape harvest, visit the Divine Llama Vineyards website, www.divinellamavineyards.com, and sign up to receive e-mail announcements.

● Anyone interested in llama fiber or products made from it should visit the Mill Stone General Store & Gallery, owned by Patricia West. The store is in the Bethania Mill & Village Shoppes at 5455 Bethania Road in Winston-Salem. To learn more, call 336-922-0374 or visit www.bethaniamillandvillageshoppes.com.

~~~~~~

SciWorks

400 West Hanes Mill Road
Winston-Salem, N.C. 27105
Phone: 336-767-6730
Website: www.sciworks.org
E-mail: info@sciworks.org

Hours: Spring, fall, and winter hours are Monday through Friday from 10 A.M. to 4 P.M. and Saturday from 11 A.M. to 5 P.M. Summer hours (June 1 through Labor Day) are Monday through Saturday from 10 A.M. to 5 P.M.

Directions: From U.S. 52 North at Winston-Salem in Forsyth County, take Exit 116. Turn right on Hanes Mill Road. SciWorks is on the left after approximately 0.5 mile.

~~~~~~

"You'll love meeting our farmyard animals, white-tailed deer, waterfowl and our playful river otters."
SciWorks website

In 2008, *Parents* magazine named SciWorks one of the top twenty-five science centers in the United States. SciWorks, the Science Center and Environmental Park of Forsyth County, was one of only two North Carolina facilities listed, along with Discovery Place in Charlotte. Never ceasing in its efforts to improve programs and experiences for the public, SciWorks has since renovated displays, introduced new exhibits, and begun construction on a new Outdoor Science Park.

In 1964, SciWorks opened as the Nature Science Center in the barn at Reynolda Village, the collection of buildings that once supported the estate of tobacco magnate R. J. Reynolds. Ten years later, the center moved to its current location. In 1992, the name was changed to SciWorks. Along with the new name came the Environmental Park, a fifteen-acre outdoor exhibit.

Visitors arriving at SciWorks should perhaps tour the Environmental Park first, as it closes a half-hour before the building. Inside the Environmental Park, they will see domestic livestock and native wildlife.

Red-roofed gray barns surrounded by a landscape of artistic sculptures create a charming residence for the domesticated animals. The cast of characters to be met in and around the barns includes May and Tess, sister goats; Annabelle and Cocoa, two

The remora is an interesting fish not often seen on display.

Visitors can safely study the details of a black widow spider behind glass.

sheep; Snowflake, a miniature horse; Hazel and Peanut, mother-and-son donkeys; and Teenie and Edy, a couple of cows. Most of the barnyard animals enjoy being petted, although the cows seem a little skittish of grabby hands. The goats are the entertainers, but the vocal one in the crowd is Peanut, whom visitors will likely hear prior to arriving at the barns.

Continuing on the path beyond the barns, guests will pass an herb garden and a pond that is often alive with ducks and turtles. Past the pond, a large forested habitat houses several white-tailed deer. The deer are accustomed to people and are generally in the vicinity of the viewing station. Following the paved trail, which winds through a wooded area, guests will happen upon Mollie and Ollie, two energetic river otters. Large glass panels surround the otters' habitat and provide excellent underwater viewing. As at other otter exhibits, the playful and skillful swimmers always attract a crowd. From the otter exhibit, the trail passes a hummingbird and butterfly garden, circles back to the barnyard, and reaches the exit.

Visitors who would like to learn more about the animals in the Environmental Park should visit SciWorks on a Monday or Saturday, as an educational tour is offered at 1:30 P.M.

In the Science Center building, visitors—particularly children—will find a number of interactive exhibits that promote hands-on, object-based science learning. In PhysicsWorks, children can learn about aerodynamics, Newton's laws of motion, and the earth's rotation. SoundWorks illustrates the principles of sound through the use of stringless harps and an extremely popular walk on a piano. HealthWorks demonstrates the inner workings of the human body and contains a giant game of Operation. KidsWorks explores science on a level appropriate for the youngest visitors, while TotSpots—placed throughout the Science Center—offer activities for children ages two to five. In Millennium Plaza, visitors will marvel as they rotate a four-foot, fifty-three-hundred-pound granite sphere to demonstrate the physics of water pressure and the principles of hydrology. SciWorks also has a planetarium that offers shows for all ages daily.

The remaining exhibits are again designed for children but also appeal to adults. The Mountains to Sea exhibit explores the state's natural treasures. Visitors can crawl inside a replicated beaver lodge, step inside a twenty-foot tree, and listen to a series of animal sounds. The aquariums featured in the exhibit showcase hermit crabs, arrow crabs, sea stars, coral banded shrimp, trout, and other sea life. A touch tank allows guests to examine whelks, horseshoe crabs, and spider crabs. One resident, the remora, is not typically seen in touch tanks. For many visitors, this may be their first encounter with this unusual-looking species. The suction pad on the back of the remora's head—which allows it to attach itself to other marine life—makes the fish appear to be swimming upside down. Feeding demonstrations are presented at the touch tank on Tuesdays, Thursdays, and Saturdays at 11:30 A.M. Those in attendance will learn about habitats, feeding behavior, food chains, and other marine topics. Located in the same room as the Mountains to Sea exhibit is the Science Lab, which allows visitors to explore fossils, shells, and other natural collections. One large collection showcases mounted animals from around the world.

BioWorks, a recently renovated exhibit, is a highlight of the Science Center, as it offers a look at a host of interesting animals native to the Western Hemisphere. A rather long red-tailed boa is the first animal to greet tourists, followed by several other snakes including a Northern pine snake, a rat snake, a corn snake, and a copperhead. Among the unique and interesting creatures in the exhibit are zebra roaches, a marine toad, a Cope's gray treefrog, a Chilean rose tarantula, a tiger salamander, Northern walking sticks, a giant desert hairy scorpion, and a black widow spider. The accompanying educational text panels are fascinating. For example, guests will learn that the marine toad is native to South America but was introduced into North America during 1955 in an effort to control sugar-cane pests. BioWorks offers one of the best displays of the deadly black widow spider in the state. Other animals visitors will enjoy seeing are a chinchilla, a raccoon, a green iguana, a painted turtle, a red-eared slider, an Eastern screech owl, bobwhite quail, and a blue-and-gold macaw. The macaw's name is Huey, and he celebrated his twenty-fifth birthday in 2010. According to Kelli Isenhour, vice president of programs and education, in "Naturalist Notes" in the Winter 2010 edition of *SciNews*, "Huey was a captive-bred bird. . . . He can say:

hi, hello, hola, bye-bye, and cracker, among other words. He also dances, laughs, and meows." Huey is able to "converse" with visitors through speakers placed inside and outside his enclosure. Guests should not hesitate to stop and chat with him. Those interested in learning more about these animals or who would like a personal encounter with one should check the daily program calendar, as "Animal Encounters" are offered Monday through Friday in SciWorks' Little Theater.

When Debbie Cesta, vice president of development and marketing, was asked what SciWorks hoped guests would take away with them, she responded, "We want our visitors to be good 'consumers' of science and to strive to be good stewards of the earth, because all things are connected and there is a purpose for every living thing." After touring the Environmental Park, the Mountains to Sea exhibit, and BioWorks and participating in one of SciWorks' daily or weekly programs, visitors will no doubt have a better understanding of those connections and leave with a desire to learn more.

Tips

• Adults without children should not dismiss a visit to SciWorks, as several exhibits are not age-specific. Even ones that are can be fun to explore.

• Pay close attention to SciWorks' calendar of events. "Family Fridays" are typically offered on the second Fridays of June, July, and August. During these events, admission is only two dollars per person between 4 P.M. and 8 P.M.

• If you have time, you may want to drive approximately three miles to Historic Bethabara Park. There, you will find the 1753 site of the first Moravian settlement in North Carolina. The grounds, gardens, trails, and six-acre wetland are open free of charge year-round. The park is located at 2147 Bethabara Road in Winston-Salem. To learn more, call 336-924-8191 or visit www.cityofws.org; click on "Departments," then "Recreation & Parks."

all-a-flutter Butterfly Farm

7850-B Clinard Farms Road
High Point, N.C. 27265
Phone: 336-454-5651
Website: www.all-a-flutter.com
E-mail: buttersare@aol.com

Hours: Open seasonally from April to October. Phone or visit the website for exact dates and hours.

Directions: From I-40 in Guilford County, take Exit 210 (the High Point/Piedmont Triad International Airport exit), travel approximately 1.5 miles on N.C. 68 South, turn right on Clinard Farms Road, and drive about 1 mile. The farm is on the right.

Guests can observe and feed monarch butterflies at all-a-flutter Butterfly Farm.

". . . see and experience a real butterfly farm up close!"
all-a-flutter Butterfly Farm brochure

Butterflies are welcome guests at flower gardens throughout the state. Their delicate beauty delights, while their aerial acrobatics entertain all who behold them. But beyond the appeal of bright-colored, individually patterned wings, the life cycle of these fluttering sky dancers astounds the human mind. That life cycle involves the transformation of a caterpillar into a winged insect. Most people are aware of this metamorphosis, but many have never viewed the process in its various stages. The opportunity exists at all-a flutter Butterfly Farm in High Point.

In 2001, Donna and Tim Pless decided to raise butterflies on their twenty-seven-acre Guilford County farm to sell to individuals and businesses for release at weddings, birthdays, graduations, funerals, and other special events. As the surrounding community learned of the butterflies, Donna began offering show-and-tell presentations for their enjoyment. The popularity of the butterflies made it apparent the farm should be opened to the public. But the family wanted to offer more than a sightseeing tour. The Plesses desired to educate their visitors about North American butterflies—particularly the monarch, the main butterfly raised on the farm. Their hope is to see each visitor leave with a greater appreciation and understanding of what a butterfly had to endure to become the beautiful creature it is. They also want to enlighten guests about the plight of the monarch and how habitat destruction is affecting its survival.

The farm sells butterflies for release and provides tours from April through October. Group tours must be scheduled by advance reservation, while "Family Days" are offered to the public on Saturdays. During Family Days, butterfly showings are presented in the morning and afternoon. The exact dates and times of the presentations can be found on the farm's website. Visitors who attend Family Days are not required to make reservations, but the farm does recommend arriving ten minutes early. After paying the admission fee, guests are directed to an outdoor seating area. There, Nora Cammer, the farm manager, uses props *and* members of the audience to demonstrate the life cycle of a monarch butterfly. Visitors will journey with the monarch as it begins life in the form of an egg, hatches into a tiny caterpillar (larva), creates its chrysalis, and at last emerges in the form of an orange-and-black butterfly. Cammer also discusses the monarch's food sources, migration pattern, and anatomy. Guests learn such things as how to distinguish a butterfly from a moth.

After the presentation, visitors are taken to the "flighthouse," the farm's main attraction. Inside the flighthouse, which holds hundreds of free-flying monarchs (and sometimes a few other species), speckles of orange and black flitter around each visitor. Guests eagerly wait to see if any of the butterflies will land on them. The farm provides each guest a sugar pad from which to feed a butterfly. Instructions are given on how to coax a butterfly to the pad. Every guest is guaranteed to feed a butterfly out of his or her own hand. Visitors delight when the butterfly rolls out its proboscis (much like a garden hose) to drink the sugar water. This activity offers a perfect opportunity for photographs.

The flighthouse is truly an incredible place. It not only holds hundreds of butterflies but is also the location where the entire life cycle of a monarch can be viewed. Guests can see newly laid eggs on milkweed plants and watch caterpillars in various stages of growth heartily devouring those plants. A caterpillar that has formed its chrysalis is a special sight to see; its enclosure is lime green and appears to have been sealed with beads of gold. Especially fortunate visitors may actually see a monarch emerge. Guests are given at least a half-hour to enjoy the flighthouse, which is ample time to view the eggs, caterpillars, chrysalises, and butterflies.

On Family Days, the farm typically offers additional activities—provided by local businesses and performers—to make the event more entertaining. "Art to Zebras," typically on-site once or twice a month, offers face painting and crafts for children.

Hundreds of free-flying monarch butterflies await visitors inside the flighthouse.

In the past, the farm has partnered with the Harmony Grove Dulcimer Ensemble for musical entertainment and the Double-C Horse Farm for pony rides. Visitors can check the farm's website to see who will be providing entertainment at upcoming Family Days and schedule a visit accordingly.

All-a-flutter Butterfly Farm remains a family endeavor. In 2008, Donna and Tim turned the operation over to their son, Brandon, whose ideas for future growth are exactly as they envisioned. The family would eventually like to expand the hours of operation and perhaps offer a pick-your-own pumpkin farm or other attraction that can engage the public during the cool months. As the farm continues to grow, however, the Pless family will remain dedicated to educating the public to be respectful of nature, to realize the importance of preserving natural habitats, and to prevent the monarch from ever becoming an endangered species.

Tips

- It may be stated during your tour that butterflies particularly like purple, white, and yellow. Try wearing a shirt in one of those colors and see if a butterfly will land on you!

- At the end of the tour, you will have an opportunity to purchase a caterpillar castle. Take my advice and buy one! Castles are not typically available the day of your visit; instead, orders are taken and guests are required to pick them up at a later date. If you are not local, call in advance to see if the farm can have one ready for pickup the day of your visit. A caterpillar castle, which is a milkweed plant wrapped in netting, will allow you and your family to observe a miracle of nature within your own home. The milkweed plant contains one or two monarch eggs. If you look hard enough, you might be able to find them; a monarch egg looks like a little white dot on the underside of a leaf. After several days, the egg will hatch and an itty-bitty caterpillar will appear. Although the larva comes out *very* hungry, you might at first see only tiny holes on the leaves, especially since the caterpillar is green. However, it's not long before it eats itself into a larger size and begins forming its chrysalis. About a week later, a delicate monarch butterfly will emerge from the chrysalis and can be released outside.

● After touring all-a-flutter Butterfly Farm, you may want to stop by the Piedmont Triad Farmers Market, located approximately two miles away. There, you can purchase plants that will attract butterflies, bees, and hummingbirds to your backyard. The market also has a variety of local fruits and vegetables, as well as a full-service restaurant. It is located at 2914 Sandy Ridge Road in Colfax. To learn more, call 336-605-9157 or visit www.ncagr.gov/markets/facilities/markets/triad/.

Natural Science Center of Greensboro

4301 Lawndale Drive
Greensboro, N.C. 27455
Phone: 336-288-3769
Website: www.natsci.org
E-mail: info@natsci.org

Hours: Open daily year-round from 9 A.M. to 5 P.M. Closed Thanksgiving, Christmas, and New Year's.

Directions: From U.S. 220 South (Battleground Avenue) in Greensboro, turn left on Pisgah Church Road, drive 0.5 mile, and turn left on Lawndale Drive. The center is on the left after about a mile.

~~~~~~~~~~~~~~~~~~~~~

". . . become immersed in a world of up-close creature encounters . . ."
Natural Science Center of Greensboro brochure

The Natural Science Center of Greensboro offers visitors a chance to explore science, technology, and animals at one place, in one day! Located on approximately twenty-five acres in Guilford County, the center opened in 1957 as the Greensboro Junior Museum. It has expanded ever since. The center opened its Animal Discovery Zoological Park in 2007.

Visitors may want to begin their exploration on the lower level, as the stairs and elevator are located directly beside the admission desk. The exciting exhibits on the lower level include the Science ROCKS! Classroom, the Physics Lab, the Biology Lab, and the Herpetology Lab, which houses a variety of snakes, lizards, and turtles. Visitors can also enter the Greensboro Jaycees Herpetarium to see an outstanding collection of snakes. Two specimens of note are the sidewinder and the Sinaloan milk snake. Sidewinders, venomous snakes found in the southwestern United States, acquired their name from the unique way they move. The Sinaloan milk snake was named after an old wives' tale that stated the reptile would sneak into barns and milk cows dry. Found in western Mexico, the Sinaloan milk snake is nonvenomous. Poison dart frogs, a hellbender, and various other animals are also displayed in the herpetarium.

In the Marine Gallery, visitors can meet sea creatures such as red lionfish, a spiny lobster, a nurse shark, and a tessellated moray eel. The tessellated moray eel is beautiful. As its name suggests, its body has a checkered pattern. Native to the Indian and South Pacific oceans, it averages four to five feet in length.

Next to the Marine Gallery is the Kiwanis Kids' Cove, where visitors will find a

Natural Science Center of Greensboro is the only facility in North Carolina to exhibit maned wolves. PHOTOGRAPH COURTESY OF NATURAL SCIENCE CENTER OF GREENSBORO

The white-handed gibbon is an endangered species.

touch tank containing sea urchins and other marine life. Staff is on hand to assist and answer questions.

On the main level is the Paleontology Gallery, where guests will be astounded to see the thirty-six-foot *Tyrannosaurus rex* model. They can also learn about rocks and gems in the Mineral Science Gallery, study atmospheric conditions in the Weather Gallery, and attend one of the daily presentations in the OmniSphere, where visitors can "take a trip to space and beyond!" as stated in the museum's brochure.

Once guests have enjoyed the inside exhibits, they can step outside to meet a plethora of animals. The Animal Discovery Zoological Park is a large, nicely designed, well-landscaped facility. Guests will likely be surprised—and impressed—to find such a considerable animal park on the grounds.

Entering Animal Discovery, tourists will see—and likely smell—the Junior League Discovery Gardens, which include oak trees, flowering annuals, perennials, rhododendrons, roses, ferns, and cattails in the swampy areas. While guests enjoy the gardens, a gigantic praying mantis may catch their eyes, as the insect appears to be crawling out of the Kavanagh Discovery House's upstairs window. The insect is most appropriate, as the building contains the fascinating Bug Discovery exhibit. The interesting specimens on display include a goliath birdeater tarantula, a black widow spider, a brown recluse spider, Northern walking sticks, Madagascar hissing cockroaches, and a whip scorpion. Native to South America, the goliath birdeater tarantula gets the most attention, as it is possibly the world's largest spider. Visitors should take time to examine the black widow and brown recluse and learn how to recognize both of them. Both of these highly venomous spiders are found in North Carolina. Also in the Kavanagh Discovery House are several small mammals including a hedgehog, ferrets, rabbits, and an armadillo. Many of the animals are brought out of their enclosures on a regular basis for hands-on encounters with the public.

Behind the Kavanagh Discovery House is the Davis Kelly Fountain of Youth and Discovery. The display features an interactive fountain complete with dancing water and music. It was built in memory of Davis Kelly, a three-year-old who was tragically killed on I-85. Beyond the fountain, the remaining exhibits showcase a stunning collection of animals. Visitors will walk a paved path to meet Nile crocodiles and tortoises—unless it is winter, when they are off-exhibit. They will also encounter three species of lemurs, white-handed gibbons, and black howler monkeys. Found in Southeast Asia, white-handed gibbons are an endangered species. The gibbons draw a crowd, as they can often be seen swinging on the ropes and branches within their habitat.

A fair distance down the path is the popular tiger exhibit. Here, visitors can observe tigers on a face-to-face basis through large glass panels. Just beyond the tiger exhibit are the maned wolves. For many visitors, this may be their first time seeing these animals, as the Natural Science Center of Greensboro is the only facility in North Carolina to exhibit the species. It is also the only facility in the nation with a green, solar, and sustainable maned wolf breeding center. Native to South America, maned wolves are an endangered species. They do not travel in packs but are solitary hunters. When they are threatened or need to display aggression, they raise their black manes in an attempt to look larger. At the maned wolf habitat, visitors can observe the animals by way of an elevated boardwalk. Staff stationed on the boardwalk instruct people not to run or talk loudly. The well-planned exhibit allows visitors to capture quality photographs of these exquisite animals.

After retracing their steps up the path, visitors can behold—and listen to— green-naped lorikeets or mimic the motion of birds in the Forward Flight Simulator. Those who want to get hands-on with animals should enter the Wallaby Walkthrough, where they can greet Jupiter, a Bennett's wallaby. Should Jupiter be so inclined, he may acknowledge guests' greetings by coming to the fence. If he does, visitors are welcome to pet him. Unfortunately, Jupiter sometimes keeps to himself. If that is the case, guests can head over to the Friendly Farm, where several animals are more than happy to be petted and admired. Animals at the Friendly Farm include Guinea forest hogs, donkeys, miniature horses, Tunis sheep, alpacas, and Nigerian dwarf goats. Visitors who take the opportunity to brush the goats find it to be a pleasurable activity.

Other animals to be observed within the park include white-nosed coatis, a groundhog, meerkats, and Asian small-clawed otters, a type of otter not commonly seen at animal facilities in the state. The center participates in the Species Survival Plan for this breed of otter and displays a lively pair named Jelly and Olin. Just like river otters at other facilities, Asian small-clawed otters entertain visitors by swiftly climbing over rocks and maneuvering through water.

Before leaving the Animal Discovery area, visitors should make sure they have not missed any exciting programs scheduled for the day. "Keeper Talks," typically held several times a day, allow guests to learn additional facts about particular animals. During "Friendly Farm Keeper Talks," visitors are allowed to feed goats and sheep.

After completing the trek through Animal Discovery, visitors will return to the main building, where they can visit the Thesaurus Shoppe and purchase nature- or science-related items before ending their day.

In November 2009, the citizens of Greensboro passed a $20 million bond that will allow the center to renovate its science museum, double the size of its Animal Discovery Zoological Park, and construct the Carolina Sciquarium.

Roxanna Burkhart, director of marketing, says that the Natural Science Center of Greensboro wants everyone to leave with "an appreciation for the vast opportunities in science." The center's goal, she says, is to "ignite sparks that [push visitors] to open a book, research the internet, or do more in school." As the facility moves forward with its expansions, it will no doubt meet the challenges of addressing the public's interests and continually exciting visitors about science and nature.

Tips

- Note that Animal Discovery closes one hour earlier than the exhibits in the building.

- The center is located next to Country Park, which offers two fishing lakes, hiking and biking trails, playgrounds, picnic facilities, and paddleboat rentals. You may want to allow time to partake of some of the park's activities before leaving the area. To learn more about Country Park, visit www.greensboro-nc.gov. Click on "Departments," then "Parks & Recreation," then "Parks," and finally "Country Park."

Huacaya alpacas have a fluffy "teddy bear" appearance.

Caraway Alpacas

1079 Jarvis Miller Road
Asheboro, N.C. 27205
Phone: 336-629-6767
Website: www.carawayalpaca.com
E-mail: carawayalpacas@embarqmail.com

Hours: Open to the public once a year on the third Saturday in November from 10 A.M. to 3 P.M. Phone or visit the website for the exact date.

Directions: From U.S. 64 East in Randolph County west of Asheboro, turn left on Old Lexington Road. Stay straight on Jarvis Miller Road. Caraway Alpacas is on the left in about 2 miles.

"... one of the most beautiful, peaceful animals you can imagine."
Southeastern Alpaca Association website

If you have never had the opportunity to meet an alpaca, then mark your calendar for the third Saturday in November. On that day, Caraway Alpacas invites the public to attend its annual "Open Barn."

Tucked away in the rolling hills of Randolph County, Caraway Alpacas is the perfect venue for an autumn afternoon. Visitors will delight in the picturesque beau-

Caraway Alpacas Research Learning Center and Gift Shop

ty of the farm, as well as the numerous alpacas traipsing the property. Bobby and Ann Poole and Mike and Teresa Johnson established the family-owned and -operated farm in 1997. After beginning with six alpacas on two acres of pastureland, they soon found it necessary to clear fifteen more acres for their growing herd.

Currently, twenty-eight alpacas reside at the farm. Both breeds of alpacas—huacaya and suri—are represented. According to the brochure *Meet the Alpaca*, produced by the Alpaca Owners and Breeders Association and The Alpaca Registry, "Although both types of alpacas are physiologically nearly identical, one main physical difference is clearly identifiable: the fleece. Huacaya fleece has a degree of 'waviness,' or 'crimp,' thus giving huacayas a fluffy, 'teddy bear-like' appearance. Suris, on the other hand, have no crimp in their fleeces, so their fiber clings to itself, forming beautiful 'pencil locks' that hang down from the body in gentle silky cascades."

Although the appearance of the two breeds' fleeces is different, visitors will quickly discover a common trait: both are amazingly soft. Guests have the opportunity to view and purchase handcrafted items made from the fleece of both resident and nonresident alpacas. The owners of Caraway Alpacas hope visitors will leave with an appreciation for this type of fiber and understand its durability. Teresa Johnson stresses the fact that a sweater made from synthetic yarn will likely wear out in a year or two, whereas a sweater created from alpaca fiber will in all probability pass from one generation to the next.

Educating the public about alpacas and their quality fiber is important to the owners of Caraway Alpacas. They remain on-site throughout the day and are happy to answer questions. One question they are likely to be asked is, what is the difference between an alpaca and a llama? Alpacas are smaller than llamas, have shorter ears, and possess tails that sit lower on their backs. Visitors who browse the facility's Resource Learning Center can uncover interesting facts about alpacas through a variety of educational materials. For instance, they will learn that alpacas are members of the camelid, or camel, family and are native to the Andes Mountains of

South America. The Resource Learning Center also houses exclusive items available for purchase.

While it is informative to learn facts about alpacas, nothing can compare to being in their presence. Such gentle and inquisitive creatures, they stand along the fence seemingly for the sole purpose of greeting guests and appear to relish the hand that holds a cup of food (a specially prepared treat is given to each visitor to feed to the animals). Being up close to the alpacas, guests will have the chance to hear the variety of sounds they make. The one made most frequently can be compared to a soft humming sound. Generally, it means an alpaca is content with its surroundings.

Another noise—one not so soft but more familiar—can also be heard on the farm. Caraway Alpacas has four Great Pyrenees dogs that stand guard over the herd. Alpacas are flight animals but are unable to run away from predators in a confined pasture, which can make for a dangerous situation. For the herd at Caraway Alpacas, the most threatening predators are neighborhood dogs and coyotes. The guard dogs are therefore an essential component of the farm's operation.

Caraway Alpacas has been "loving and caring for alpacas since 1997." The alpacas, the guard dogs, and the farm owners make every visitor feel welcome and leave a lasting impression upon all.

Tips

- Check the website to verify date and hours. Caraway Alpacas warns that MapQuest directions are currently inaccurate. The correct directions are on the website.

- For the best selection of products, especially socks and stuffed animals, try to arrive early in the day. If you plan to purchase Christmas presents, note that Caraway Alpacas does not currently accept credit cards.

North Carolina Zoo

4401 Zoo Parkway
Asheboro, N.C. 27205
Phone: 800-488-0444 or 336-879-7000
Website: www.nczoo.org
E-mail: Online form

The polar bear is one of the zoo's most popular animals.
PHOTOGRAPH COURTESY OF NORTH CAROLINA ZOO

Hours: Open daily year-round except for Christmas. The hours are 9 A.M. to 5 P.M. from April to October and 9 A.M. to 4 P.M. from November to March.

Directions: From I-73 South in Randolph County, exit onto West Dixie Drive (U.S. 64 East). Travel approximately 1.5 miles, turn right on Zoo Parkway (N.C. 159), and drive about 4.5 miles. The zoo is on the left.

**"Connect with wildlife from the two continents
of Africa and North America."**
North Carolina Zoo 2010 Visitor Guide

When the words *animal* and *adventures* are used in the same sentence in this state, most people immediately think of the North Carolina Zoo in Asheboro. That is fitting, as the North Carolina Zoo, according to its website, is "nationally recognized

Red river hogs are native to western and central Africa.
PHOTOGRAPH COURTESY OF
NORTH CAROLINA ZOO

as one of the nation's finest zoos." North Carolina has achieved many "firsts" throughout its history, and the zoo added another to the list when it opened in 1974, becoming the nation's first state-supported zoo. Today, it remains the country's largest walk-through natural-habitat zoo. In terms of acreage, the zoo encompasses over two thousand acres in Randolph County, five hundred of which are currently developed.

The zoo showcases animals from two continents: North America and Africa. When visitors arrive, they can enter at whichever continent they choose. The North America continent has three miles of pathways; the zoo recommends three hours for a visit. In Africa, visitors will find two miles of pathways; the zoo recommends two hours. During their exploration of the continents, visitors will observe countless animals, many of which cannot be seen anywhere else in the state. The educational text panels accompanying each exhibit inform guests about the animals, the zoo's role in conservation, and ways in which people can protect wildlife and the environment.

Without a doubt, Africa as a whole is the highlight of the zoo. The vast landscape, buildings with African motifs or architectural elements, and animals that most people will never experience in the wild bring the continent vividly to life. Visitors who enter the zoo through Africa will do so across a tall and fairly long wooden bridge. The first area to be explored inside is the Forest Edge Habitat, where Grant's zebras, ostriches, and giraffes roam a large, open woodland. At the Acacia Station Giraffe Deck, visitors can get at eye level with giraffes and offer them food.

A favorite of many visitors is the Watani Grasslands Reserve. Here, viewing stations allow them to observe and photograph African elephants across a large expanse of land. Also in this area are ostriches, Southern white rhinoceroses, and eight species of antelopes.

At the Forest Glade Habitat, visitors will be astounded to observe the Western lowland gorilla. One silverback male and two females can be viewed through large glass panels. Often, the gorillas sit directly next to the glass, which allows observers an intimate look at these remarkable animals.

Likely the most entertaining of the habitats is the Kitera Forest Chimpanzee Reserve. Thirteen chimpanzees climb trees, interact with one another, and examine visitors through the viewing glass. According to the zoo's website, the chimpanzees inside this habitat are the largest such troop at any United States zoo.

Leapin' Lemurs is a fairly new habitat that features ring-tailed and red-ruffed lemurs. Beyond the lemurs are the Lion Habitat and the Red River Hogs Habitat. Visitors will not want to miss the red river hogs. Their name comes from the facts that they are reddish in color and are often found near water. For many, this may be their first encounter with red river hogs, as only twelve other zoos in the United States exhibit them.

The last exhibit in Africa is the Forest Aviary, which re-creates a tropical forest. A host of exotic birds can be observed flying through the interior. Visitors will both enjoy trying to glimpse each bird and delight in seeing the variety of tropical plants. When exiting the aviary, guests may want to use the restroom or purchase a drink, as the next outpost where these amenities can be found is a good distance away.

Entering North America, visitors will discover the Honey Bee Garden. This exhibit teaches the importance of pollinating insects such as bees, butterflies, and hummingbirds. Guests can peer inside a working beehive and see these amazing creatures at work. They can also enjoy flower gardens specifically designed to attract pollinators. Most importantly, they can learn how to attract these insects to their own backyards.

Beyond the Honey Bee Garden is the Sonora Desert, the first animal habitat to open in the North America region of the zoo. Inside, various desert animals and plants re-create the environment of the Southwest so clearly that visitors can easily imagine being there. Birds fly freely about the building, while other animals such as tarantulas, lizards, desert tortoises, and ocelots are housed in their own enclosures. A darkened area features nocturnal animals such as vampire bats and coatis. Needless to say, the vampire bats get considerable attention. Two other animals that visitors find particularly interesting are the greater roadrunner and the Gambel's quail. Many have seen only the cartoon version of the "speedy" roadrunner and are amazed to encounter the real animal. The Gambel's quail, although a relatively small bird, leaves a big impression on visitors, thanks to its colorful feathers and head plume.

Continuing the trek into North America, visitors will pass the Red Wolves Habitat and the Grizzly Bears Habitat. Although the red wolves may be difficult to see, guests should not have a problem locating the grizzly bears. The two males on display came to the North Carolina Zoo by way of Montana, where they were deemed "nuisance bears by the Grizzly Bear Recovery Program and U.S. Fish and Wildlife Service," according to the zoo's website. "They would have been destroyed if an appropriate home had not been found."

Several viewpoints allow visitors to scan the Prairie Habitat and observe the natural behaviors of American elk and American bison. The next exhibit is the Black Bears Habitat. The American black bears, two of which were rescued from roadside zoos, can typically be seen wading in their pools and lounging on rocks.

At Streamside, visitors will learn about species native to North Carolina. They will encounter river otters, bobcats, frogs, snakes, turtles, a barred owl, and aquariums full of fish. They will also have an opportunity to view some of the state's endangered plants. An interesting educational text panel teaches guests what to do should they encounter a snake.

Just past Streamside, visitors may suddenly feel a chill in the air, as the next exhibit explores animals of the Arctic region. Rocky Coast is probably *the* most popular exhibit at the North Carolina Zoo. Here, visitors have the rare chance to come face to face with a polar bear. This is made possible through an exhibit that provides both above- and below-water viewing opportunities. Standing in front of the glass panel as the polar bear swims by or stops in front of them is an unforgettable experience for guests. Other animals in the Rocky Coast exhibit include California sea lions, harbor seals, Arctic foxes, horned puffins, and a bald eagle.

Warming back up again, visitors can walk through the Marsh Habitat to see several species of native wildlife. Or they can walk down the boardwalk among bald cypress trees toward the Cypress Swamp Habitat, where they can view various species of ducks as well as numerous American alligators, whose size and prehistoric look are awe-inspiring. Visitors will also see turtles, snakes, frogs, and cougars. They should not overlook the carnivorous plant garden, where pitcher plants and Venus flytraps are on display.

Upon reaching the end of North America, visitors can take a tram or bus back to Africa or walk through the exhibits once again, although few are up to more walking at this point. Guests have a large variety of gift shops to explore, where items relevant to the exhibits are available for purchase. They can also attend a short program at the Adventure 4-D Theatre or take a relaxing spin on the zoo's carousel. Daily events such as animal feedings should not be missed, as they present the opportunity to learn more about particular species. The zoo also offers special events throughout the year. Some of the most popular are the Earth Day Celebration (April), Migratory Bird Day (May), and "Boo at the Zoo" (October).

The North Carolina Zoo is a work of art where the public can explore the wildlife of two continents in one day. Because animals are displayed in habitats made to resemble their native environments, visitors can imagine they are observing them in the wild. They will relish their time spent at the nation's largest—and perhaps most beautiful—walk-through natural-habitat zoo.

Tips

* Wear your most comfortable shoes, as the zoo requires a considerable amount of walking. Although trams and buses are available to take you back and forth between the parking lots and the two continents, animals *cannot* be viewed from either. Strollers, wheelchairs, and electric mobility chairs are available for rent.

* To fully enjoy the zoo, especially if you are a first-time visitor, make plans to spend the entire day. Also, be sure to study the visitor guide—which will be given to you when you purchase a ticket—before heading out. That way, you can plan your day and make the most of your time. Don't forget to pick up a daily schedule of events!

Sunny Slopes Farm

2994 Fairview Farm Road
Asheboro, N.C. 27205
Phone: 336-879-5996 or 336-879-1606
Website: www.sunnyslopesfarm.com
E-mail: info@sunnyslopesfarm.com

Hours: The farm typically offers its annual Heritage Day Festival on the first Saturday in May from 10 A.M. to 5 P.M. The event is open to the public. Phone or visit the website for exact date and hours. Otherwise, advance reservations are required. Same-day reservations are available; call the office between 8 A.M. and 8 P.M.

Directions: From U.S. 64 East (Dixie Drive) in Asheboro in Randolph County, turn right on N.C. 42 East. Drive about 4 miles and turn right on Fairview Farm Road. Sunny Slopes Farm is on the right in about 1.5 miles.

 (On Heritage Day, food is available from vendors.)

"... see beautiful land features ... as well as
domesticated animals in natural settings."
Sunny Slopes Farm website

Igor is a Brahma bull with the personality of a puppy dog.

Purgatory. By definition, it is a place of temporary torture or suffering. Hearing the word elicits dark and foreboding images. But Purgatory Mountain—part of the Uwharrie Mountains in Randolph County—fails to satisfy its name. It is a magnificent natural attraction with a colorful heritage that encompasses, according to the Sunny Slopes Farm brochure, "farming, hunting, gold mining . . . and . . . even moonshining." Sunny Slopes Farm, located in Asheboro on nearly 220 acres along the northeast face of Purgatory Mountain, seeks to preserve that heritage.

In 2007, Roger Pritchard opened the farm as an "outdoor classroom." His classroom consists of over two hundred animals—representing a variety of species—that can be observed in their natural setting. Some of his animals were donated, several were purchased, and a few were born on the farm. The majority are typical of those expected on a farm: cows, sheep, llamas, goats, miniature donkeys, horses, a mule, rabbits, chickens, fish, ducks, and a turkey. However, several personalities within the group are anything *but* typical, and visitors will be delighted to meet them. One such character is Ramses, the Painted Desert ram that is the farm's mascot. Ramses is charged with keeping order among the sheep and goats. According to staff, "When Ramses speaks, sheep listen." Bucky, a black and white pygmy goat, "loves to be petted" and insists on being the center of attention. Visitors will enjoy feeding Bucky and all his barnyard friends.

Other animals not so common at local farms include Texas longhorn cattle (one of which, Bunyon, has a stately pair of horns worthy of a photograph), Scottish Highland cattle, American bison, a Brahma bull, emus, and peacocks. Out of this assemblage, Igor, an *enormous* black Brahma bull, is the resident celebrity. Said to have the disposition of a puppy dog, Igor often travels the Eastern Seaboard attending fairs and other agricultural events.

Visitors will find that the animals are best viewed from a seat on one of Sun-

A cria (baby llama) and its mother at Sunny Slopes Farm

ny Slopes' wagons, as the farm is rather large and the ride is most enjoyable. After meandering around the farm—and stopping on occasion to get a good look at the animals—the hayride eventually ascends to the top of Purgatory Mountain, where a breathtaking view awaits. As guests stand atop the mountain, identify animals in the distance, see countless acres of land, and hear nothing more than the wind, they are instantaneously removed from the hustle and bustle of everyday life. It is this feeling—this vestige of the nineteenth century—that the farm is committed to sharing with its visitors.

That commitment is best seen during the farm's Heritage Day Festival, an annual event that typically takes place on the first Saturday in May. In addition to participating in the farm's regular offerings, visitors can watch men tilling the land behind Belgian draft horses; ride ponies or a mule train; observe quilting, knitting, and crocheting; see pottery being made; and examine a cider mill in action. They can also listen to bluegrass and gospel music, discover the art of making arrowheads and spears, taste a variety of foods, meet historical characters presented by the Bethel Friends Meeting, and converse with authors.

The farm also has other attractions visitors will find appealing: gem mining and a view of the Ghost Gold Mine. Gold was discovered in several places in North Carolina, and the Ghost Gold Mine was one of them. Although staff members are not sure how the mine got its name, they believe it might date back to the Civil War, when a ruthless recruiter named Skully abducted several boys for enlistment in the Confederate army. A despised man, Skully was eventually murdered, purportedly near the entrance of the mine. Local stories say his ghost still haunts the area. Many have reported seeing unexplained lights coming from the mine.

Sunny Slopes Farm's welcoming staff, friendly animals, and pastoral setting ensure that guests of all ages will have a memorable experience at this "great outdoor adventure."

Tips

● Although Sunny Slopes is open by advance reservation only, do not hesitate to contact the farm on the spur of the moment, as reservations can often be scheduled the same day.

● If attending the Heritage Day Festival, make sure you take a ride on the wagon to see the view from the mountain, which is absolutely spectacular.

● Adventurous travelers may want to make a reservation at Richland Creek Zip Line Canopy Tours the same day as their farm visit. The zip line is located about a half-mile from the farm at 2728 Fairview Farm Road in Asheboro. To learn more, call 336-629-9440 or visit www.richland-creekzipline.com.

Conservators' Center

P.O. Box 882
Mebane, N.C. 27302
Phone: 336-421-0883
Website: www.conservatorscenter.org
E-mail: tours@conservatorscenter.org

Hours: Open year-round. Advance reservations are required.

Directions: From the junction of N.C. 119 and N.C. 49 near the Alamance County–Orange County line, travel north on N.C. 119 into Caswell County. Turn left on Huffines Road and follow it to where it dead-ends at Hughes Mill Road. Turn left, then take an immediate right into the Conservators' Center driveway.

~~~~~~~~~~~~~~~~~~~~~~~

"You get so close to these amazing animals you can feel their power."
Conservators' Center website

When tourists enter the gates that lead into Conservators' Center, they may feel as though they are no longer in North Carolina. The impression as they step out of their vehicles is that they have arrived at a remote outpost. They hear the sounds of wild animals nearby and continually catch glimpses of movement. It is an exciting moment, as they know an adventure is about to begin.

In 1999, Mindy Stinner and Doug Evans founded Conservators' Center to preserve threatened species "through responsible captive breeding, rescuing wildlife in need, and providing educational programs and support worldwide," according to their mission statement. Years later, the facility moved to its current location—forty-five-acres in Caswell County. In September 2007, it opened to the public.

Conservators' Center provides refuge to approximately one hundred animals. It is dedicated to educating the public about individual species and their conservation needs. Animals at Conservators' Center are ambassadors that Mindy Stinner and Doug Evans believe "contribute to the survival of their species because people who learn about them come to understand why it is important to protect them, and their habitats."

Visitors arriving for their tours are escorted along a trail where they can observe—from a distance of four to five feet—numerous species. At each habitat, they

Conservators' Center maintains the largest population of lions in North Carolina.

*Tigers at Conservators' Center
are ambassadors for their species.*

will learn the natural history of the animal, its role in the environment, and the story of how it came to live at the facility. They can expect to see caracals, bobcats, ring-tailed lemurs, jungle cats, a lynx, servals, binturongs, wolves, New Guinea singing dogs, lions, and tigers.

One of the first animals on the tour is Aretha Franklin, a caracal. Beginning the tour at the habitat of this lovely creature is most appropriate, as she was Conservators' Center's first intake. Caracals, whose range is Africa and the Middle East, are medium-sized wildcats easily identified by their long black ear tufts.

Next, visitors may have an opportunity to meet Roy, an elderly bobcat. Bobcats are native to North Carolina. Twenty-four-year-old Roy is deaf and suffers from a cataract in one eye. He originally resided at a zoo in Maggie Valley, but the facility closed after fifty-one years. Visitors should be warned about Roy—he is more than capable of stealing their hearts.

Conservators' Center initially had only carnivores on-site. In 2007, however, it received a phone call from someone needing help with an aggressive lemur. After serious consideration, it was determined the center would take in Jeremiah, a ring-tailed lemur. With assistance from Duke Lemur Center—and the introduction of Cookie, another ring-tailed lemur—Jeremiah found a happy home and a lifelong companion. Jeremiah and Cookie are the only primates at Conservators' Center. Visitors are able to greet both of them.

Some of the most intriguing animals at the center—and members of a species many visitors have never seen—are the jungle cats. Jungle cats look very much like domestic cats but are bigger and have larger teeth. Found in Africa, southeastern Europe, and Southeast Asia, they appear to be declining in population. Visitors will greatly enjoy seeing and hearing about these intriguing animals and may meet Tarzan, Little One, or Sahara.

Another fascinating animal to behold is Taz the Eurasian lynx. Taz is believed to have once been a pet, as he arrived at Conservators' Center both neutered and declawed.

Beyond Taz's habitat are numerous servals, which are native to Africa and are important in controlling rodent populations. Visitors will also encounter several binturongs, another species they have likely never examined on an up-close basis. Even guests who have *seen* a binturong have probably not been close enough to *smell* one. But after visiting Conservators' Center, they can add this to their list of experiences. Guests should not be concerned about the smell, which is used to mark the binturong's territory. It closely resembles the smell of popcorn.

Following their guide, visitors will next approach an area where larger animals come into view. Several wolves are housed at the center. Guests will learn how wolves are beneficial to the environment and how they even help manage erosion by controlling the overpopulation of deer and elk. Past the wolves are the New Guinea singing dogs. Not commonly on display at wildlife parks or zoos, New Guinea singing dogs are an extremely rare species with a unique, almost spectral-sounding vocalization. Guests will be amazed should they have the chance to hear it.

The next sounds to be heard on the tour will likely make visitors' hearts beat faster. Conservators' Center has the largest population of lions (twenty-one) in North Carolina. Seeing these massive animals from such close proximity and feeling their powerful roars constitute an experience that cannot adequately be described. Visitors learn how these incredible animals came to live—some unexpectedly—at the center and will savor the time spent in their presence.

The last animals on the tour are tigers. Each one has a compelling story. Arthur, for example, is a white tiger that began life as a photo-booth animal. For a fee, people could feed Arthur a bottle of food while having their photograph taken with him. The owner kept the cub hungry so he would focus on the bottle rather than on biting someone. Due to this terrible abuse, Arthur weighed only a fraction of what he should have. He was eventually seized and brought to Conservators' Center, where today he has ample food, a lion friend named Kira, and an all-around contented life.

A tour of the center typically lasts around two hours. Afterward, visitors may wonder how they can see and learn more. Three specialty tours—a private tour, a twilight tour, and a photography tour—allow guests to have different encounters with the animals and perhaps a chance to view some of the other species housed at the center. These may include leopards, red foxes, kinkajous, chausies, genets, a Geoffroy's cat, and an ocelot.

Conservators' Center is a "home of last resort, providing a haven for elderly animals, animals with behavioral problems, or those with extensive injuries," according to the center's website. Each animal, no matter what its previous circumstances, now displays a countenance of contentment. Those who visit this one-of-a-kind facility will relish all they have seen, heard, smelled, and learned. Conservators' Center is a special place that provides an adventure no animal lover should miss.

Tips

● Remember to schedule an appointment in advance, as those without reservations will not be allowed on-site. Also note that you will not be allowed to pet, touch, or feed any of the animals at any point on the tour. Wear comfortable shoes you do not mind getting dirty.

● Conservators' Center does not have a physical address that can be input into a GPS. It is located near the intersection of Huffines Road (S.R. 1763) and East Hughes Mill Road (S.R. 1762). For a map and complete directions, visit the website.

Thompson's Prawn Farm

5919 Allie Mae Road
Cedar Grove, N.C. 27231
Phone: 919-563-3220
Website: www.thompsonprawnfarm.com
E-mail: thompsonprawnfarm@hotmail.com

Hours: The prawn harvest generally occurs two days a year. Phone or visit the website for dates and hours.

Directions: From N.C. 49 North near Cedar Grove in Orange County, turn right on Carr Store Road. Travel approximately 2 miles and turn right on Allie Mae Road. The farm is on the right within 0.5 mile.

"You've had the rest . . . Now try the best!!"
Thompson's Prawn Farm

Something big is growing in the small community of Cedar Grove. Located in northern Orange County approximately twenty-five miles from Chapel Hill, Cedar Grove is home to Thompson's Prawn Farm, where giant Malaysian freshwater prawns are grown yearly from May to September. If you're wondering what this creature is,

Joe Thompson displays a handful of freshly harvested prawns.
PHOTOGRAPH BY DENNIS P. DELONG

you are not alone. Many North Carolinians have never seen or heard about this particular crustacean. Giant Malaysian freshwater prawns are similar to shrimp but grow larger, their lengths ranging from eight to ten inches. Their meat, according to information provided by the prawn farm, is close in taste to the sweet, buttery flavor of lobster. Low in fat and lacking the iodine content of marine shrimp, prawns are prized among gourmet chefs.

Joe Thompson, the farm's owner, likely never imagined he would one day harvest such a unique product. For twenty-three years, Thompson and his wife, Geraldine, raised tobacco. Several hip replacements, however, led Thompson to cease growing the labor-intensive crop and seek new possibilities for his farm.

Thompson's son came across information on the Internet regarding prawn farming and presented it as a prospect. Intrigued, Thompson attended a seminar to learn about the industry. Upon discovering no other farmers in the North Carolina Piedmont were in the prawn business, Thompson, who "loves a challenge," decided to "go for it."

Clearly, it was a challenge. Thompson tried not only to establish a new business for himself but to help create a new aquaculture market in the state. After much research, he was ready to begin. In 2006, he successfully farmed and harvested his first prawns.

According to Thompson, the Piedmont allows for one prawn growing season a year. For prawns to survive, the water temperature of their habitat must remain above seventy degrees. The Piedmont's mild climate can therefore support a growing season from May to September. When autumn approaches and temperatures begin to cool, the time for harvest nears.

The prawn harvest usually occurs on two days, typically one week apart from

Joe Thompson feeding his prawns
PHOTOGRAPH BY DENNIS P. DELONG

each other. Thompson has a pair of two-acre ponds and drains one pond per harvest day; it would not be feasible to drain both the same day. The harvest commences around nine in the morning when Thompson and his workers begin draining a pond. As it drains, the prawns collect in a basin or trough. Thompson's workers divide the prawns into smaller bins and place them on ice. The area from the pond to Thompson's front lawn is a scene of much activity as he and his workers drive trailer loads of fresh prawns back and forth between the two. Thompson's wife and her assistants await the arrival of the prawns on the front lawn, where they are sold by the pound and cooked on fiery grills.

Visitors to the prawn harvest will have the rare opportunity to view North Carolina aquaculture production. Thompson encourages guests to drive to the ponds—located just past his house—park their cars, and walk around the operation.

Those who attend the first day of the prawn harvest have the opportunity to see a pond before and after it is drained. Once the pond is drained, its floor is exposed. Workers wearing knee-high waders tread through thick brown muck searching for prawns that were left behind. Visitors standing on the banks above the pond will be amazed to spy the prawns' large antennae sticking out like periscopes from the mud. They watch the workers pull the prawn out one after another, collecting them in their baskets. Interestingly, they will also see the workers pulling out turtles. "Turtles in the pond are a big problem," Thompson says. "They eat the prawns."

Despite the turtles, Thompson's Prawn Farm yields approximately sixteen hundred to two thousand pounds of prawns per pond each year. Any prawns not sold fresh or hot off the grill from Thompson's front lawn the days of the harvest are frozen and can be purchased year-round at the farm.

Joe Thompson personally welcomes each visitor and is happy to answer any questions relating to giant Malaysian freshwater prawns or prawn farming. Geraldine is glad to provide information pertaining to the storage, preparation, and cooking of prawns.

Those who experience the prawn harvest will indeed get a firsthand look at an uncommon North Carolina industry. They might even discover a creature they never knew existed.

Tips

- If you plan to purchase prawns, bring a cooler or a freezer bag. Although the prawns are placed in bags with ice, it may melt before you arrive home.

- The harvest does not last all day. It generally begins around nine in the morning and ends approximately four hours later. Call or e-mail Joe Thompson to verify the schedule. Bring hand sanitizer in the event you handle prawns.

- Those interested in additional North Carolina prawn farms should visit www.americanprawncoop.com, the website of the American Prawn Cooperative, for locations and dates of harvests.

Maple View Agricultural Center

3501 Dairyland Road
Hillsborough, N.C. 27278
Phone 919-942-6122
Website: www.mapleviewagcenter.com
E-mail: Allison@MapleViewFarm.com

Hours: Open on weekends during spring and fall. Phone or visit the website for dates and hours.

Directions: From I-40 East in Orange County, take Exit 261 and turn right on Hillsborough Road. Travel approximately 3 miles, turn right on

Arthur Minnis Road, drive about 2 miles, turn left on Rocky Ridge Road, go 1 mile, and turn right on Dairyland Road. The center is on the right in less than 1 mile.

"Come visit our barnyard, enjoy the hayride, relax in our picnic area, explore the working garden, and play on our brand new playground."
Maple View Agricultural Center website

Allison Nichols was born on a farm and maintains a love for agriculture. A former kindergarten teacher, she also has a passion for education. Bob Nutter is a lifelong dairyman who in 1963 moved Maple View Farm from Corrina, Maine, to Hillsborough. Together, Nichols and Nutter opened Maple View Agricultural Center—which adjoins Maple View Farm—in April 2009. They "hope to instill in all . . . visitors conservation practices, science education and an appreciation for farming life." The center, according to its website, "is an Agritourism facility designed by educators to teach children about agriculture in relation to the North Carolina Standard Course of Study in Science." It serves public and private schools, home-schoolers, and preschool groups.

Four interactive classrooms provide hands-on learning related to dairies, seeds and plants, insects, and conservation practices. In the center's "All About the Dairy" classroom, children learn how milk and ice cream are produced, as well as interesting facts about Holstein cows. The "Plants, Crops & Nutrition" classroom educates them about seeds and the process by which they become plants. Children also learn about nutrition and how to make healthy food choices. The popular "Insects" classroom lets students examine several live specimens and discover why bugs are important to agriculture. The "Soil Science, Recycling & Composting" classroom instills valuable knowledge students can use at home. Outside the classrooms, children interact with barnyard animals (by milking a Jersey cow, for example), learn about gardening, take an educational hayride, enjoy ice cream, and have fun on the playground.

School groups are not the only ones able to take part in the center's offerings. On weekends during spring and fall, Nichols and Nutter open the center to the public. Maple View Agricultural Center consists of twenty-four acres, while Maple View Farm encompasses over four hundred acres. Weekend visitors are able to explore areas of *both* facilities. After paying their admission at a freestanding welcome booth located next to the center's parking lot, they are free to walk the property and partake of activities in the order of their choosing.

Some of the farm's Holstein cows

A hayride gives visitors a fun and educational tour of a working dairy.

The first area they will see is the barnyard, where a host of super-friendly animals waits to greet guests. A staff member is always on-site to answer questions about the animals or perhaps provide visitors a treat to share with them. Animals most likely to be seen include Coco the miniature horse; Guapo the llama (*guapo* means "handsome"); Maple, a Jersey cow; Don Quixote, a miniature donkey; a Nubian goat; a Nigerian dwarf goat; pigs; sheep; rabbits; chickens; ducks; and geese. In the spring, visitors can expect to see newborn animals and may even have the opportunity to bottle-feed a calf!

A trail beside the barnyard leads visitors to a pond, where they will see ducks and geese. If the birds are quiet, the pond is a nice place to enjoy a tranquil moment. Visitors can also take a walk through a North Carolina garden where tobacco, soybeans, cotton, sweet potatoes, and peanuts may be growing.

The highlight of a trip to the center, and the activity that sets this facility apart from other agritourism sites, is its hayride. Yes, a tractor pulls the hayride, and visitors do sit on hay, but it is where they go and what they see that make the difference.

Visitors begin on the center property and then head over to Maple View Farm. The hayride lasts twenty-five to forty minutes, during which the driver—who is also the narrator—makes four stops.

At the first stop, the driver calls up a herd of Holstein cows. While tourists are getting an up-close look at these large ladies, the driver provides information about the breed. For example, he explains why Holsteins are used at the dairy and how much food and water the cows consume each day. Maple View Farm has over three hundred Holsteins. Each cow eats a hundred pounds of food daily. Depending on the weather, each can drink as much as fifty to one hundred gallons of water per day.

Continuing the ride toward the farm, visitors will see equipment, tools, and all types of machinery necessary for the operation of a dairy. Arriving at the calf pens, the driver stops again to show guests a calf and explain the breeding and birthing process. Visitors never leave the hayride during the trip, as they can clearly observe everything from their seats.

Around the back of the farm, the hayride stops near a three-trench silo where food for the cows is kept. Here, visitors will learn what types of food cows eat and how they are cared for. Approaching the barn, they will see countless black-and-white cows; for most visitors, this will be the most cows they have ever seen at one time.

The last stop is in front of the milking parlor, where the driver discusses the milking and bottling process. Every Holstein at Maple View Farm is milked three times a day—at 3 A.M., noon, and 8 P.M.—and each one produces nine gallons of milk per day. The farm has a twelve-stall milking parlor, and it takes four minutes to milk each cow. Only milk produced on the farm is bottled here, in returnable glass bottles.

By the end of the tour, visitors will know a great deal about dairy farms and milk production. The driver is more than happy to answer any questions related to the farm or the center.

Maple View Agricultural Center is a unique educational facility where visitors gain an understanding and appreciation of agriculture by seeing crops in production, interacting with farm animals, and learning where milk comes from and how it is produced. Together, the center and the farm champion the work of American farmers and impart knowledge about the hard work required to produce healthy products.

Tip

- Maple View Farm Country Store is located within sight of the center. After your tour, be sure to visit to store, where farm-fresh milk, ice cream, butter, and other goodies are sold. A large front porch filled with rocking chairs allows customers to eat and drink their purchases while enjoying a picturesque view of the farm. Pack a freezer bag or cooler if you plan on bringing extra dairy products home.

~~~~~~

Duke Lemur Center

3705 Erwin Road
Durham, N.C. 27705
Phone: 919-489-3364
Website: http://lemur.duke.edu
E-mail: Online form

Hours: Open year-round. Advance reservations are required.

Directions: From U.S. 70 East in Durham County, turn right on N.C. 751. Drive about 3 miles and turn right on Erwin Road. The center is on the left.

~~~~~~~~~~~~~~~~~~~~~~~~~~~~~

"Learn . . . what makes lemurs some of the most
fascinating animals in the world."
Duke Lemur Center website

When visitors arrive at Duke Lemur Center in Durham, the first thing they notice is the unusually tall perimeter fencing. It is so high that scenes from *Jurassic Park* might pop into their minds. After all, lemurs are relatively small, so the fencing may make some wonder what else is housed at the center. In reality, the largest of the enclosures surrounds thirteen acres of the center's eighty-five-acre property in Duke Forest. Lemurs roam their small area of the Durham County countryside at large. Their jumping ability—the coquerel sifaka can cover twenty-five feet in one leap—makes the reason for the tall fence obvious.

Duke Lemur Center was founded in 1966 and opened for public tours in the 1980s. According to its website, the center "is the world's largest sanctuary for rare and endangered prosimian primates." Prosimian primates—lemurs—are "ancient relatives of monkeys, apes and humans."

Lemurs are found in the wild only on Madagascar, an island off the coast of

Native to Madagascar, the Aye Aye is the largest nocturnal primate.
PHOTOGRAPH BY DAVID HARING,
COURTESY OF DUKE LEMUR CENTER

Africa. Over the course of millions of years, the species evolved there. Today, seventy different kinds of lemurs reside on the island. About two thousand years ago, humans began clear-cutting forests on Madagascar in search of land to grow crops. Since their arrival, according to the center, "one-third of the lemur species have become extinct and more teeter on the brink of extinction." In an effort to help solve this crisis, "the Duke Lemur Center (DLC) has had an active conservation program for twenty years, both at the DLC and in Madagascar."

Duke Lemur Center has the world's largest collection of lemurs outside Madagascar. It houses nearly 250 animals. This includes 233 lemurs, which represent fifteen species, as well as lorises from India and Southeast Asia and bushbabies from Africa. Visitors who wish to tour the center and learn about these incredible animals can do so only if they make an advance reservation. Three tour options are available: "Lemurs Live," "Walking with Lemurs," and "Learning with Lemurs."

"Lemurs Live" is a guided tour in which visitors observe several lemur species. The tour begins with a history of lemurs and the island of Madagascar. Visitors are then led to different habitats to view and discuss various lemur species. The first lemurs to be examined are ones that are diurnal—meaning they are active during the day and sleep at night. One of the most beautiful and intriguing is the blue-eyed lemur. These lemurs are the only primates besides humans with blue eyes. The completely black male blue-eyed lemur is a most impressive sight, thanks to his stark eyes. Another diurnal species of lemur is the coquerel sifaka. Children on the tour might shout, "Zoboo!" when they see a coquerel sifaka, as this particular species was featured in the PBS kids' show *Zoboomafoo*. In fact, Jovian, a resident coquerel sifaka,

It is thought the slow loris can produce toxic saliva and will lick its young to protect them from predators.
PHOTOGRAPH BY DAVID HARING,
COURTESY OF DUKE LEMUR CENTER

portrayed Zoboomafoo. A small segment of the filming actually occurred on-site. Although Jovian still resides at Duke Lemur Center, he is not seen on tours. However, visitors will see numerous other species of diurnal lemurs. If they arrive at the right time, they may witness a training session or feeding.

The next stop, and what some consider the highlight, is the building that houses nocturnal lemurs—those that are active at night and sleep during the day. The nocturnal building is a fascinating place. The keeper actually keeps a check on the sun in Madagascar and makes sure the animals get the same hours of sunlight they would in the wild. The lights in the building are on a timer in order to tell the animals when to wake up and when to go to sleep. Visitors enter at "night." The lighting is red, which represents moonlight. As the room is dark, they have to look hard to find the animals in their habitat. Eventually, their eyes adjust so they can see the animals—except perhaps the Aye Aye. The Aye Aye is the lemur all visitors hope to see and the one hardest to find. The largest nocturnal primate, the Aye Aye is a peculiar-looking creature "considered by many to be the strangest primate in the world," according to the center's website. Another interesting animal is the slow loris. It is believed that the slow loris will cover its young with toxic saliva to protect them from predators.

"Lemurs Live" typically lasts an hour but varies depending on the interest level of the participants. Tour groups are divided into small numbers to ensure that everyone has an equal chance to see the lemurs, hear the presentation, and ask questions. The personal nature of the tour makes "Lemurs Live" an incredibly informative experience.

Visitors who desire an up-close and personal experience should make a reservation for the "Walking with Lemurs" tour, which lasts approximately one hour and takes place inside Duke Forest. Participants have the rare chance to observe lemurs partaking in natural behaviors like eating, running, and jumping, all from a few inches away. As there are no barriers on this tour, visitors have the opportunity for excellent photographs. The tour is limited to eight participants and is available to persons age ten and older. Before reserving a spot, visitors should note that they will not be allowed to touch the animals at any point during the tour.

"Learning with Lemurs" allows visitors to attend a training and research session. Participants assist staff as they demonstrate how positive reinforcements are used to teach lemurs certain behaviors. This training is most important, as lemurs must learn behaviors that allow staff to care for them. For example, they are taught how to sit on a scale, hold their tails, and remain motionless, so staff can accurately take their weights. They are also taught to enter crates, which is important should they need to be transported for veterinary care. Participants should note that they will not enter a lemur's habitat but will assist from outside its enclosure.

Although tourists can see lemurs on display at other animal attractions, they will not find this many species at any other location in the United States. In fact, they won't see this many lemurs anywhere unless they travel to Madagascar! This once-in-a-lifetime chance to observe ancient and extraordinary primates is an animal adventure not to be missed.

Tips

- When scheduling a "Lemurs Live" tour, ask when training sessions and feedings take place and see if you can arrange a tour near those times. Parents should note that "Lemurs Live" is not recommended for children under age three.

- Although photography is welcome on tours, flash systems may not be used, as they can damage lemurs' eyes.

- The Museum of Life and Science (see pages 149–54) is only five miles away, so consider visiting both facilities in one day.

An observation platform, complete with a zoom camera, provides exceptional views of American black bears.
PHOTOGRAPH COURTESY OF
THE MUSEUM OF LIFE AND SCIENCE

Museum of Life and Science

433 Murray Avenue
Durham, N.C. 27704
Phone: 919-220-5429
Website: www.lifeandscience.org or www.ncmls.org
E-mail: Online form

Hours: Open Monday through Saturday from 10 A.M. to 5 P.M. and Sunday from noon to 5 P.M.; closed Mondays from mid-September to mid-December. Also closed Thanksgiving, Christmas, and New Year's.

Directions: From I-85 North at Durham, take Exit 176B onto U.S. 501 North. Travel approximately 1.5 miles and turn right on West Murray Avenue. The museum is on the left in about 0.5 mile.

"Study live bears, lemurs and endangered red wolves."
Museum of Life and Science brochure

The Museum of Life and Science offers visitors, as proclaimed in its brochure, "an unforgettable adventure." Considered one of the state's top visitor attractions, the museum opened in 1946 as a small trail-side nature center. Over time, it has evolved into a science park encompassing eighty-four acres in Durham County. Today, numerous indoor and outdoor exhibits—many of which display live animals—offer a fun and educational experience for visitors no matter what their ages.

The adventure begins with the science-related exhibits in the main building. On the first floor, visitors can observe a tornado forming in the weather exhibit and study rocks and minerals as well as an earthquake in the geology exhibit. In soundSpace: Hear Motion, visitors create sounds by their movements; the faster they move, the more sounds they make. Life's Devices illustrates the concepts of physics through the use of skeletons and mechanical tools, while Contraptions teaches visitors to build something that *does* something by using pulleys, ramps, balls, etc. In the Aerospace exhibit, visitors can sit inside an Apollo space capsule, see a meteorite, and view authentic NASA space suits. For children six and under, the Play to Learn exhibit offers painting, building blocks, and an animal-care corner, where—through the use of stuffed animals and other toys—they can pretend to be veterinarians or farmers.

Another exhibit on the first floor, and likely one of the most popular, is Carolina Wildlife. All of the animals in the exhibit are native to North Carolina; several can no longer survive in the wild. The large number of animals in Carolina Wildlife includes several species of venomous and nonvenomous snakes, American alligators, and turtles. Visitors especially interested in reptiles should tour the museum on a Thursday, when the "Snake and Alligator Feeding" program is presented. A good-sized aquarium in Carolina Wildlife showcases three species of sunfish (hybrid bluegill, black crappie, and redear), while an aviary houses a mourning dove, an American robin, and a house sparrow. Several barred owls, all of which suffered wing or eye injuries, have their own habitat and always draw a crowd hoping to hear their familiar hoots. Mammals in the exhibit include a Virginia opossum that came to the museum after being rehabilitated, a groundhog (also known as a woodchuck) that is blind, and a muskrat. The muskrat habitat is a highlight of the exhibit. Because they are usually viewed from a distance, muskrats are sometimes mistaken for beavers. Visitors will enjoy watching the muskrat swimming and working within its habitat.

The second floor offers additional exhibits such as Flip It, Fold It, Figure It Out! and Investigate Health!

After enjoying the indoor exhibits, visitors can proceed outside, where a paved trail leads to a new series of adventures. Loblolly Park is the first area they will encounter. This playground for children offers a caboose to climb on and musical instruments to play. Beyond Loblolly Park is the Farmyard, a surprisingly clean area that houses kid-friendly animals including a Jersey steer, a Boer goat, Nigerian dwarf goats, Gulf Coast sheep, a donkey, a rabbit, pot-bellied pigs, a Muscovy duck, and a

The Farmyard is home to many animals, including this Muscovy duck.

royal palm turkey. Visitors wishing to learn more about these animals should attend the "Farmyard Up-Close" program. Presented daily except on Thursdays, the program allows visitors to ask an animal keeper questions and watch the animals being cared for and being put to bed. Participants may have the chance to give an animal its evening treat or meal. This outdoor exhibit is a wonderful place for anyone who enjoys seeing, petting, and learning about animals typically found on a farm.

The next stop on the trail takes visitors inside an *amazing* building. The Magic Wings Butterfly House is one of the largest butterfly conservatories in the Southeast, according to Taneka Bennet, marketing director. Visitors who enter will enjoy the climate of a rainforest, see hundreds of tropical plants, and find themselves surrounded by a thousand tropical butterflies. Butterfly releases occur twice daily except on Sunday; visitors should be sure to check the daily schedule if they want to witness this spectacular event. The full-color identification charts available for guests to carry through the conservatory encourage them to try to find each species on the list—an impossible feat! Although each of the butterflies is beautiful and unique, visitors might agree that the most interesting species is the owl butterfly. Native to Central and South America, it has spots on its wings that resemble owls' eyes, hence the name. The owl butterfly is quite large, so visitors should not have to look hard to find one. Guests will also delight in the fact that the conservatory contains several species of birds, which help control pests. Speaking of pest control, visitors who come to the conservatory on weekends can help a horticulturalist release ladybugs, a fun and educational experience.

The building that houses the conservatory also contains the Bayer CropScience Insectarium, which "features a rare assortment of exotic insects from around the globe" and is "one of the top destinations in the Southeast to admire entomological life cycles," according to the museum's website. Indeed, a large variety of intriguing insects is on view. Although the insectarium holds too many to mention by name, several stand out. The Malaysian thorny stick and moving leaf insects, both native to Southeast Asia, look like the trees and plants on which they live. They are therefore camouflaged from predators wanting to eat them *and* from visitors trying to see them. Another insect that looks like its surroundings is the giant prickly stick. Found in northern Australia and New Guinea, this insect is considered tasty by many animals and some humans. The best and most innovative exhibit in the insectarium is one in which visitors can view a tobacco hornworm on a leaf. Native to the United States, these little green caterpillars have a voracious appetite for tobacco leaves. At the exhibit, visitors can not only use a moveable camera to get an up-close look at a tobacco hornworm but also hear the sound it makes munching on leaves. The only word that can describe the exhibit is *awesome*. Visitors may also enjoy the daily program "Spiders, Frogs, and Other Feeding Frenzies," in which they can observe predators eating their prey. Participants in the program have an opportunity to ask questions of an entomologist.

After exiting the insectarium, visitors can take a ten-minute ride on the Ellerbe Creek Railway, grab a bite to eat at Grayson's Café, or embark on a journey back in time. On the Dinosaur Trail, they will trek a wooded path leading to a number of life-sized dinosaurs from the Late Cretaceous period. At the end of the trail, a fossil site with a variety of prehistoric treasures awaits.

They will next encounter Explore the Wild, accurately described by the museum as a "one-of-a-kind outdoor natural science experience!" The exhibit is entered by way of a boardwalk that leads through a wetland environment. Guests can stop at overlooks that provide opportunities to explore animals and plants that thrive in a wetland habitat.

Continuing along the boardwalk, they will reach the Bear Yard, where four American black bears can be observed in a natural environment. The bears reside at the museum because they interacted with humans at an early age and were deemed unsuitable to be released into the wild. Visitors can use remote-controlled cameras to scan the habitat and zoom in on interesting locations or activities. The Bear Yard also includes interactive displays. For example, visitors can squeeze a bottle to release scent and try to determine what type of bear food it is. Educational text panels allow them to feel a bear's fur and touch a bear's claw.

The next large animal habitat in Explore the Wild showcases the red wolf, one of the most endangered animals in the world. In an effort to ensure the survival of red wolves, the museum participates in the Red Wolf Species Survival Plan. According to Bennett, the first red wolf arrived in November 1992. The habitat then welcomed a litter of pups in May 1993 and a second in April 2002. As with other institutions that participate in the program, the goal is to certify the genetic purity of wild-caught wolves, increase the number of genetically pure wolves in captivity, distribute them to select zoos, and maintain a viable red wolf gene pool to reestablish the species in the wild. Most visitors will never see a red wolf in the wild, which makes this a great opportunity. Just like in the Bear Yard, visitors to the Red Wolf Habitat can explore several hands-on displays.

Ring-tailed lemurs and red-ruffed lemurs—on loan to the museum from Duke Lemur Center—are the last animals featured in Explore the Wild. Lemurs are native to Madagascar. All species are on the endangered list. Visitors greatly enjoy watching the lemurs, as they are highly active and playful. Remote-controlled cameras, computers, and other interactive displays make the Lemur Habitat even more pleasurable. Visitors who would like to learn more about the lemurs or any of the other animals in Explore the Wild should attend a "Meet the Keeper" program, offered daily.

The last outdoor exhibit is Catch the Wind, where several attractions—the most popular of which is a sailboat pond—allow visitors to explore the power of wind and understand its role in nature.

After returning inside, visitors can browse the gift shop or wait for one of the end-of-the-day programs.

Considering the variety of exhibits, hands-on activities, and programs, it is no wonder Taneka Bennett stated that one of the museum's greatest challenges is trying to close at the end of the day. Visitors are never quite ready to leave. A statement in the museum's membership brochure proclaims it to be "a place like no other!" Anyone who visits will declare that assertion to be true.

Tips

- Check the daily program schedule as soon as you arrive, as something may be offered that you will not want to miss.

- If you will be visiting without children, avoid coming on a school holiday, as the museum will be extremely crowded. If you *do* visit on a school holiday, consider packing a picnic lunch, as long lines will likely be the norm at Grayson's Café.

- Plan to spend the entire day in Durham by also making a reservation to tour Duke Lemur Center (see pages 145–48), located approximately six miles from the museum. Try to schedule an early-morning tour at Duke

Lemur Center, which will leave the rest of the day to explore the Museum of Life and Science.

~~~~~~

North Carolina Museum of Natural Sciences

11 West Jones Street
Raleigh, N.C. 27601
Phone: 919-733-7450
Website: www.naturalsciences.org
E-mail: Staff directory available online

Hours: Open year-round Monday through Saturday from 9 A.M. to 5 P.M. and Sunday from noon to 5 P.M.; open until 9 P.M. on the first Friday of every month. Closed Thanksgiving, Christmas, and New Year's.

Directions: From U.S. 401 North/ U.S. 70 West in the center of Raleigh, turn right on West Jones Street. The museum is on the right in the second block.

A two-toed sloth in the museum's Living Conservatory
PHOTOGRAPH BY PEGGY BOONE, COURTESY OF NC MUSEUM OF NATURAL SCIENCES

~~~~~~~~~~~~~~~~~~~~~~~~~~~~~~~~

"Explore North Carolina's diverse habitats, meet live animals and discover your connections to the natural world . . ."
North Carolina Museum of Natural Sciences website

According to the Greater Raleigh Convention and Visitors Bureau website, the city has been labeled "the Smithsonian of the South." With its twenty highly esteemed museums, most of which are free to the public, Raleigh certainly warrants the distinction. One of those facilities—the North Carolina Museum of Natural Sciences—is recognized as "the largest museum of its kind in the Southeast," as stated on the museum's website. The museum began in 1879, when the North Carolina General Assembly combined "the collections of State Geologist Washington Caruthers Kerr (rocks, minerals, fossils, and woods) and Commissioner of Agriculture Col. Leonidas LaFayette Polk (agricultural products) under one roof." Over time and through the work of dedicated staff, the museum amassed an amazing collection. Today, visitors have four floors to explore.

On the first floor are numerous exhibit cases that provide a sampling of—or perhaps an introduction to—the state's natural treasures. Also located on this floor is the WRAL Digital Theater and Auditorium, where visitors can attend daily showings of movies including the award-winning *Wilderness North Carolina*. A highlight is the Coastal North Carolina exhibit hall, which features aquariums that allow guests to observe a variety of North Carolina sea life including eelgrass animals like seahorses; salt-marsh fish such as sheepshead; and belted sandfish, a hard-bottom fish. Another popular attraction on the first floor is the Museum Store and Nature Gallery.

A twenty-foot waterfall is the first thing to catch visitors' eyes on the second floor. It is the focal point of the Mountains to the Sea exhibit, which uses animals and plants to take visitors on a journey across the state's mountain, Piedmont, and coastal regions. The numerous fish on display in the exhibit include dace, longnose gar, largemouth bass, bowfin, and various species of sunfish. Turtles, salamanders, and treefrogs can also be examined. Several interesting species of treefrogs are exhibited, among them a green treefrog, a pine woods treefrog, a squirrel treefrog, and a barking treefrog. Visitors can likely guess how the barking treefrog acquired its name; when mature male barking treefrogs are at rest, they make a call that sounds like a dog. Another exhibit on this floor is Nature's Explorers, which explains the museum's history and highlights items from its early days. Other areas of interest include Underground North Carolina, which provides visitors a look at the world beneath their feet, and Discovery Room, where young children can engage in hands-on exploration with live animals and various objects.

On the third floor, visitors will venture back in time when they enter the Prehistoric North Carolina exhibit hall. They will be most excited to see the fossil remains and fossilized heart of Willo, a small, 66-million-year-old plant-eating *Thescelosaurus*. Next is the Terror of the South exhibit, where guests will come face to face with an *Acrocanthosaurus*, a predatory dinosaur; its remains are stated by the museum to constitute the "most complete specimen of its kind on display in the world." Other exhibits on the third floor include Tropical Connections, Snakes, and Mountain Cove. In the Tropical Connections exhibit hall, visitors can examine the relationship between North Carolina and the tropics and observe tropical reptiles and amphibians. Some interesting animals in the exhibit are emerald tree boas, acacia ants, and poison dart frogs. The Snakes exhibit showcases numerous venomous

Visitors can study the intricate details of a seahorse while exploring the Coastal North Carolina exhibit hall.
PHOTOGRAPH BY STEVE EXUM,
COURTESY OF NC MUSEUM OF NATURAL SCIENCES

and nonvenomous species. At the Mountain Cove exhibit, visitors will see live displays of salamanders—including a hellbender—turtles, and frogs. A highlight is an interactive display entitled, "Things That Go Bump in the Night." Visitors press a button, hear a random animal call, and press another button beside the animal they think made the sound. The Windows on the World Demonstration Theater, also on the third floor, is likely the most popular area in the museum. Daily programs in the theater give visitors a chance to learn about nature and meet live animals. Jonathan Pishney, communications manager, says that he often sees "parents introducing their kids to nature through those programs." Pishney also enjoys seeing children touch a live turtle, rabbit, snake, or cockroach for the first time. "Sometimes," he says, "it's the first time for parents, too."

Visitors may want to relax by the time they reach the fourth floor. The perfect place to do so is in the Acro Café. Or they may be eager to enter the Anthropod Zoo, where an enormous praying mantis stands at the entrance. The Anthropod Zoo houses a countless number of bugs including Eastern Hercules beetles, Madagascar hissing cockroaches, emperor scorpions, giant millipedes, giant centipedes, milkweed bugs, a black widow spider, and Eastern lubber grasshoppers. Visitors can learn fascinating facts by reading the educational text panels. For example, they will discover that milkweed bugs do not need to hide, as their bright colors warn predators to stay away. They will also learn how giant centipedes use their pair of venomous claws to defeat their prey. Upon departing the Anthropod Zoo, guests will enter the Living Conservatory, where they will find themselves surrounded by free-flying butterflies. Other animals including a snake, a tarantula, a turtle, and a two-toed sloth also reside in the conservatory. Giant ground sloths once roamed North Carolina. A skeleton of one can be seen on the third floor!

The museum offers a number of special events that will have visitors returning over and over again. Annual events include "Astronomy Days" (January), "Reptile and Amphibian Day" (March), "Planet Earth Celebration" (April), and "BugFest" (September). According to Pishney, "BugFest" is the museum's biggest event. It generally attracts over thirty thousand visitors in one day. During the event, Café Insecta serves up food containing bugs. Items on the menu have included Szechuan stir-fry scorpion and chocolate chip cookies with crickets.

The North Carolina Museum of Natural Sciences has been educating and exciting the public for over a hundred years. Its success is a result of constantly adhering to the words of its first curator and director, Herbert Hutchinson Brimley. "The building of a museum is a never-ending work," Brimley said, according to the museum's website. "A finished museum is a dead museum, and such a one must deteriorate and begin to lose usefulness from the time its growth stops."

In 2011, the facility will expand again when it opens a new wing to be called the Nature Research Center. According to current plans, the wing will be connected to the museum by a bridge. It will feature live animal programs; a hard-bottom reef tank with sharks and other fish; two wetland exhibits; a biodiversity exhibit with Asian turtles, milk snakes, and mussels; an aquarium featuring glowfish (genetically altered zebra fish used in genetics research); and "Window on Animal Health," where the public will be able to watch a veterinarian perform exams and surgeries.

Never ceasing in its efforts to establish original programs and exhibits, the North Carolina Museum of Natural Sciences offers something new each and every visit.

Tips

- Note that the Discovery Room, the Naturalist Center, and the Living Conservatory are closed on Mondays.

- After touring the museum, you may enjoy visiting Prairie Ridge Ecostation. Located six miles away, the museum's forty-five-acre off-site field station features several walking trails through a Piedmont prairie and a bottom-land forest. Visitors can view several species of native wildlife. To learn more about the ecostation, stop by the museum's information desk or visit the website.

Banks Miniature Horse Farm

145 Peele Road
Clayton, N.C. 27520
Phone: 919-553-7216
Website: www.banksminiaturehorsefarm.com
E-mail: bill@banksminiaturehorsefarm.com

Hours: Advance reservations are required.

Directions: From U.S. 70 Business East near Clayton in Johnston County, turn right on Pony Farm Road. After 1 mile, turn left on Little Creek Church Road. In less than 0.5 mile, turn left on Peele Road. The farm is on the right after 0.5 mile. If you are using a GPS, input 2667 Peele Road for the address or you *will* get lost.

"Little Horses with Big Hearts"
Banks Miniature Horse Farm website

Horse farms are not a rarity. Visit any county in North Carolina and you are sure to find stables offering tours, riding lessons, and trail rides. On the other hand, *miniature* horse farms, particularly ones that offer individual and group tours to the public, are not so common.

In Clayton, Banks Miniature Horse Farm—one of the largest breeders of miniature horses in the southeastern United States—welcomes visitors to "meet and play with all the horses."

Owned by Bill and Pam Banks, the fifty-acre Johnston County farm is home to over eighty miniature horses. Bill raised thoroughbred horses for eleven years. Due to his wife's apprehension of the large animals, he decided to purchase three miniatures. The two fell in love with the breed and expanded their farm. It wasn't long before the couple was known for raising miniature blue-eyed black-and-white pintos. Since the Bankses raise the horses they breed, guests can see generations of the animals on the farm. Without hesitation, Bill can tell visitors which horse is the grandparent, parent, aunt, or cousin to any other horse on the property. He has a bond with each of his horses; when he calls one's name, even at a distance, it comes running.

Numerous foals enliven the farm in late spring.

Miniature horses are bred and sold for show, as family pets, and as service animals for people with disabilities. Their heights vary. According to the American Miniature Horse Registry, those measuring thirty-four to thirty-eight inches are "B" division horses, while those thirty-four inches and under are classified as "A" division horses. In order for a miniature horse to meet the criteria set forth by the Guide Horse Foundation to become a service animal, it has to measure less than twenty-six inches. Such horses must also undergo physical examinations and intelligence testing before being accepted into the guide-horse training program.

During the tour, the Bankses impart interesting facts about miniature horses, including information visitors should know if they are considering purchasing one as a pet. For example, a miniature horse needs less acreage than a full-sized horse but still requires the same care and accommodations. It eats the same type of food, only in less quantity. And because miniature horses are social animals, they should always be kept in pairs. In regard to being saddled, miniature horses *are* capable of carrying children under eighty pounds. They can also learn to pull carts.

Visitors in late spring get a special treat, as many of the mares have had foals. At birth, foals are approximately eighteen inches tall and weigh twenty to twenty-five pounds. The fuzzy little newborns with their charming personalities and dainty features leave a lasting impression. Without a doubt, they are the feature attraction at Banks Miniature Horse Farm.

Besides miniature horses, two other animals—a llama (which looks like a giraffe in comparison to its pasture pals) and a donkey (whose priority is to greet each

Banks Miniature Horse Farm boasts over eighty miniature horses.

visitor)—reside at the farm. Both hold important positions, as they protect the herd from predators such as coyotes.

An afternoon at Banks Miniature Horse Farm is guaranteed to put a smile on any visitor's face. The little horses display a variety of colorful coats and markings, as well as unique personalities that have guests quickly picking favorites among the herd. Bill and Pam Banks have an undeniable passion for their miniature horses and enthusiastically share it with all who visit.

Tips

- Remember, if you want a tour of the farm, you must make an advance reservation. However, if you would simply like to view the horses, the Bankses welcome visitors to park in the driveway and admire the herd.

- If you would like to explore more of Johnston County's natural heritage, travel approximately thirty miles south to Four Oaks, where you will discover Howell Woods Environmental Learning Center, staffed and operated by Johnston Community College. The center has several live birds of prey on display, as well as reptiles and amphibians. Howell Woods also offers hiking trails, fishing, hunting, camping, picnicking, horse and mountain-bike trails, and educational programs and activities. It is located at 6601 Devils Racetrack Road in Four Oaks. To learn more, call 919-938-0115 or visit www.howellwoods.org.

Mule teams pull weighted sleds during the Mule Pulling Contest.

Benson Mule Days™

Benson Area Chamber of Commerce
303 East Church Street
Benson, N.C. 27504
Phone: 919-894-3825
Website: www.bensonmuledays.com
E-mail: info@benson-chamber.com

Hours: The festival is held annually on the fourth weekend of September, beginning on Thursday. Mule events occur on Friday starting around 9:30 A.M.

Directions: The East Church Street address above is the location of the chamber of commerce and is listed for contact purposes. Chamber Park and Nowell Smith Arena are located at 355 J. Lee Road. To reach them from I-95 South at Benson, take Exit 77 and turn left on Hodges Chapel Road. Travel approximately 2 miles and turn right on U.S. 301. Drive about 1 mile and turn left on J. Lee Road. Chamber Park and Nowell Smith Arena are on the left after approximately 0.5 mile.

"**Benson Mule Days™ is rated as one of the Top Festivals in the Southeast.**"
Benson Mule Days™ brochure

Coon-Jumping illustrates the mule's ability to perform a high jump from a standing position.
PHOTOGRAPH BY PAUL DUNN, COURTESY OF THE BENSON AREA CHAMBER OF COMMERCE

Once a year on the fourth weekend of September, nearly everyone and everything in Benson moves at a four-legged pace. Mules, horses, and animal-drawn conveyances fill the town's streets, sidewalks, parking lots, and fields. The happening is Benson Mule Days™, a festival that originated in 1950 as a way of celebrating the local farm community and its working mules—animals that are the offspring of male donkeys and female horses. The largest event in Johnston County, it is sponsored by the Benson Area Chamber of Commerce and attracts well over fifty thousand people a year. The profits are used to support various community programs and services.

The festival gets under way on Thursday morning when campgrounds open for check-in. That evening, carnival rides swing into action and a free outdoor concert is presented at the Benson Singing Grove.

On Friday, mules take center stage in Nowell Smith Arena, where an incredible showcase of competitions takes place throughout the day. First-time attendees may arrive with preconceived notions about mules—perhaps ones that suggest stubborn or unintelligent creatures—but will quickly discern highly perceptive and dedicated animals. At 9:30 A.M. on Friday, the mule competitions commence with a Halter Show. The winner will have the distinguished honor of leading the festival parade (held on Saturday morning) with the red "Grand Champion" blanket proudly displayed over its back. After the Halter Show is the Children's Stick Mule Race, followed by the Performance Show. During the show, spectators will observe one of the mule's most remarkable abilities—that of performing a high jump from a standing position. The Coon-Jumping Competition best demonstrates this talent. In this event, a mule is led into an area marked off as a twelve-foot box. On one side of the box are two poles with a bar stretching between them. The mule, if so inclined, will depart the boxed area by way of jumping the bar. Handlers must get their mules to walk up to the bar, pause, and then jump from a standing position. Should the mule step out of the box, it is disqualified. Mules are given two attempts to jump the bar and a maximum of ninety seconds to jump per height. Mules that successfully hurdle the bar will continue to the next round, during which the bar is raised three inches. The competition continues until the highest-jumping mule is declared the winner. Seeing a mule walk up to a chest-high bar and leap it without touching is a truly amazing sight. Attendees are guaranteed to be impressed.

Other competitions in the Performance Show include Single-Hitch Driving, Multiple-Hitch Driving, Pleasure Driving, the Barrel Race, the Egg and Spoon Race, the Key Hole Race, the Flag Race, and Sit-A-Buck. Spectators will no doubt have a chuckle or two while watching these events. In the Egg and Spoon Race, participants must carry an egg on a spoon while riding their mules around the arena. During Sit-A-Buck, a piece of paper about the size of a dollar bill is placed under each rider's leg. As the riders, who are on their mules bareback, begin circling the arena, instructions are given over the loudspeaker for them to walk, canter, trot, back up, or turn around. These commands are given over and over until, one by one, the "bucks" begin falling to the arena floor. The person who manages to hold on to his or her "buck" wins the competition.

The Mule Pulling Contest and Mule Races take place in the afternoon. During the Mule Pulling Contest, the brute strength of these working animals is put on display. Hitched mules—single animals and teams, divided into lightweight and heavyweight categories—are harnessed to sleds containing a set amount of weight. On command, they pull the sleds fifteen feet. The winning mule or team is the one that pulls the most weight. Spectators will find it interesting to watch the mules' expressions, as they sometimes appear to ready themselves for the pull even before they are harnessed. By midafternoon, the highly popular Mule Races begin. Mules and riders circle the arena as fast as they can while staying on the outside of four barrels. Some mules go and some don't. Hats go flying. It is quite a sight to behold. Among the several different races held during the event are a one-lapper, a two-lapper, and a grand finale suicide race.

On Saturday, the big event is the parade. Mules, horses, wagons, and even "animated animals" (Shriners dressed as animals) line the streets. Other attractions include an arts-and-crafts show on Main Street, carnival rides, fresh-cooked barbecue in the Benson Singing Grove, musical concerts, the Benson Mule Days™ Rodeo (no mule events) in Nowell Smith Arena, and a street dance on South Market Street.

The final day of the festival offers carnival rides and an afternoon high-school rodeo (again, no mule events) in Nowell Smith Arena. By late Sunday afternoon, thousands of mules, horses, wagons, and other animal-drawn vehicles are loaded into trailers, and Benson returns to a modern pace.

In an article by Elizabeth Barnes in the *60th Annual Benson Mule Days* newspaper, a supplement to the *News in Review*, Cynthia Dunn, a 2009 festival grand marshal, stated why people should attend the festival: "If you don't come, you miss a chance to let your kids see what they won't see anywhere else." Indeed, Benson Mule Days™ is unlike any other festival in North Carolina.

Tips

● Note that mule events occur *only* on Friday and that a small fee is charged. (Fees are also charged for carnival rides and other attractions including rodeos and the street dance.) Bring a stadium seat or a cushion to Nowell Smith Arena so you can watch in comfort. It will likely be hot the day of your visit, so consider packing a hand-held fan or an umbrella.

● Visit the website prior to arriving for a complete schedule of events.

Noah's Landing

1489 Live Oak Road
Coats, N.C. 27521
Phone: 910-897-6624
Website: www.noahslanding2x2.com
E-mail: info@noahslanding2x2.com

Hours: Open seasonally. Weekdays are reserved for scheduled groups. Public tours are offered Saturday at 11 A.M. and 2 P.M. Phone or visit the website for exact dates and hours.

Directions: From I-40 East in Johnston County, take Exit 319 onto N.C. 210 toward Benson. Travel approximately 1.5 miles and turn left on N.C. 50. Drive 2 miles, turn right on Stephenson Road, proceed about 2 miles, and turn left on Old Fairground Road. After 1 mile, turn right on Benson-Hardee Road. In 2 miles, turn right on Johnston County Road. In less than 0.5 mile, turn left on Live Oak Road. Noah's Landing is on the right after 0.5 mile.

"A world of animals at your fingertips."
Noah's Landing website

Animals have always fascinated Dora Turner. As a child, she kept rare fish in her aquarium and a skunk for a pet. As an adult, she became one of the first llama breeders on the East Coast. During that time, Turner worked with children, educating them about llamas and wool. She realized they learned best when allowed to meet llamas face to face, to touch them, and to examine their wool. The value of hands-on education was clear. That realization inspired Turner to create a place where children could be educated about animals in an environment dedicated to hands-on learning. In 1995, she opened the Two by Two Petting Zoo in Middlesex, North Carolina. Originally, its collection consisted of a few exotic animals and several rare domestic breeds. However, as the zoo's reputation grew, so did its collection of animals. Pet owners and other facilities seeking to donate animals often turned to Turner. To accommodate the increasing number of animals, she relocated the zoo to a twelve-acre farm in Harnett County in 2002 and reopened it as Noah's Landing in 2004.

Unlike most animal attractions in North Carolina, self-guided tours are not an option at Noah's Landing. Visitors who tour the facility must do so in the company of a guide. In accordance with Turner's vision, the guide—often Turner herself—presents fun and educational facts about the animals. The guide also removes several kid-friendly critters from their enclosures for hands-on encounters.

When the tour begins, visitors are led to the Feeding Zone, where they are encouraged to feed miniature Sicilian donkeys, llamas, and Victoria, a Grant's zebra. The guide, who walks around with a basket of carrots, makes sure guests are evenly supplied with food. The donkeys do not nudge each other out of the way but stand politely side by side. While feeding the animals, visitors are taught about conservation, particularly in regard to the miniature Sicilian donkeys, as their numbers are decreasing in the Mediterranean—where they are a native species—but increasing in North America. Other animals in the vicinity of the Feeding Zone include an emu,

Willing tourists are allowed to "pet" Rosie, a rose-haired tarantula.

Noah's Landing is the only facility in North Carolina to exhibit an African springhare.

pot-bellied pigs, a horse, a wild horse, and a yak. The wild horse, Diego, came to Noah's Landing from Shackleford Banks by way of the North Carolina State University College of Veterinary Medicine. Diego became separated from his herd and was unable to survive on his own. After receiving care, he required a permanent place to live.

Leaving the Feeding Zone and following a dirt path, the tour guide takes visitors to meet ring-tailed lemurs and vervet monkeys. After that comes a visit with African spur thigh and leopard tortoises. Guests are given the opportunity to touch tortoises' shells and examine them up close. Stepping inside a large building, guests will see another reptile—a large snapping turtle named Big Mama that was removed from a block of ice. Visitors are *not* permitted to touch Big Mama.

An assortment of intriguing animals including an African springhare can be seen inside the building. Noah's Landing is the only facility in North Carolina to exhibit an African springhare, which means many visitors will likely be seeing this animal for the first time. In describing the African springhare—which resembles both a kangaroo and a rat—the word that comes to mind is *cute*. Apparently, the staff at Noah's Landing thought so, too, as they named their specimen Cutie. Both animals and humans hunt African springhares in the wild. To avoid capture, they never sleep in the same burrow twice and emerge only at night. Cutie does not have those worries but instead enjoys a life filled with Mazuri primate biscuits, lettuce, apples, and sweet potatoes, according to Carie Page, who manages the Junior Zookeeper program. While in the building, visitors can expect a considerable amount of interaction with the animals. They are permitted to touch Shrek, an armadillo, and Zippy, a fennec fox. Animals brought out for interaction are not selected by happenstance. They are chosen because of their tame natures and because they have lessons to teach. Zippy, for example, is allowed to interact with guests because he illustrates how animals are able to adapt in hot and arid climates.

Before leaving the building, visitors will view other animals including a serval,

Bengal cats, and prehensile tail porcupines. A ball python is removed from its enclosure to allow a closer inspection. Guests are permitted to touch *and* hold the python with the assistance of the tour guide. This experience is a must for photographs.

Back outside, visitors stop at several habitats to meet animals such as a Bennett's wallaby, a wallaroo, gray wolves, muntjac deer, Patagonian cavies, a coati, African crested porcupines, prairie dogs, a New Guinea singing dog, raccoons, rabbits, an East African crowned crane, pigeons, a turkey, and peacocks. Among other fascinating facts, they will learn that African crested porcupines *cannot* throw their quills but *can* kill a lion. Most of these animals cannot be touched. An exception is the pigeons, which guests can touch as the guide discusses their physical characteristics and homing capabilities.

Inside the Rainforest Room, just the opposite is true, as visitors will be introduced to nearly all of the inhabitants. An air of excitement permeates the room, as children *and* adults anticipate the next animal to be brought forth from its enclosure. Rosie, a rose-haired tarantula, elicits comments such as "Yikes" and "Oh, my goodness"—mainly from the adults—when presented for examination. Children, on the other hand, are anxious to touch and learn about the spider. A large number of reptiles are removed for discussion and inspection, the most notable being a fat tail gecko and an American alligator—a juvenile one, of course. Three of the mammals in the room are especially popular. Arthur the "awesome" opossum is a large, gentle creature that is truly a star. Many people are unaware that opossums are the only marsupials in North America and simply view them as unintelligent creatures that usually end up on the side of the road. The tour guide sets the record straight by presenting facts about this oft-misunderstood animal while allowing visitors to pet Arthur and feel his tail. After meeting Arthur, visitors will likely have a new appreciation for his species. The guide also introduces a kinkajou and an amazingly soft chinchilla, both of which can be touched and examined up close. Guests can also view—but not touch—a two-toed sloth, Jamaican fruit bats, and various birds. If she is so inclined, one of those birds—Molly the Moluccan cockatoo—may entertain visitors with her version of "Old MacDonald."

A tour of Noah's Landing typically lasts about two hours. Depending on the interest level of the group, it could run shorter or longer. The guides are in no rush and make sure each person has an opportunity to examine the animals. According to Page, Noah's Landing's goal is for the public to "walk away with a greater awareness of the diversity of the animal kingdom and the unique place that every species holds in our global ecosystem." She says the facility wants people to "be surprised by nature's creative adaptations or animals they weren't even aware existed . . . and leave motivated to protect the environment." By showcasing a variety of animals and allowing people to connect with them through touch, Noah's Landing is fulfilling its goals by creating irreplaceable memories.

Noah's Landing also offers special-event programs and Junior Zookeeper Camp. Among its goals for the future are increasing the number of Junior Zookeeper Camps, becoming certified to rehabilitate raptors, constructing a rehabilitation center, creating a natural bog area, and establishing an active connection with the community by reaching out to underserved populations and developing volunteer programs.

Dora Turner has indeed brought a world of animals to the public's fingertips.

Tips

● Bring a meal to enjoy before or after your tour. Several picnic tables offer views of the animals.

● Duffie's Exotic Bird Ranch (see pages 168–71) is about twelve miles from Noah's Landing. You may want to plan your trip to enjoy both animal adventures in one day.

~~~~~~~~~~~~~~~~~~~~~~~~~~~~~~~~~~~~~~

Duffie's Exotic Bird Ranch

242 Bryan McLamb Lane
Dunn, N.C. 28334
Phone: 910-892-4755 or 910-658-2262
Website: www.duffies.net
E-mail: info@duffies.net

Hours: Open year-round Monday through Saturday from 10 A.M. to 5 P.M. and Sunday from 1:30 P.M. to 5 P.M. Group tours are by advance reservation only.

Directions: From U.S. 301 North in eastern Harnett County between Dunn and Benson, turn left on Bryan McLamb Lane. The ranch is on the right.

 (Limited availablility of snacks and drinks)

~~~~~~~~~~~~~~~~~~~~~~~

"... up-close viewing and photo opportunities."
Duffie's Exotic Bird Ranch brochure

The helmeted curassow has a bluish gray growth on its head that resembles a helmet, hence the name.

To say Bo McLamb loves birds is an understatement. He has spent over forty years collecting wild birds from around the world. On his eight-acre breeding facility in Dunn, McLamb displays over a thousand birds representing seventy-five to one hundred species. After purchasing a wood duck and a Canada goose when he was eight years old, he "has been loving birds nonstop ever since," McLamb says.

In May 2009, he opened Duffie's Exotic Bird Ranch to the public—Duffie is McLamb's nickname. He did so to share his collection and to create an awareness of the extreme diversity among bird species. He also hoped visitors would see the birds' intricate designs and colorations as examples of God's artistry. The layout of his facility allows guests a superior view of each bird.

Upon arriving, visitors may assume the facility is small, as the majority of the property cannot be seen from the parking area. They should not be fooled, however, as it takes several hours to take in all the birds. After paying admission, visitors begin a self-guided tour. One of the first birds they will see is the endangered helmeted curassow. A native of South America, this peculiar-looking bird has a bluish gray growth on its head that resembles a helmet, hence the name. Nearby is a Reeve's pheasant, a bird native to China that is distinguished by its tail feathers, which can reach lengths of up to eight feet. Other birds located near the parking area include a greater curassow, additional pheasants—the Lady Amherst pheasant with its metallic-colored feathers is a must-see—guineafowl, conures, and parrots. The parrots vie for attention by demonstrating their ability to "dance" and "talk." Conures, on the other hand, steal the spotlight with their loud, high-pitched squawks.

Large numbers of ducks—McLamb's favorite type of bird—are located

Black swans, with their velvety black feathers and red bills, are among the most popular birds at the ranch.

throughout the property. Although there are too many to list by name, three duck species are especially intriguing. The silver wood duck—a mutation of the common wood duck—is a North American bird not often seen in the wild, as its feathers are light in color and make it an easy target for prey. The white-faced whistling duck, found in Africa and South America, resembles a person standing at attention when it is fully upright. This duck has tall legs, a long neck, and a small head. The white-faced whistling duck has a distinct three-note whistle and can often be seen in flocks of a thousand or more in the wild. The Australian shelduck—particularly the female— can be described only with words that address its beauty. The duck's feathers are primarily black with a hint of metallic green. Its chest feathers are brown to orange, while the feathers of the neck and head are again black. The female, unlike the male, exhibits a patch of white around her eyes and bill, which creates an impressive display.

As guests walk farther into the property and down toward a pond, they will begin to see several species of swans. McLamb currently has seven of the eight worldwide species in his collection. Swans are amazing to watch. Should visitors arrive while any are nesting, they may get to witness a male's territorial display, which involves threatening wing and neck movements. The mute swan, found in Europe and Asia, is not silent as its name suggests; it was given the name because it is less vocal than other swan species. Visitors will discover that silence is not a virtue for the whooper swan; this species makes itself known with loud honking sounds. At first glance, guests may think the text panel at its enclosure should identify it as the *whopper* swan, given its incredible size. Found in Europe and Asia, the whooper swan requires a large body of water in which to swim, as its legs cannot support its body weight for long periods. The black swans garner the most attention. With their ruffled black feathers and bright red bills, these swans are likely the most-photographed birds on the property. Native to Australia, they have long S-shaped necks.

Reaching the far end of the property and the last part of the tour, visitors will enter an open area that includes a central pond. The various birds in this area include emus, rheas, peacocks, additional ducks, a Sandhill crane, and a multitude of geese. The geese seem quite curious about their "guests." For example, several Cape Barren geese will likely approach the fence of their enclosures when visitors come near, as if to greet them. Guests are greatly amused by this species, as its vocalizations sound like those of a grunting pig. Native to Australia, the Cape Barren goose has another unique trait: it can fly but doesn't. The fluffy, white Sebastopol goose can fly but has a difficult time taking off. When it does get off the ground, its curly feathers prevent it from flying well. By contrast, one bird at the ranch is worthy of a supreme flier award. The bar-headed goose, which breeds in central Asia, is the world's highest-flying bird. It has been seen at altitudes over thirty-three thousand feet!

At the end of the tour, visitors will likely say they never knew such a variety of birds existed. Bo McLamb has collected a world of birds in Harnett County, where he provides an opportunity for the public to see and learn about these remarkably diverse creatures. He wants his bird ranch to be enjoyable and educational for everyone who visits and is constantly working to improve the facility. He plans to build additional duck enclosures and to add new duck species to his collection. He also hopes to eventually construct an aviary solely for his pheasants.

When planning a trip to the bird ranch, visitors should consider the guided tour, as they will learn much information that cannot be gleaned otherwise. The tour lasts about two hours and must be scheduled in advance. But no matter how guests choose to tour Duffie's Exotic Bird Ranch, they are guaranteed an informative and gratifying visit.

Tips

- You will see birds behind a house; pull into the driveway and park, as you are at the right place. If no one is visible on the grounds, simply knock at the door. As the ranch is for the most part a one-man operation, call in advance to confirm it will be open.

- Noah's Landing (see pages 164–68) is about twelve miles from the ranch. You may want to plan your trip to enjoy both animal adventures in one day.

The camel at Jambbas Ranch brings a smile to every visitor's face.

Jambbas Ranch

5386 Tabor Church Road
Fayetteville, N.C. 28312
Phone: 910-484-4808 or 910-484-2798
Website: www.jambbas.com

Hours: Open year-round Monday through Saturday from 9 A.M. to 5 P.M. and Sunday from 1 P.M. to 5 P.M., weather permitting.

Directions: From I-95 near Fayetteville in Cumberland County, take Exit 49 and travel approximately 6 miles east on N.C. 53. At the flashing light at Cedar Creek, turn right onto Tabor Church Road. The ranch is on the right after 2 miles.

 (Limited availablility of snacks and drinks)

"A bunch of fun for everyone!"
Jambbas Ranch brochure

Visitors to Jambbas Ranch might find themselves singing the familiar lyrics, "Oh, give me a home where the buffalo roam,/Where the deer and the antelope play," as they explore this exceptional 155-acre zoo. A must-see Cumberland County attraction, Jambbas Ranch allows tourists to come face to face with a variety of exotic and domestic animals.

Owned and operated by Milton and Anna Bass, Jambbas Ranch opened to the public in 1994. The unique name honors each member of the Bass family: **J**ames (son), **A**nna (mother), **M**ilton (father), **B**eth (daughter), **B**ecky (daughter), **A**nita (daughter), and **S**abrina (daughter).

Upon their arrival, visitors will at once see the welcome center, which resembles a Western outpost. Inside, they can purchase admission tickets and minimally priced food buckets and bear treats. They can also view snakes, tortoises, and small animals. Guests are permitted to feed all animals at Jambbas Ranch except the snakes and alligator.

The self-guided road leads from the back door of the welcome center through the ranch. One of the stops, and a favorite of many, is Ben the bear. Other animals along the walk include a horse, a miniature horse, several varieties of goats, an ostrich, an alligator, a miniature pot-bellied pig, white-tailed deer, blackbuck antelopes, African sheep (an interesting breed that does not need shearing), a gray fox, a red fox, llamas, a dromedary camel, elk, cows, rabbits, and an array of ducks, geese, peacocks, and chickens.

The most incredible sight at Jambbas Ranch, and one that will make guests imagine they have ventured out west, is a magnificent herd of American bison. Once numbering in the millions, these stunning animals were nearly brought to extinction during the nineteenth century. Thanks to conservation efforts, their numbers are increasing. The bison at Jambbas Ranch reside in a vast field spotted with stately pine trees. However, even if grazing at a distance, these iconic figures of the American West will promptly approach the fence when visitors are near. This rare opportunity

A herd of bison imparts a vision of the American West.

to observe the largest land mammals in North America alone demands a visit to the ranch.

In keeping with the ranch's Western theme, visitors will pass the "No Chance Gold Mine," "Fort Rest," and "Fort Leisure." The two "forts" provide covered and uncovered picnic facilities and a place for guests to rest their feet.

The scenery is beautiful, especially in the spring, as the ranch borders the Cape Fear River. A covered bridge provides a splendid backdrop for photographs. Ponds filled with fish, crayfish, and a variety of ducks create a serene atmosphere. Next to one pond, guests can purchase food from a vending machine to toss to fish from a small bridge.

Speaking of bridges . . .

As visitors continue their walk through the varied collection of animals, they will arrive at a swinging bridge that immediately brings to mind adventure movies. The bridge, which crosses a ravine, indeed swings and bounces. A sign warning, "Maximum Capacity 1500 pounds," leads groups to cautiously add up their weights before crossing. Anyone afraid of heights should choose to walk *around* the ravine instead of crossing over it. In the future, this area of the ranch may include a zip line and perhaps a monkey exhibit.

Visitors eventually return to the welcome center. Upon completing their tour of Jambbas Ranch, they will likely agree that a day spent at this Sandhills attraction is a unique, relaxing, and enjoyable experience for all.

Tips

- To ensure interaction with all the animals, try to arrive before 2 P.M. By midafternoon, especially on crowded weekends, some animals may become satiated and take naps.

- The cost of food treats is minimal, and I recommend *at least* one bucket per person. That is enough food to get you around the ranch unless you have to feed *every* goat and sheep that asks, in which case you should probably purchase an extra bucket.

- Visitors are permitted to drive through the ranch if the roads are not muddy, so feel free to ask.

- Once you have visited Jambbas Ranch, head over to Clark Park Nature Center, approximately twenty miles away, where you can learn about

North Carolina's diverse plants and wildlife. You'll enjoy mounted displays and see live reptiles and amphibians. The center also offers access to the Cape Fear River Trail. It is located at 631 Sherman Drive in Fayetteville. To learn more, call 910-433-1579 or visit www.fcpr.us/outdoor_programs/clark_park.aspx.

Talamore Golf Resort

48 Talamore Drive
Southern Pines, N.C. 28387
Phone: 910-692-5884
Website: www.talamoregolfresort.com
E-mail: tag@talamore.com

Hours: The resort is open year-round. The llamas are available seasonally. Call for information.

Directions: Follow N.C. 211 East to the traffic circle in Pinehurst in Moore County. Take the exit off the circle marked for Southern Pines/N.C. 2. Follow N.C. 2 (Midland Road) for 1.5 miles and turn left on Talamore Drive to reach the resort.

"Talamore is Home to the World Famous Llama Caddies."
Talamore Golf Resort website

Tag Leon and Dollie llama at Talamore Golf Resort
PHOTOGRAPH COURTESY OF TALAMORE GOLF RESORT

Dollie llama in Talamore Golf Resort
PHOTOGRAPH COURTESY OF TALAMORE GOLF RESORT

Golf resorts typically do not allow animals on their fairways and often take action to keep them away. But at Talamore Golf Resort, one animal—the llama—is welcome. The owner wanted something that would set his course apart from all others. He read how golf great Chi-Chi Rodriguez had used a donkey for a caddie when he was a young boy. A friend of the owner's suggested using llamas instead, stating they were better pack animals. Thus, an idea was born.

In 1991, Talamore Golf Resort opened as the first course in the *world* to use llamas as caddies. According to Tag Leon, head golf professional at Talamore, the course is actually an answer to a Trivial Pursuit question: "What is the only golf course in the world to utilize llama caddies?" Interestingly, a common question asked not by a board game but by members of the public regards who cleans up after the llamas on the course. "They are very particular about where they go to the bathroom," says Leon, "and . . . almost always wait until they are back in their pen."

The llama caddies fascinated the public and became an overnight media sensation. Over five thousand articles were written about the Talamore llamas. They were featured in popular magazines such as *Golf, Golf Digest, Sports Illustrated, Time,* and *Life.* Thanks to the llamas, the resort found its place on the international golf map.

After years of service, the llama caddies were recently given a six-year hiatus. Now, they are available to golfers once again. But because llamas are cool-weather animals, they are on the course only during certain months. Unfortunately, llama caddies cannot assist with club selection or offer other advice, but their gentle manner and adorable faces may help golfers remain calm in spite of bad swings or putts.

Talamore Golf Resort is no longer the only course to offer llama caddies. No matter, though. It was the first in Moore County—and the world—to do so.

Tip

● Since the course is just beginning to offer llama caddies again, and since llamas are used only in cool weather, call to make sure they are indeed available.

Aloha Safari Zoo

159 Mini Lane
Cameron, N.C. 28326
Phone: 919-770-7109 or 919-770-4257
Website: www.AlohaSafariZoo.com
E-mail: alohasafarizoo@gmail.com

Hours: Open year-round Saturday and Sunday from 10 A.M. to 5 P.M. Weekday tours are by advance reservation only.

Directions: From N.C. 87 South between Olivia and Pineview in Harnett County, turn right on Milton Welch Road. After about 1.5 miles, turn left on Mini Lane. The zoo is on the left.

> "... take the 'Safari Tour' ... where all of our big animals are ..."
> **Aloha Safari Zoo website**

S. Lee Crutchfield is passionate about animals. On sixty acres in Harnett County, he built a home, a business, and a sanctuary for animals. Ninety percent of the animals residing on his property are rescues. Many came from game ranches; others are from owners who could no longer care for them; and some were once used in photo booths. In January 2010, Crutchfield opened Aloha Safari Zoo to the public. He did so because he felt families in his community needed something to do and because he believed interaction with people would be beneficial to his animals.

When visitors arrive at the zoo, they are greeted by a large sculpture of a friendly-looking elephant. Upon parking, they are immediately in the presence of animals. Guests can see miniature horses and cows even before entering the zoo. In addition,

The Safari Tour stops beside an Asian water buffalo.

they will see beautiful ponds populated by ducks and black swans and manicured lawns that are enjoyed by free-roaming peacocks and rabbits, which occupy a large area created just for them.

Inside the zoo, visitors will at once see Spartacus, a white Bengal tiger. They will also see a Russian grizzly bear. In the future, these two youngsters will be in another location on the property, as new habitats are currently being constructed for them. Other animals to be met in the building include a caiman, a green iguana, an African spur thigh tortoise, a bearded dragon, an emperor scorpion, an emerald tree boa, ball pythons, corn snakes, two-toed sloths, and tamarins. Visitors should be sure to see the tamarins—small, unique-looking primates native to Central and South America. The zoo also has tarantulas. Crutchfield's collection consists of a goliath birdeater tarantula, a Brazilian stripe knee tarantula, a king baboon tarantula, a rose-haired tarantula, and a Chaco golden stripe tarantula. The building also houses Connie's Café and a gift shop, where visitors can purchase food for the animals before proceeding outside.

Exiting the back of the building, guests will find a large petting area, habitats for several species of monkeys, an aviary, an incredible view of the property, and the Safari Tour loading area.

The petting area is full of kid-friendly, kid-sized animals like goats, cows, an alpaca, rabbits, ferrets, and even a young camel.

Although visitors cannot touch the monkeys, Crutchfield is frequently on-site with Jackson, his infant spider monkey, whose adorable face and mannerisms make him a star attraction.

In the aviary, guests can listen and talk to a variety of birds such as parrots and macaws.

The pastures near the aviary hold numerous horses, including one that truly makes a trip to the zoo worthwhile. Fletch, a spotted draft horse—who according to the zoo is the nation's largest—makes regular-sized horses look like miniatures when

Aloha Safari Zoo is home to the nation's largest spotted draft horse.

standing in his shadow. A retired workhorse from Ohio, this massive animal is a sight to behold.

When they hear that the Safari Tour will soon be leaving, guests should grab their animal food and a seat. Pulled by a tractor, a wagon takes visitors to the lower section of the property, where large animals—ones requiring considerable space—can be seen. A tour guide provides interesting facts about the animals and the zoo. As the journey begins, visitors will pass numerous animals including several Asian water buffaloes. Midway through the tour, the driver will stop so visitors can disembark to feed animals that approach the fence. Animals likely to be seen here are donkeys, Watusi cattle, miniature pot-bellied pigs, a variety of goats and sheep, miniature zebus, a hog, American bison, nilgais, chickens, and turkeys. When the animal food is gone, the guide gathers everyone back on board to continue the tour. Coatis, blackbuck antelopes, dromedary camels, mammoth mules, a zebra, emus, and ostriches are all in view as the driver heads back to the loading area. Although visitors will have opportunities to take lots of pictures, they will see the most photographed—and most intriguing—of the zoo's animals near the end of the tour. Cinnamon, a zorse, is the offspring of a male zebra and a female horse. This will likely be the first and only time visitors have seen this particular species.

After the Safari Tour, guests can revisit areas of the zoo, converse with the friendly staff, have a bite to eat at Connie's Café, or browse the gift shop. They will no doubt agree that Aloha Safari Zoo is a wonderful place to spend an afternoon or an entire day.

Tips

● Don't forget to purchase a bucket of food before departing on the Safari Tour. The trip will be much more fun if you have food for the animals!

● When you are ready to feed yourself, grab a bite at Connie's Café—the hot dogs are quite delicious—and take it outside to a picnic table for an enjoyable lunch or snack.

● Parents with children who are fascinated by animals should talk to the staff about the weekday "Keeper for a Day" program.

San-Lee Park Nature Center

572 Pumping Station Road
Sanford, N.C. 27330
Phone: 919-776-6221
Website: www.leecountync.gov/Departments/SanLeePark.aspx

Hours: Open daily year-round; hours are seasonal. The park closes for various holidays. Phone or visit the website for exact dates and hours.

Directions: From U.S. 421 South at Sanford in Lee County, take the ramp onto U.S. 1 North. In 1 mile, take Exit 70A onto U.S. 421 Bypass South (Oscar Keller Jr. Highway). Travel approximately 4 miles, take Exit 145, turn left on Kelly Drive, go 0.5 mile, and turn right on Pumping Station Road. The park is on the right after less than 0.5 mile.

"See your wild neighbors up close and learn more about them."
San-Lee Park Nature Center website

Tourists traveling near Sanford should absolutely make plans to visit San-Lee Park, a picturesque 160-acre park that opened in June 1978. A division of Lee Coun-

Yellowbelly sliders are abundant throughout the Piedmont and coastal regions of North Carolina.

ty Parks and Recreation, it offers visitors an abundance of options including tent and recreational vehicle camping, several miles of hiking and mountain-bike trails, picnic facilities, a playground, two stocked lakes for fishing—lakes that, according to the park's website, "have been stocked with over 29,600 fish in the past 5 years"— and paddleboat rentals. It also gives guests a chance to explore native North Carolina wildlife in Lee County's one and *only* nature center.

San-Lee Park Nature Center houses native nonreleasable wildlife. Most of the animals arrived with injuries and were rehabilitated but remain incapable of surviving in the wild. For example, the center's Eastern gray squirrel survived a head injury but cannot be released because his eyes do not dilate properly. Some animals at the center were confiscated from people who kept them illegally as pets. Visitors may not realize that some species, like the spotted turtle, are protected by the state of North Carolina and are illegal to possess without special permission. Interesting facts such as this and information about the animals can be found on the educational text panels beside each exhibit.

Guests will be intrigued to see the spotted turtle, a yellowbelly slider, a painted turtle, a common snapping turtle, an Eastern mud turtle, an Eastern box turtle, and a common musk turtle—which acquired its name from the odor it emits when threatened. Other reptiles on display include a variety of venomous and nonvenomous snakes. Visitors may encounter cottonmouths, a copperhead, watersnakes, rat snakes, an Eastern kingsnake, a corn snake, and a timber rattlesnake. The timber rattlesnake is four and a half feet long and four to five inches around. According to Jaime Osborne, the park's outdoor education specialist, it is this impressive specimen guests seem to talk about most when visiting the center.

Other wildlife exhibits include gray treefrogs, a flying squirrel, and a crayfish. Guests who can't locate the crayfish in its habitat should look closely in the hollow

San-Lee Park Nature Center showcases numerous snakes native to North Carolina.

log, as it is said to hide there frequently. Staff at the center feed the crayfish a healthy diet of mealworms, earthworms, and crickets every other day.

Visitors also have the opportunity to see several species of North Carolina raptors, including a red-shouldered hawk, a red-tailed hawk, a great horned owl, a turkey vulture, and a black vulture. The red-tailed hawk is one of the most recognizable birds of prey in North Carolina. A text panel beside its habitat explains that, although protected today, "these birds were once persecuted by people for fear that they fed on poultry." In reality, their diet consists of "rodents, rabbits, amphibians, and insects."

San-Lee Park Nature Center is a great place to see and learn about North Carolina wildlife. It offers a variety of programs throughout the year, some of which involve live animal presentations. Those who are interested can read the park's newsletter, *The Raptor*, online for news, information, and upcoming events. Those who visit will be glad they discovered this small but undisturbed Piedmont getaway. As its website and brochure proclaim, "You are assured a wonderful time at San-Lee Park!"

Tips

- Although the park exhibits rehabilitated and nonreleasable wildlife, you should not drop off injured animals.

- Fishing is permitted year-round. San-Lee Park participates in the North Carolina Wildlife Resources Commission's Community Fishing Program and Fishing Tackle Loaner Program. A fishing license is required.

❋ A lovely waterfall, creek, and open field are in the San-Lee Park meadow. Together, they create the perfect background for a photograph. Take advantage of it!

Carolina Tiger Rescue

1940 Hanks Chapel Road
Pittsboro, N.C. 27312
Phone: 919-542-4684
Website: www.CarolinaTigerRescue.org
E-mail: Online form

Hours: Tours are offered Saturday and Sunday at 10 A.M. and 1 P.M. Advance reservations are required.

Directions: From U.S. 64 East near Pittsboro in Chatham County, turn right on Foxfire Trace. In 0.5 mile, turn left on Dee Farrell Road. Drive about 1 mile and turn left on Hanks Chapel Road. Carolina Tiger Rescue is on the right in less than 1 mile.

Visitors can meet tigers like Kaela and hear the story of her rescue.
PHOTOGRAPH COURTESY OF CAROLINA TIGER RESCUE

". . . learn to talk to a tiger."
Carolina Tiger Rescue brochure

The mission of Carolina Tiger Rescue is "saving and protecting wildcats in captivity and in the wild." Situated on fifty-five acres in Chatham County, it was founded in the 1970s as the Carnivore Evolutionary Research Institute. Dr. Michael Bleyman, a University of North Carolina geneticist, established the facility to "ensure the survival of specific keystone species from threatened/endangered ecosystems," according to the facility's website. He began a breeding program for "caracals, servals,

Tours of Carolina Tiger Rescue are available by reservation only.
PHOTOGRAPH COURTESY OF CAROLINA TIGER RESCUE

ocelots, and binturongs" and later began "rescuing big cats."

In 1981, the institute was incorporated as a nonprofit. Later, its name was changed to Carnivore Preservation Trust. Its breeding program was halted in 2000. In 2009, the name became Carolina Tiger Rescue. This is the only wildcat sanctuary in North Carolina. To qualify as a sanctuary, a facility must meet criteria established by the U.S. Fish & Wildlife Service and the Captive Wildlife Safety Act. Those criteria can be found on the Carolina Tiger Rescue website.

The facility began offering public tours—by reservation only—in 2003. Visitors who attend will see seven species of animals: tigers, servals, ocelots, caracals, bobcats, binturongs, and kinkajous. In total, approximately seventy animals are on-site. Although the facility is a *tiger* rescue, smaller carnivores remain from the breeding program for keystone species, while others have been rescued from individuals or transferred from other facilities.

Upon arrival, visitors will be educated about Carolina Tiger Rescue's mission and then led on a guided tour. The tour takes them across an expanse of land where several of the world's most endangered species abound. The tour guide will present facts about the species—particularly their roles in the environment and current threats to their survival. One of the carnivores likely to grab the attention of visitors is a serval named Elvis, who literally showed up on Carolina Tiger Rescue's doorstep in April 2009. Elvis had a few health issues but quickly recovered and made friends with another serval and his caretakers.

Tigers are the main attraction. In most cases, visitors will be able to view them from a distance of four or five feet. Meanwhile, the tour guide will explain the circumstances under which the animals came to live at the sanctuary. Some of the tigers have especially touching stories. Nitro is a male tiger rescued from a junkyard in Kansas. When he arrived, it was discovered he was blind. Visitors will quickly notice that the perimeter of Nitro's enclosure is lined in sand. This allows him to know when he is nearing the fence, so he will not run into it. A happy and trusting tiger, Nitro can now "navigate his home like a pro," according to his online biography. Kaela, a female tiger, and Rajah, a male, have an interesting story. The two tigers were found as cubs wandering along a highway near Charlotte. Wounds on the animals were consistent with being pushed out of a car. After being brought to the sanctuary in 2005, the two cubs "adjusted to their new home almost immediately, and wasted no time before they were playing with toys in their new habitat," as stated in their online biography. Kaela and Rajah will be lifelong residents of Carolina Tiger Rescue. These are just a couple of the stories to be told.

Besides weekend public tours, Carolina Tiger Rescue offers private and group tours, "Twilight Tours," "Feeding with a Keeper," and "Behavior Training with a Keeper." "Twilight Tours" occur seasonally on Saturday evenings when the animals are most active. "Feeding with a Keeper" allows participants to learn what a carnivore's diet consists of, to assist an animal keeper with the preparation of food, and to observe distribution. Visitors who attend "Behavior Training with a Keeper" will be educated about animal behavior and given the chance to watch a training session. These special tours require advance reservations; many are age-specific. Special-event programs are also offered throughout the year. Two of them—"Kids' Enrichment Day" and "Teen Enrichment Day"—are specially designed for young participants. Visitors interested in these programs should visit the website for a listing of dates and hours.

According to volunteer coordinator Scott Miller, Carolina Tiger Rescue hopes visitors will "gain a better appreciation for wildcats as unique individual beings who make valuable contributions to our quality of life on earth, and who deserve the protection required so that they can thrive in their native environments." Because tours are divided into small groups, visitors are able to ask questions, observe animals up close, and acquire considerable knowledge about each species. They will therefore leave with a greater understanding of tigers and other carnivores, particularly regarding threats to their survival, be it in the wild or captivity.

Tips

- To ensure a tour on a particular weekend, call several weeks in advance, as spots fill up quickly.

● If you wish to take photographs, you will be required to sign a photo release and pay a small additional fee.

Celebrity Dairy

144 Celebrity Dairy Way
Siler City, N.C. 27344
Phone: 877-742-5176 or 919-742-5176
Website: www.celebritydairy.com
E-mail: theinn@celebritydairy.com

Hours: "Open Barns" are held several times a year—two in the spring (typically the first weekends in February and March from noon to 5 P.M.) and one in the fall (usually the Sunday of Thanksgiving weekend from 1 P.M. to 5 P.M.). Phone or visit the website for exact dates and hours.

Visitors can see kids (baby goats) in February and return in November to observe their growth.

Directions: From U.S. 421 South in Chatham County, take Exit 171 (the Siler City/Pittsboro exit). Turn left on U.S. 64, travel approximately 4 miles, turn left on Mount Vernon–Hickory Mountain Road, and drive about 2 miles. The dairy is on the right.

 (Limited availablility of snacks and drinks during the Open Barns)

"Kids are always eager for attention, and even the blasé older 'hoofers' will amble over to be admired and have their ears scratched."
The Inn at Celebrity Dairy brochure

For anyone who enjoys being in the company of goats, Celebrity Dairy is *the* place to visit. Owned and operated by Brit and Fleming Pfann, the dairy encompasses 300 acres in Chatham County. The couple took up residence on their Siler City property—a farmstead that had not been worked in twenty-five years—in 1987. To

The Inn at Celebrity Dairy

aid in the removal of brush, they bought several goats, one of which was in milk. Fleming was intolerant of cow's milk but discovered she had no trouble digesting goat's milk. For that reason, the Pfanns acquired more goats and soon had more milk than they knew what to do with—until they discovered the art of cheese making. In 1991, the Pfanns were licensed and began, according to their website, "ongoing efforts to make consistently good cheese—and learning to manage the many facets of herd nutrition & health, dairy equipment operation & maintenance, developing & adapting cheese making techniques to complement seasonal variations in climate and milk characteristics."

Since then, they have increased their herd to over sixty does and have become quite the experts at cheese making. To produce goat cheese, they use traditional French farmstead methods. The dairy has attained regional and national recognition, and its cheeses have received several awards. Celebrity Dairy goat cheese is sold at the farm's "Open Barn" events and at farmers' markets, stores, and restaurants.

Several weekends a year, the dairy is opened to the public. Visitors can learn about the operation, meet the goats, and taste the award-winning goat cheese. Since the farm is located in a rural area, visitors may feel they have returned to a simpler time. A large farmhouse is the focal point of the dairy. Surrounding it are pastures and wooded areas—and a number of free-roaming chickens, ducks, peacocks, and cats.

Visitors who attend an Open Barn event should first check in at the farmhouse using the side entrance next to the parking area. Inside, they can learn the events of the day and purchase a cup of warm soup, a johnnycake, brownies, a hot drink, or Celebrity Dairy goat cheese or eggs. They can also purchase items from local farmers on-site during the Open Barn event.

Behind the farmhouse is the place most guests are eager to visit—the area known as "Goat Hilton," home of the Celebrity Dairy goats. Visitors at the spring Open Barn events will find the area alive with the sights and sounds of kids. As a hundred or so baby goats will likely be clamoring for attention, guests may be overwhelmed. The goats at Celebrity Dairy are Alpines, which are known for their good temperaments and excellent milk. The mature does at the dairy have all been named—after celebrities, of course—and enjoy being admired and petted just as much as the kids. Therefore, visitors should not overlook the adults!

Many visitors who attend an Open Barn event hope to see a milking demonstration. However, milking takes place only at 6 A.M. and 6 P.M. Although milking is not part of the Open Barn events, drop-in visitors are allowed to watch the process if they show up at one of the scheduled times. Brit and Fleming will be happy to answer any questions relating to goats, cheese, their business, or other scheduled events. The two have a great love for their animals and enjoy sharing what they do with others.

Visitors who do not want to leave at the end of the day will be happy to learn they don't have to! The farmhouse at Celebrity Dairy is also an inn. Guests who spend the night have greater access to the farm and its activities. The Inn at Celebrity Dairy offers a choice of seven rooms and one suite. Guests are free to stroll the grounds during the day and are also welcome to attend the scheduled milkings. The ten miles of trails on the property offer guests an opportunity to hike and to see native wildlife. Inside the inn, they can view a collection of artwork that includes original etchings, watercolors, photographs, pottery, ceramics, and metal sculptures. In the morning, they are treated to a hearty breakfast created from a host of farm-fresh ingredients.

Brit and Fleming Pfann provide their guests—whether visiting for an afternoon or longer—a tranquil retreat and the unique opportunity to explore a working goat dairy. The world seems a bit slower at Celebrity Dairy. Visitors will be glad they stopped in to meet a goat, or two, or three . . .

Tips

- The best time to visit is during a spring Open Barn event, as nothing is more delightful than seeing, hearing, and touching hundreds of recently born goats. If you are interested in purchasing fresh eggs during an Open Barn event, try to arrive early, as they sell out quickly.

- If you enjoy gourmet meals, you might want to attend one of the dairy's third-Sunday dinners. See the website for information.

- The dairy requests donations for Heifer Project International.

Wildwood Learning Farm

133 Star Lane
Hollister, N.C. 27844
Phone: 252-257-5575
Website: www.ncagr.gov/ncproducts/ShowSite.asp?ID=101143
E-mail: wildwoodfarm@live.com

Hours: Open year-round on weekends, weather permitting. The hours are Saturday from 9 A.M. to 5 P.M. and Sunday from noon to 5 P.M. Weekday tours are by advance reservation only.

Directions: From Louisburg in Franklin County, take N.C. 561 toward Hollister. Drive approximately 20 miles and turn left on Capps Farm Road. In 0.5 mile, turn left on Star Lane. The entrance is on the left.

> **"Learn about rabbits, llamas, mini horses,**
> **pigs, tortoises, and lots more . . ."**
> **Wildwood Learning Farm flier**

In 2001, Bill and Sherry Boncek settled on a fifty-acre farm in Hollister. A year later, they were presented with their first farm animal—a calf named Brutus, who had been rejected by his mother. Without hesitation, the Bonceks took on the responsibility of bottle-feeding the little calf and welcoming him to their Warren County farm. Today, as a full-grown bull, Brutus still thinks he is the couple's baby.

Shortly after receiving Brutus, the couple took in another abandoned calf. Thereafter, word evidently spread that the Bonceks would rescue or house unwanted animals. People around the area began calling in regard to *all* types of animals. On one occasion, the Bonceks were alerted to a pot-bellied pig in need of rescue. When they arrived to pick up the pig, they discovered that a macaw—the largest member of the parrot family—also needed a home. The macaw, whose name is Pepper, had a habit of plucking feathers from her chest, the result of which was a bare-breasted bird. The Bonceks immediately bonded with Pepper and continue to spend a great deal of time with her. Bill designed and attached a special pole to his golf cart that allows Pepper to accompany him and Sherry as they ride around the farm. Pepper, who likes to say

Scottish highland cattle are among the many animals at Wildwood Learning Farm.

her name loudly and repeatedly, seems to enjoy being the star of Wildwood Learning Farm.

After years of rescuing and sheltering unwanted animals and making several purchases, the Bonceks saw their operation grow from a single calf to approximately 150 animals. In 2010, they opened their farm to the public, as they wanted to share their animals with the community. Sherry says, "When folks leave our farm, we hope they have a better understanding of how to care for animals, the upkeep and feeding, and a little knowledge about each one here, and most of all, the pleasure of seeing these animals up close and personal. Each of our animals are unique in their own way and are loved."

Visitors will indeed gain knowledge about the animals at Wildwood Learning Farm. Upon their arrival, they will be greeted by the bleating of goats and sheep. Guests can park at the farm's office, which is also the Bonceks' residence. If the goats and sheep have not gotten the couple's attention, visitors should knock at the door.

During the guided tour, the Bonceks present interesting facts about each animal. Visitors can purchase food from vending machines to feed the residents. Nearly every animal on the farm is available for feeding and petting, except perhaps Betty the pig. Betty was found running along a highway when only a piglet. Now, she is older and several *hundred* pounds larger. Animals likely to be encountered on the tour include Scottish highland cattle, cows, bulls (Brutus is still on-site), donkeys, miniature donkeys, miniature horses, a pony, sheep, goats, llamas, Betty the pig, pot-bellied pigs, rabbits, a prairie dog, sugar gliders, tortoises, a gecko, various exotic birds (including Pepper), chickens, ducks, geese, turkeys, guineafowl, and a peacock.

As the Bonceks have only recently opened to the public, their farm is a work in progress. Current efforts involve building new facilities and erecting fences. Future goals include seasonal programs and nature trails. Bill and Sherry have no plans to cease rescuing and taking in unwanted animals; therefore, additional furry faces are

Guests can feed and pet llamas and other animals at Wildwood Learning Farm.

also in Wildwood Learning Farm's future.

Those traveling near Hollister should stop for a tour with the Bonceks. For anyone considering purchasing an animal, a visit to the farm might be helpful in understanding the level of care involved in ownership. After all, Wildwood Learning Farm is not just a place to interact with animals but also, as its name implies, an educational facility that provides an up-close look at how to care for a variety of animals.

Tips

- When you turn onto the road leading into the farm, follow the driveway all the way to the end. It may look as though you are going into an area that is off-limits, but you are in the right place. The house to the right of the large cream-colored barn is *not* where you need to park or go for directions.

- If you have time, make plans to visit Medoc Mountain State Park. In contrast to the peaks of western North Carolina, Medoc Mountain reaches an elevation of only 325 feet. Throughout history, the mountain and its surrounding land were used primarily for agriculture; in the nineteenth century, it was used for the cultivation of grapes. Today, the 2,300-acre state park is a great place to go for canoeing, fishing, hiking, picnicking, bridle trails, bird watching, and wildlife observation. Lucky visitors with a keen eye may catch a glimpse of the rare Carolina mudpuppy, a large aquatic salamander that has been spotted in Little Fishing Creek. If you see a Carolina mudpuppy, do not touch, harass, or harm it. The park is located at 1541 Medoc State Park Road in

Hollister. To learn more, call 252-586-6588 or 252-586-6476 or visit www.ncparks.gov.

Sylvan Heights Waterfowl Park

1829 Lees Meadow Road
Scotland Neck, N.C. 27874
Phone: 252-826-3186
Website: www.shwpark.com
E-mail: info@shwpark.com

Hours: Open year-round Tuesday through Sunday. From April through September, the hours are 9 A.M. to 5 P.M. From October through March, the hours are 9 A.M. to 4 P.M. Closed Thanksgiving and Christmas.

Directions: From N.C. 125 South at Scotland Neck in southeastern Halifax County, turn left on Main Street (U.S. 258). Drive approximately 2 miles and turn right on Lees Meadow Road. Look for the entrance sign on the right in less than 0.5 mile.

The Mandarin duck is an exquisite bird.
PHOTOGRAPH COURTESY OF
SYLVAN HEIGHTS WATERFOWL PARK

$ 🚻 ⛩ 🏕 (Limited availablility of snacks and drinks)

"Meet more than 1,500 birds from around the world."
Sylvan Heights Waterfowl Park brochure

Scotland Neck is a small North Carolina town where stoplights do not exist. But it is in this unassuming locale where visitors will discover "the largest and most biologically significant waterfowl collection in the world," according to Sylvan Heights Waterfowl Park's website. Founded by Mike Lubbock in 1989, the park opened in October 2006. Lubbock, according to the website, is "considered by many avian bi-

The white-winged wood duck is a highly endangered species.
PHOTOGRAPH COURTESY OF SYLVAN HEIGHTS WATERFOWL PARK

ologists to be the most intuitive and prolific waterfowl aviculturalist in the world." Through breeding and conservation efforts, he is intent on assuring "the survival of . . . species . . . disappearing in the wild, and those in peril even in managed collections around the world." In opening the park to the public, Lubbock seeks "not only . . . to entertain and engage visitors, but to inspire and educate them about the importance of waterfowl, wildlife and wetland conservation."

Arriving at the park, guests may expect to see familiar-looking ducks and geese and other common birds. They have little idea of the *variety* and *number* of birds they will soon encounter. Inside the visitor center, guests immediately come face to face with wildlife. An incubator allows them to view eggs in the process of hatching. A sign alerts guests to what's "Hatching Today." Typically, the various species of bird eggs exhibit a wide range of shapes, sizes, and colors. The same can be said for the hatched chicks, which are an incredible sight to behold.

Before heading out to explore the eighteen-acre facility, guests can watch a short video about the park that explains its founding and purpose. Afterward, they can proceed out the back door into an enchanting world. Sounds will enter their ears from all directions. Many are what would be expected from birds: squawks, whistles, chirps, honks, and coos. But others are not so common. Some birds in the park make sounds that resemble pigs grunting, while others bring to mind people talking or laughing. A few birds make eerie sounds for which there is no description.

A self-guided loop trail leads through the park. Along the way, guests enter large walk-through aviaries representing Australia, Africa, Eurasia, North America, and South America. When birds fly inside the aviaries, they are often so close that visitors can feel the breeze created by their wings. Educational text panels provide fascinating facts about each bird. Inside and around the aviaries, ponds, landscaped gardens, and picnic areas enhance the beauty of the park.

Guests will see too many birds to mention from the continent of Africa. Several—including the old world comb duck, the Egyptian goose, and the Madagascar teal—should not be missed. The old world comb duck is an odd-looking bird, as it has a fatty comb atop its bill, hence its name. The Egyptian goose has dark areas surrounding its eyes that make it easy to recognize. This particular goose was considered sacred by ancient Egyptians and can often be seen in their artwork. The Madagascar teal, according to the park, "is among the rarest of all waterfowl" and "was thought to be extinct until 1969, when stragglers were rediscovered on the island of Madagascar. Biologists believe the bird faces a very high risk of extinction in the wild." Visitors will definitely not want to miss seeing the Madagascar teal.

While examining species from Australia, visitors will meet the star of Sylvan Heights Waterfowl Park. Matilda, a Cape Barren goose, has appeared on television, on radio, in magazines, and in numerous newspaper articles. Although Matilda's stout gray body, pink legs, and greenish yellow bill make her stand out in a crowd, her pig-sounding vocalizations and amiable character are what astound visitors. Matilda shares the spotlight with other intriguing birds such as black swans and Australian brush turkeys. Black swans, with their black bodies, red eyes, and red bills, are visions of elegance. Australian brush turkeys, also known as "thermometer birds," do not use body heat for egg incubation but instead mound their nests with soil and leaf litter. The decomposition of the organic matter heats the eggs for them.

The Multinational Aviaries contain an assortment of fascinating species—small birds, curassows, pheasants, and raptors. Many the birds are strange looking, bizarre sounding, and brightly plumed. A few birds to be seen here are Lady Ross's turacos, a Toco toucan, Northern rosellas, sun conures, rainbow lorikeets, a Javan pond heron, a crested wood-partridge, various macaws, a Himalayan monal pheasant, a silvery-cheeked hornbill, a red-wattled curassow, a temminck's tragopan, and a Eurasian eagle-owl. The male red-wattled curassow has a bright orange-red knob and wattle. Curassows, native to South America, are heavily hunted, making them some of the most threatened birds on their continent. Visitors will not want to miss seeing the Lady Ross's turacos, as they exhibit a spectacular display of color. Native to Africa, they get their brilliant color from two copper pigments unique to their species. The Eurasian eagle-owl, one of the largest owls, teaches visitors an important lesson regarding captive breeding, as this particular species has been successfully reintroduced into the wild.

After exploring the Multinational Aviaries, visitors will pass the Endangered Species Aviary, where they can gaze upon the highly endangered white-winged wood duck, which once thrived in parts of India and Asia. The International Union for Conservation of Nature now "qualifies this forest duck as critically endangered because it has a very small, rapidly declining, severely fragmented population as a result of deforestation, wetland drainage and exploitation," according to the park's website. Thanks to captive breeding at Sylvan Heights Waterfowl Park, white-winged wood ducks are, as stated on the website, "well established in managed preserves."

Continuing their journey through the park, visitors will find they have traveled halfway around the globe when they reach the birds from Eurasia. Among these, they may find themselves drawn to the smew, the white-headed duck, and the Mandarin duck. The smew, the whitest of ducks, has stark black patterns that create a stunning contrast. White-headed ducks are brown except for their white heads and bright blue bills. Once uncommon, they now have a relatively stable population. Mandarin ducks are so exquisite they cannot be adequately described. Highly regarded in Japanese culture, they were once given in pairs as a traditional wedding present.

Visitors will next pass an area that showcases sizable swans, geese, and cranes. Depending on whether or not the trumpeter swans are vocalizing, the stroll through this section could be a bit loud. Trumpeter swans are one of the largest birds in North America and also have the loudest call of all waterfowl. The highly endangered whooping crane can also be seen in this area. Only one flock exists in the wild. Viewing this bird and learning about its near-extinction and successful reintroduction into the wild are highlights of the tour.

Countless species are on display from North America. Many like the black-necked stilt immediately grab the attention of visitors. A shorebird, it has a black-and-white body, a skinny black bill, and long pink legs that allow it to stand in deep water. Only two types of whistling ducks are found in the United States, and both—the fulvous and black-bellied whistling ducks—can be seen at the park. These birds make high-pitched whistling calls, hence their names.

The area of the park that showcases species from South America is perhaps the nicest. A paved walkway leads through the aviary and between two ponds. The layout and the fact that birds often cross the walkway make this a perfect location for photographs. Birds that cameras find particularly stunning include the scarlet ibis and the Chiloe wigeon. The scarlet ibis has a long, curved bill for probing mud and a distinct dark pink coloration that is a result of the aquatic food it eats. The Chiloe wigeon also has striking plumage; it was named after Isla Chiloe in Chile.

Visitors can next proceed down a trail to the wetland area. Even if they do not need to use the facilities, they should enter the building that contains restrooms, as it also houses a small exhibit of honey bees, poison dart frogs, and carnivorous plants. Back on the trail, guests can relax in the park's handicapped-accessible tree house, which overlooks a natural wetland area. Beyond the tree house, they can explore the wetland area from the Beaver Pond Blind. Small slats in the blind allow guests to discreetly look out on the area and see native wildlife in a natural habitat.

Heading back toward the visitor center, guests will pass another aviary, a playground, a fossil dig, and a picnic area. They will also see areas marked for new exhibits, one of which is to be called The Landing Zone. This aviary will give guests an opportunity to feed birds in a free-flight atmosphere. Back at their starting point, visitors will likely want to relax on the deck that overlooks the Multinational Pond and have one last listen to the amazing sounds echoing through the park.

Visitors to Sylvan Heights Waterfowl Park will embark on a whirlwind tour around the globe and discover birds they have never seen before—and probably cannot see anywhere else. Featuring more than fifteen hundred ducks, geese, swans, and other exotic birds, the park offers much to see *and* hear. Learning about endangered and threatened birds and discovering how the Sylvan Heights Survival Breeding Program helps ensure their survival make for an incredible way to spend a day. A few well-known naturalists claim that "without the dedicated efforts of Mike Lubbock and the staff at Sylvan Heights, a number of waterfowl species would already be extinct today," according to the park's website. When visiting Halifax County, travelers should not bypass the park, as "an unforgettable up-close experience" with some of the world's most intriguing birds awaits.

Tips

- Be sure to purchase several bags of food at the admission desk before heading out on your tour, as some birds expect a treat.

- If you think you may be unable to walk around the entire park, or if you would like to be accompanied by a guide who can answer questions, you can schedule a golf-cart tour in advance for an additional fee.

- Several local businesses, including Hardee's and Scotland Neck Inn, give discounts for showing a Sylvan Heights Waterfowl Park paid receipt. For information about the offers, see the "Dining, Lodging and Local Attractions" section of the park's website. In regard to food, however, you should consider bringing your lunch to the park, as several nice picnic areas are available.

- If you like festivals, schedule your trip to coincide with Scotland Neck's Crepe Myrtle Festival. Typically held the second Saturday in August, the event features food, music, games, vendors, and a petting zoo. To learn more, visit www.townofscotlandneck.com.

Coast

Coast Adventures

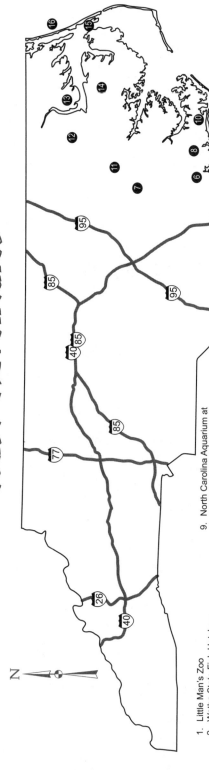

1. Little Man's Zoo
2. Watha State Fish Hatchery
3. Cape Fear Serpentarium
4. North Carolina Aquarium at Fort Fisher
5. The Karen Beasley Sea Turtle Rescue and Rehabilitation Center
6. Lynnwood Park Zoo
7. Exchange Nature Center at Neuseway Nature Park
8. Outer Banks Wildlife Shelter
9. North Carolina Aquarium at Pine Knoll Shores
10. Wild Horses of Shackleford Banks
11. The Walter L. Stasavich Science and Nature Center at River Park North
12. Livermon Park & Mini-Zoo
13. Edenton National Fish Hatchery
14. Red Wolf Howling Safaris
15. North Carolina Aquarium on Roanoke Island
16. Wild Horses of Corolla

Little Man's Zoo

222 Faircloth Drive
Chadbourn, N.C. 28431
Phone: 910-654-5725
Website: www.littlemanszoo.com

Bandit is an infant spider monkey and a new arrival at Little Man's Zoo.

Hours: Open seasonally Monday through Saturday from 9 A.M. until dark. Phone or visit the website for exact dates and hours.

Directions: From U.S. 74 East near Chadbourn in Columbus County, turn left on Tommie Wooten Road. In about a mile, bear right on North Colony Road. After another mile, turn right on Peacock Road. Drive 0.5 mile and turn left on Merritt Road. In approximately 0.5 mile, turn right on Faircloth Drive. The zoo is on the right.

 (Limited availablility of snacks and drinks)

"Come and See Us"
Little Man's Zoo website

Pat and Herlar Faircloth have a special affinity for spider monkeys. Their first was a three-week-old crippled male they named Jake but affectionately called "Little Man." Jake was fortunate, as the Faircloths provided him an enriching and loving environment in their Chadbourn home. However, some spider monkeys are not so lucky, the Faircloths discovered.

After hearing stories about abuse and neglect, they traveled across the United States to retrieve or rescue spider monkeys. A typical problem occurs when people without proper knowledge of primates acquire spider monkeys. Such situations can

One of Little Man's Zoo's most intriguing animals is a Z-donk, an offspring of a male zebra and a female donkey.

cause the animals to be mistreated, which in turn compels them to bite. Biting is indeed a prevailing reason many spider monkeys are in need of rescue.

In 1998, the couple opened Little Man's Zoo—named for Jake—in Columbus County. The zoo's focal point is a large habitat for nearly thirty spider monkeys. Native to parts of Central and South America, spider monkeys are easy to recognize by their elongated limbs and prehensile tails. Visitors will likely spend most of their time walking around the different sections of this habitat, as spider monkeys' antics and acrobatics are most enthralling. Swinging from ropes and playing with a variety of objects in their enclosure, the spider monkeys evidently enjoy entertaining themselves and their visitors.

Jake had numerous friends. Walking the nicely landscaped grounds—where grand pink azaleas bloom in spring—visitors will encounter a large assortment of animals. Many may be fed (treats are available for purchase at the entrance), which provides the opportunity for an up-close view of several species.

Beyond the spider monkey habitat is another primate enclosure, where two snow macaques reside. Guests will delight in seeing these primates, as one has a rather comic personality. Other animals include a Bennett's wallaby, a nilgai, blackbuck antelopes, ring-tailed lemurs, a dromedary camel, a pot-bellied pig, a zebra, llamas, LaMancha goats, sheep, donkeys, African crested porcupines, Himalayan bears, a black leopard, and a Z-donk—also referred to as a "zedonk" or "zonkey." Perhaps the most-photographed animal at the zoo, the Z-donk is an offspring of a male zebra and a female donkey. Its facial characteristics and light brown coloration show the animal's donkey ancestry, while the pronounced stripes on its legs and the vague stripes across its midsection clearly denote its zebra heritage. Beautiful and intriguing, the Z-donk alone demands a visit to Little Man's Zoo, as few facilities in North Carolina exhibit this particular animal. Among the countless birds at the zoo are pigeons, doves, parakeets, cockatiels, peafowl, turkeys, and a cockatoo.

In 2005, Pat and Herlar Faircloth's beloved Jake passed away. Fortunately, they had promised Jake they would "take care of his friends till the end." The couple maintains that promise by working hard to make the zoo better for both its animal residents and human patrons. Little Man's Zoo currently encompasses fourteen acres. However, an expansion is under way that will enlarge the property to forty acres. Upon completion of the project, certain elements of the zoo may change. These may include a new location for parking spaces, a new entranceway, redesigned enclosures, and additional animal exhibits. Despite any changes, the Faircloths' goal will be the same. They hope visitors who come to their zoo will acquire a greater appreciation for animals and understand they all should "be loved and taken care of."

Tips

● Pack a lunch to enjoy at one of the zoo's picnic tables.

● As the zoo operates on a seasonal schedule, call first to make sure it is open. Should it open in mid-April as usual, you may want to plan your visit to coincide with the North Carolina Strawberry Festival in Chadbourn. Held the first weekend in May, it is the largest agricultural festival in the state, according to its website. To learn more, visit www.ncstrawberryfestival.com.

Watha State Fish Hatchery

4945 Shiloh Road
Watha, N.C. 28478
Phone: 910-283-5099
Website: www.ncwildlife.org
E-mail: jeff.evans@ncwildlife.org

Hours: Open weekdays from 8 A.M. to 3 P.M. Advance reservations are requested for hatchery tours.

Directions: From the junction of N.C. 11 and U.S. 421 in Pender County, follow U.S. 421 South for 2.5 miles and turn left on Shiloh Road. The hatchery is on the right after about 3 miles. When inputting directions into your GPS, use Willard as the city.

Holding tank for 450,000 fry (newly hatched fish)

> "... the Watha State Fish Hatchery is a warmwater
> hatchery ... covering more than 45 acres of water."
> **North Carolina Wildlife Resources Commission website**

The search for Watha State Fish Hatchery offers tourists a fascinating glimpse at eastern North Carolina's rural heritage and landscape. At times, the road to Watha may seem long and desolate. But those who complete the journey at the correct time of year and who schedule a tour will be rewarded with an astonishing sight.

The North Carolina Wildlife Resources Commission purchased the facility—originally called the Cape Fear Fish Farm—in 1992 and began operating it as a warmwater fish hatchery. Today, according to the commission's website, Watha State Fish Hatchery "is used to produce channel catfish, largemouth bass, Atlantic striped bass, Bodie bass (striped bass hybrids), bluegill sunfish, redear sunfish, redbreast sunfish, hybrid sunfish and American shad for stocking public waters across the entire state of North Carolina." Included in those waters are Community Fishing Program lakes, reservoirs, and rivers.

When visitors arrive at the hatchery, they will see what appear to be two large warehouses and thirty-eight ponds. At first glance, they may wonder if there is anything significant to do at the site. Guests are allowed to walk around the ponds. Although they will enjoy a nice stroll, they are not likely to see any fish unless they are being fed or are swimming near the surface. However, fisheries technicians will be expecting those guests who have scheduled tours. A technician will escort them inside the hatchery building—one of the large warehouse-like structures—which will prove *the* memorable part of their trip.

Upon entering the hatchery building, visitors will step inside an amazing world where fish—whichever species are being raised—can be examined in all stages of life. The hatchery may bring to mind a scientific laboratory, as clear cylinders and containers filled with eggs and hatching or newly hatched fish are arranged in perfect rows. Large holding tanks fill the extensive room; pipes, drains, and valves can be seen throughout the building.

The fisheries technician will explain how the eggs are gathered from on-site adult fish and the process by which they evolve into fish. Through the glass cylinders and containers, visitors can examine the eggs closely and see a multitude that have "eyed"—meaning the eggs have developed identifiable eyes—and many that are in the process of hatching.

As they move toward the large, round holding tanks, they may notice a tank with glass cylinders above it. At first glance, it may appear empty. But upon closer examination, visitors will see that the tank is completely full of fry (newly hatched fish)—450,000 of them, to be precise. The technician knows exactly how many fry are in the tank, as an infrared eye counts each one. It is hard for a human eye to even *see* each tiny fish, much less count them. Visitors will be astounded to see nearly half a million fish in one place at one time. They will also learn about a fry's struggle to reach adulthood, as well as how and why different species of fish are raised and stocked in public waters.

They will then proceed to the tanks that hold adult fish to learn about their role at the hatchery and about how fish age and grow. Depending on visitors' interest, their time in the hatchery can vary greatly.

Visitors should be aware that fish are hatched during certain times of the year. At Watha State Fish Hatchery, newly hatched fish can be seen *only* during April and May. Although the hatchery is not like a zoo in that regard, it is a place where guests can witness a miraculous event unfolding before their eyes. A trip to Pender County

Guests can see fish eggs in various stages of development at Watha State Fish Hatchery.

should definitely include a visit to the hatchery. *Age and Growth in Fishes*, a North Carolina Wildlife Resources Commission brochure, states, "The more we learn about fish, the more we realize how little we can afford to take them for granted." After seeing nearly half a million newly hatched specimens, visitors will never again look at fish in the same way *or* take them for granted.

Tips

* When planning your trip, be sure to call the hatchery manager to schedule a tour or discuss the best day to visit. The hatchery is a long drive from anywhere, and it would be pointless to make the journey if fish cannot be seen or staff is unavailable. The months when fish hatch (April and May) are some of the busiest for staff; therefore, if you arrive without notice, it is possible no one will be available to assist you. You will learn *so* much more if a fisheries technician accompanies you; scheduling a tour ensures your questions will be answered. Note that state fish hatcheries are generally closed to visitors on state holidays.

* Plan your trip to coincide with an animal-related activity at a nearby beach. You will have several to choose from!

* Another warm-water hatchery is available to the public. McKinney Lake State Fish Hatchery, located at Hoffman in Richmond County, is open on weekdays; again, call ahead to make sure that fish are hatching and that someone will be available to assist you. McKinney Lake State Fish Hatchery raises only channel catfish and works in conjunction with the Watha hatchery to stock Community Fishing Program sites. May and June are the only months the public can see newly hatched catfish; it is a spectacular sight, as forty thousand of them can typically be witnessed at once. Staff members will open the hatchery building for visitors upon their arrival. Inside, they will explain about the holding tanks and the massive egg balls inside and tell guests how to spot the tiny fish that are hatching. Seeing the egg balls and the newly hatched fish is something you will likely never witness again. Visitors can also walk around the ponds. McKinney Lake, adjacent to the hatchery, offers boating, picnicking, and fishing opportunities. The hatchery is located at 220 McKinney Lake Road in Hoffman. To learn more, call 910-895-5330 or visit www.ncwildlife.org.

The venomous eyelash viper, named for the horny projections of scales over its eyes, is on view at Cape Fear Serpentarium.

Cape Fear Serpentarium

20 Orange Street
Wilmington, N.C. 28401
Phone: 910-762-1669
Website: www.capefearserpentarium.com

Hours: Open year-round. Hours are seasonal. Phone or visit the website for exact dates and hours.

Directions: From where I-40 East ends at Wilmington, continue straight on U.S. 117 South for about 1.5 miles. Turn right on Martin Luther King Jr. Parkway (U.S. 74 West) and travel approximately 5 miles. Martin Luther King Jr. Parkway becomes North Third Street. Continue about 1.5 miles and turn right on Orange Street. The serpentarium is on the left after less than 0.5 mile.

> **"... one of the most famous reptile collections on earth!"**
> **Cape Fear Serpentarium brochure**

In historic downtown Wilmington is a facility like no other. Attractions across the state showcase exotic animals that—with enough time and money and a skilled guide—visitors could perhaps see in their native habitats. But the animals inside

*Cape Fear Serpentarium also displays reptiles like Bubble Boy,
a saltwater crocodile.*

Cape Fear Serpentarium are ones most travelers would hope to never encounter in the wild.

Founded by herpetologist Dean Ripa in 2001, the serpentarium features the "World's Rarest & Most Dangerous Snakes, Crocodiles, Dragons and More." Ripa, a Wilmington native, has traveled to more than thirty countries and explored five continents researching and capturing venomous and nonvenomous snakes. He spent years in the Neotropics studying the bushmaster and is an expert on the species. A survivor of twelve venomous snakebites—seven by the bushmaster—Ripa has created a remarkable facility where guests can examine deadly snakes on an up-close basis without the fear of being bitten.

Upon entering, visitors walk into a dimly lit area that appropriately creates a foreboding atmosphere. The numerous large, beautifully designed exhibits spaced throughout the two floors hold an incredible array of reptiles. The well-lit exhibits contain plants, streams, waterfalls, and artifacts characteristic of the reptiles' natural habitats. In all, the serpentarium houses over eighty species, several of which, as stated in its brochure, are "so rare they are not exhibited anywhere else."

The educational text panels accompanying the exhibits give facts pertaining to the reptiles. Visitors often look at the panels first, as they contain skull-and-crossbones images beside the names of the reptiles. The number of skull-and-crossbones images—from one to five—is related to the snakes' venom. For example, if one skull-and-crossbones image is shown, it is not likely a human would die from the bite. However, if five are shown, the bite may prove fatal. Many of the text panels document Ripa's encounters with the species in the wild. For instance, when examining the Western green mamba, a highly venomous snake native to Africa, visitors learn how Ripa, who was suffering from malaria at the time, almost picked one up, mistakenly thinking it was a grass snake, before his assistant stopped him. One series of panels provides a fascinating look at venom and its effect on the human body. Visitors may develop feelings of excitement or uneasiness when they remember they are standing within striking distance of the creatures capable of delivering the powerful toxins they are reading about. Fortunately, all reptiles are kept in locked enclosures with thick glass.

Guests have a rare opportunity to see venomous and nonvenomous snakes from around the world. In viewing the reptiles up close, they will likely be surprised to see such a variety of colors and patterns. Two snakes extremely beautiful in color are the eyelash viper and the emerald tree boa. The eyelash viper, named for the horny projections of scales over its eyes, is a bright yellow native of Central America and northeastern South America. The bite of this snake is usually not fatal. The emerald tree boa is brilliant green. Found in the trees of Amazonian South America, it is nonvenomous. A snake that blends in with the ground but has a striking pattern on its back is the gaboon viper—the largest viper in Africa. The unique markings spaced along its back closely resemble hourglasses. According to the text panel outside its enclosure, the gaboon viper is the world's heaviest-bodied snake and may be the world's deadliest viper.

Among the many species of snakes at the serpentarium are a king cobra, a giant anaconda, a reticulated python, blackheaded bushmasters, puff adders, a Mexican West Coast rattlesnake, a black mamba, a Western green mamba, an Eastern green mamba, a fer-de-lance, a hundred pacer, and many more. According to Scott McKenzie, assistant director, "People seem to like . . . the king cobra, especially when it stands up and spreads its hood, and the anaconda—a 350-pound snake."

The serpentarium also features several lizards and crocodiles. Visitors will long remember the Nile crocodile. The text panel beside its enclosure reads, "Man-eating crocodile." After snakes, Nile crocodiles are the reptiles responsible for killing the most humans on the African continent, according to the panel. Guests can also view a Siamese crocodile—a critically endangered species—and a saltwater crocodile.

Weekend visitors are in for a special treat, as serpentarium staff—often Dean Ripa himself—perform feeding demonstrations. No live animals are used for feeding. Visitors have the rare opportunity to observe snakes lock onto their prey, strike, and then devour it. The most exhilarating part of the demonstration comes when food is put into an enclosure and a hidden snake suddenly lunges forth from the background. A crocodile is also fed during the demonstration, but it cannot compete with the heart-stopping action of the snakes.

Those who visit New Hanover County should put Cape Fear Serpentarium on their must-see list. It is a place, according to Scott McKenzie, "for snake lovers and snake haters," a place where visitors leave "with a different outlook on snakes." Featured on the Discovery Channel and Animal Planet, the serpentarium is one of the most unique facilities in the state. Guests will be glad they chose to explore a facility that holds, according to its website, "one of the world's foremost reptile collections."

Tips

● Note that the serpentarium does not accept credit cards. An ATM is located a block or so away; staff can provide directions.

● The staff does an excellent job of keeping the glass enclosures smudge-free, particular for photographic purposes. You will have the chance to capture some amazing shots of snakes.

● If you are going to be in the area for a day or two, make plans to visit the North Carolina Aquarium at Fort Fisher (see pages 208–11), located approximately twenty-one miles south.

North Carolina Aquarium at Fort Fisher

900 Loggerhead Road
Kure Beach, N.C. 28449
Phone: 800-832-3474, ext. 2
Website: www.ncaquariums.com
E-mail: ffmail@ncaquariums.com

Hours: Open daily year-round from 9 A.M. to 5 P.M. Closed Thanksgiving, Christmas, and New Year's.

Directions: From U.S. 421 South at Kure Beach in southeastern New Hanover County, turn left on Logger-head Road. The aquarium is on the left after about 0.5 mile.

The North Carolina Aquarium at Fort Fisher is home to Luna, a rare albino alligator.

"Come face to face with alligators."
North Carolina Aquariums website

Not everyone has the ability to swim, snorkel, or dive. Even those who do will never see each plant and animal that resides in the underwater world. Fortunately, the three North Carolina Aquariums—at Fort Fisher, Pine Knoll Shores, and Roanoke Island—allow nonswimmers and experienced divers alike to view a fascinating array of sea creatures. The aquariums not only showcase intriguing marine life but also explore life on the water's edge. Opened in 1976 as Marine Resource Centers, they were established, according to their website, "to promote an awareness, understanding, appreciation, and conservation of the diverse natural and cultural resources associated with North Carolina's ocean, estuaries, rivers, streams, and other aquatic environments." In 1986, they were renamed the North Carolina Aquariums.

Each aquarium has a theme. For the North Carolina Aquarium at Fort Fisher—the largest of the three facilities—the theme is "From the Cape Fear River to the Sea." Visitors are led on a journey that takes them, as explained on the website, "down the Cape Fear River—from freshwater streams and swamps, to coastline habitats, to reefs and the open ocean."

Guests first visit the Cape Fear Conservatory. This exhibit examines freshwater life and is the aquarium's most spectacular and diverse display. Several animals—like bobwhite quail, an Eastern box turtle, and an Eastern glass lizard—are not in enclosures but either roam the area freely or are visible behind barriers in the ground cover. Also in the ground cover are carnivorous plants such as the Venus flytrap, various pitcher plants, the yellow butterwort, and the sundew. Multitudes of freshwater fish are displayed in areas that appear to be cutaways of particular wetland habitats; snake and frog exhibits are placed between them. A focal point of the conservatory is the large American alligator exhibit, where visitors can get face to face with these mesmerizing reptiles. One alligator steals the spotlight. Luna is a rare albino alligator that came to the aquarium in February 2009. Luna cannot produce color pigments. Being white makes her susceptible to burns from the sun's rays and an easy target for predators. For these reasons, Luna could not survive in the wild. She can and does, however, live well at the aquarium. According to Amy Kilgore, public-relations coordinator, Luna has nearly doubled her weight since arriving at the aquarium and has become a picky eater that prefers chicken instead of fish. She has her own exhibit, which keeps her safe and allows visitors excellent viewing opportunities. Fewer than fifty albino alligators are known to exist. Guests who view Luna can receive a special sticker reading, "I Met Luna at the NC Aquarium at Fort Fisher."

The Cape Fear Conservatory is home to free-roaming bobwhite quail.
PHOTOGRAPH COURTESY OF NC AQUARIUM AT FORT FISHER

Guests will next proceed to the Marine Building to explore the Coastal Waters Gallery, where the main attraction is the Coquina Outcrop Touch Pool. Here, they can interact with stingrays, horseshoe crabs, hermit crabs, and other marine creatures. Additional highlights of the gallery are the seahorse and loggerhead turtle exhibits. Seahorses are bred at the aquarium, which eliminates the need for collecting them in the wild. According to aquarist technician April Zilg in the article "A Tiny Life" on the aquarium's website, "Many people don't even know seahorses are real, or have never seen one. Being able to display seahorses brings more understanding, and hopefully they [visitors] like them enough that they may do a beach sweep or join an oceanic conservation association." At the loggerhead sea turtle display, guests can see a juvenile turtle, pick up brochures about nesting sites, and speak with a staff member about this endangered species.

In the Marine Building, visitors can also journey through the Open Oceans Gallery and stand in front of the two-story Cape Fear Shoals exhibit. Cape Fear Shoals, the largest of the aquarium's saltwater exhibits, holds 235,000 gallons of water. The twenty-four-foot-deep exhibit, a replica of an offshore reef, houses several species of sharks, stingrays, fish, and moray eels. Thanks to the massive sharks and the daily dive presentations, large crowds typically gather around this exhibit. Visitors interested in sharks will enjoy the aquarium's superb Sharks of North Carolina exhibit, which has a display that illustrates sharks' anatomy and also showcases the jaws of a variety of different species. The Open Oceans Gallery offers an opportunity to examine nonindigenous marine life. On display in the Exotic Aquatics exhibit are some of the brightest-colored and most interesting species, including lionfish, spiny lobsters, Pacific reef fish, and poison dart frogs.

After exiting the Marine Building, visitors can spend time in the gift shop—where a wide selection of books on marine life and the local community is available—or step outside to the SharkBites snack bar. On the walk back to the parking lot, guests exit by way of a boardwalk through the aquarium's Memorial Gardens, where they can stop to look at a pond full of turtles or enjoy the native plants and birds. From the parking lot, they can embark on a trail through a maritime forest or search for shark teeth in a fossil pit.

New Hanover County tourists should indeed visit the North Carolina Aquarium at Fort Fisher, which offers an up-close look at marine life and other animals not typically seen by beachgoers.

Tips

● To enhance your experience, check out the calendar of events prior to your visit and register for a special event or activity. Several occur off-site. Also, check the daily schedule, as "Animal Feedings," "Animal Encounters," "Creature Feature," "Dialog with a Diver," and "Tank Talk" programs are offered on a regular basis.

● If you will be in the area for a day or two, take the ferry to Oak Island and visit the Oak Island Nature Center. Although small, the center has a few animals that leave large impressions. One is a blue jay that was attacked by a crow and lost an eye when it was very young. Having been in the company of humans for so long, the blue jay is now able to mimic them. It is quite something to hear. The center also houses other birds and small mammals. It is located at Northeast Fifty-second Street and Yacht Drive. To learn more, call 910-278-5518 or visit www.oakislandnc.com/Recreation/nature_center.htm.

The Karen Beasley Sea Turtle Rescue and Rehabilitation Center

822 Carolina Boulevard
Topsail Beach, N.C. 28445
Phone: 910-328-1000
Website: www.seaturtlehospital.org
E-mail: loggrhead@aol.com

Hours: Open seasonally. Phone or visit the website for exact dates and hours.

Directions: From U.S. 17 North near the Pender County–Onslow County line, turn right on N.C. 50. Follow N.C. 50 for approximately 6 miles as it travels over the bridge to the stoplight on Topsail Island. N.C. 50 turns right at the stoplight. Continue on N.C. 50 about 6.5 miles toward the south end of the island. Turn right on Crews Avenue, then turn right on Carolina Boulevard. The center is on the left. Note that these directions are to the center's location at the time of this writing. In 2011, it will move approximately 10 miles away to the mainland portion of Surf City. The expected opening is June 3, 2011.

▉ ▉ ▉ (Will have restrooms in new facility)

~~~~~~~~~~~~~~~~~~~~~~

"Committed to the Care & Release of Sick and Injured Sea Turtles"
The Karen Beasley Sea Turtle Rescue
and Rehabilitation Center website

Jean Beasley visited Topsail Beach in 1958. She returned during the 1970s and purchased a home. It was then she met—and fell in love with—her first sea turtle. It nested beside her house. Many years later, in 1996, Beasley encountered another sea turtle. This time however, the sea turtle was injured, and she tried to find help for it. As no assistance was available, she returned home with the turtle, nursed it back to health, and released it. One year later, The Karen Beasley Sea Turtle Rescue and Rehabilitation Center opened on the southern end of Topsail Island.

The center—named in honor of Beasley's daughter—continues to be a godsend for sea turtles suffering from illness or injury. When the center opened in 1997, plans were for it to care for eight turtles. But it has never held that few. In fact, since opening, the center has released nearly three hundred sea turtles. Beasley, executive director, says she was fortunate to find an all-volunteer staff dedicated to the cause of caring for sea turtles in need. In the summer, the center has the assistance of college interns.

Sea turtles arrive at the center with a wide range of illnesses and injuries. Most often, their circumstances are associated with human factors such as fishing gear, litter, pollution, and loss of habitat. Sea turtles undergoing rehabilitation receive physicals by veterinary students. Minor surgeries are done on-site, but complicated procedures—ones that involve life support—are performed at the North Carolina State University College of Veterinary Medicine.

One of the missions of the center, beyond its main purpose of protecting all species of sea turtles in the water and on land, is to provide experiential learning to stu-

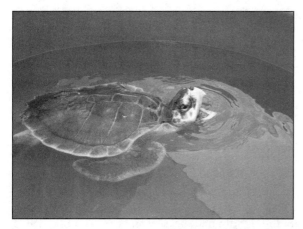

The Kemp's Ridley is the smallest and most endangered sea turtle.

A dedicated volunteer holds a green sea turtle being treated at the center.

dents, graduates, veterinarians, and researchers. It is also dedicated to educating the public about sea turtles and spreading a message of conservation. One of the best ways it provides information is by offering tours. Because the center is a hospital, tours are available only a few hours a day seasonally, as the turtles' well-being is the priority.

Entering the hospital, visitors will view several species of sea turtles, learn about their status in the wild, and hear stories of how they came to be at the center. The hospital is a large area full of massive blue holding tanks containing survivors that have beaten the odds, are now recovering, and may soon be released. Visitors will likely observe loggerhead turtles, green sea turtles, and Kemp's Ridley sea turtles. Although all three are endangered species, the Kemp's Ridley is *critically* endangered. Guests might meet inspiring sea turtles such as Ocean's Eleven, a loggerhead found with 50 percent of her carapace (shell) crushed. After enduring over two hours of surgery that required eleven surgical plates, Ocean's Eleven is now recovering and interacting with volunteers. Hopefully, she can one day be released. The same cannot be said for Lennie, a Kemp's Ridley sea turtle found with a head injury. He is now blind; no surgery can help him.

After visiting the hospital, guests will no doubt want to know of the turtles' progress and eventual release. To accommodate this "need to know," Beasley created a "Patient's Index" on the center's website, where interested parties can track each turtle.

In 2007, Jean Beasley was named Animal Planet's Hero of the Year. It is no surprise that someone who is so dedicated to educating others about sea turtles, who is so willing to provide around-the-clock rescue and rehabilitation, and who is responsible for releasing nearly three hundred turtles back into the wild should receive such an esteemed recognition.

Beasley's first intake was a turtle named Lucky, whose flippers, she says, told everyone to "get going." And get going the staff must, because as soon as one sea turtle is released from the hospital, another is admitted. Beasley and her team of devoted volunteers will not stop in their efforts to rescue, rehabilitate, and release sea turtles. In fact, they will open a new facility in 2011 that will provide better conditions for turtles and allow more opportunities to educate the public about their plight. Visitors to Pender County should plan to visit The Karen Beasley Sea Turtle Rescue and Rehabilitation Center, where they can learn why these endangered creatures are so vital to the environment and discover some easy steps they can take to protect them.

Tips

- As the center is in the process of moving to a new facility, be sure to call before visiting.

- Note that you can bring a camera to the center but that photography is not allowed inside the hospital.

- Young visitors may be interested to know that Jean Beasley is also involved with the Marine Biology Camp for Teens. During the camp, teenagers volunteer at The Karen Beasley Sea Turtle Rescue and Rehabilitation Center. For information, visit www.seaturtlecamp.com.

Guests may have an up-close encounter with Franklin, an African spur thigh tortoise.

Lynnwood Park Zoo

1071 Wells Road
Jacksonville, N.C. 28540
Phone: 910-938-5848
Website: www.lynnwoodparkzoo.com

Hours: Open year-round Friday through Monday from 10 A.M. to 5 P.M. Open Tuesday through Thursday by advance reservation only.

Directions: From U.S. 258 South/N.C. 24 South near Jacksonville in Onslow County, turn left on Wells Road. The zoo is on the left in less than 0.5 mile.

"At Lynnwood Park Zoo you will have an 'Adventure with Nature.'"
Lynnwood Park Zoo brochure

When tourists think of Jacksonville and Onslow County, military images likely come to mind, as the area is home to Marine Corps Base Camp Lejeune and Marine Corps Air Station New River. However, images of exotic, domestic, and native animals should supplement those visions, as it is also the location of Lynnwood Park Zoo. Gary Evans founded the zoo in 1994. A ten-acre facility with a half-acre pond, it showcases over fifty animals.

The blackbuck antelope, native to India, is one of the fastest animals on the planet.

Upon entering the zoo's parking area, visitors should look to the left for a small freestanding structure, where they can purchase tickets, acquire a map, and receive a complimentary bag of corn to feed the animals. Evans and a team of volunteers operate the facility, so it is likely he will be selling tickets and interacting with guests.

Visitors begin their tour by walking down a dirt path leading into the woods. On a hot day, the forested area provides a shaded escape; on overcast and autumn days, it can be a bit cool. The trail passes numerous animal enclosures housing mammals, reptiles, and birds. As many of the animals appreciate the corn, visitors may soon deplete their complimentary bags. If so, they can stop at the vending machines at various locations along the trail.

Guests will encounter various mammals including Jacob sheep, Barbary sheep, black Welsh mountain sheep, mouflons, blackbuck antelopes, a black-tailed prairie dog, an ocelot, a serval, coatis, llamas, a raccoon, grivet monkeys, a dama wallaby, a swamp wallaby, a Patagonian cavy, a capybara, pot-bellied pigs, a miniature Sicilian donkey, Scottish Highland cattle, a zebra, an African crested porcupine, a skunk, a silver fox, an Arctic fox, a squirrel, and pygmy goats. The most fascinating animals— and perhaps the most beautiful—are the silver and Arctic foxes. As these species are not common at North Carolina animal parks, visitors will likely spend considerable time admiring them. Another mammal that captures attention is a lively little gray squirrel. The squirrel, which cannot be released into the wild, originally resided at a zoo in Bolivia, North Carolina. After that facility closed, it came to live at Lynnwood Park Zoo. A lover of corn, the squirrel runs about its enclosure to bring visitors—and their treats—close by.

The zoo also has a large collection of birds. Visitors will enjoy seeing species such as emus, rheas, a barred owl, royal palm turkeys, golden Polish chickens, white crested chickens, silkie chickens, old English bantams, shelducks, wood ducks, Mandarin ducks, an Egyptian goose, pheasants, guineafowl, ring-necked doves, pigeons, bobwhite quail, a green-winged macaw, and many others. The majority of birds are located on the right side of the zoo, an area alive with sound. Reptiles—snakes, lizards, turtles, and juvenile alligators—are also located along the nature trail.

If Evans is not busy or if ample volunteers are on-site, visitors may be treated to a special showing of select animals midway along the path. Those animals might include Franklin, an African spur thigh tortoise, and Snowball, a silkie chicken. If animals are brought out, visitors are allowed to feed or pet them. When asked which animal is the star of his zoo, Evans immediately said it is his little silkie chicken, Snowball. "Snowball brings back people over and over again," he says. Children especially delight in having Snowball—a small, fluffy white chicken—peck food from their hands. After sharing the animals, Evans or one of his volunteers gives visitors another complimentary bag of food treats and sends them on their way.

Gary Evans works hard to provide everyone a little something extra when they visit Lynnwood Park Zoo. Whether it is a special bag of treats for a specific breed of animal or a meeting with Snowball and Franklin, he finds some small way to leave a big impression in the minds of his guests.

Tips

- As the walk leads through a wooded area, you may want to apply bug spray if visiting during a warm month. Also, bring quarters for the vending machines located along the walk. Hand sanitizers are located near the exit.

- After visiting the zoo, head over to Mike's Farm & Country Store to see a variety of barnyard animals, several of which can be fed or petted. Mike's Farm also serves up an incredible family-style dinner that includes the best macaroni and cheese in the state. The farm has a bakery and a country store on-site and offers special events—hayrides, a festival of lights, etc.—throughout the year. Located approximately eleven miles from the zoo at 1600 Haw Branch Road in Beulaville, Mike's Farm should not be missed. To learn more, call 910-324-3422 or visit www.mikesfarm.com.

Exchange Nature Center at Neuseway Nature Park

401 West Caswell Street
Kinston, N.C. 28501
Phone: 252-939-3367
Website: www.neusewaypark.com

Hours: Open year-round Tuesday through Saturday from 9:30 A.M. to 5 P.M. and Sunday from 1 P.M. to 5 P.M. Closed on some holidays.

Directions: From U.S. 70 Bypass East/U.S. 258 Bypass South at Kinston in Lenoir County, turn left on Old Pink Hill Road (N.C. 11). In less than 0.5 mile, turn left on West Caswell Street. The park is on the left in approximately 1 mile.

> "Get your hands wet investigating our salt-water touch tank . . ."
> **Neuseway Nature Park website**

When traveling near Kinston, make plans to visit Neuseway Nature Park. Situated on the banks of the Neuse River, this fifty-five-acre park operated by the Kinston/Lenoir County Parks and Recreation Department offers diverse attractions: a campground and meeting facility, a health and science museum that includes a planetarium, and a nature park.

At the Lenoir Memorial Hospital Health and Science Museum—which is designed for children—creative hands-on exhibits showcase the inner workings of the body. Youngsters can disappear inside a tunnel that replicates a blood vessel or inside a miniature replica of Lenoir Memorial Hospital. The museum also houses the fifty-two-seat Neuseway Planetarium, where shows are presented daily.

The multitude of entertainment options includes a playground, a fossil dig, a climbing wall, and Big Daddy's Express, a miniature train; a small fee is charged for train rides. Visitors can also partake of a variety of outdoor activities like hiking (self-guided nature trails are located near the campground), biking, picnicking, canoeing, and fishing. The park participates in the North Carolina Wildlife Resources Com-

Oliver, an umbrella cockatoo, likes visitors to sing "Happy Birthday to You."

mission's Community Fishing Program and therefore offers a pond full of channel catfish. For visitors who would like to fish but do not have a rod and reel, the park also participates in the commission's Fishing Tackle Loaner Program, which means they can simply borrow one for the day.

The focal point of the nature park is Exchange Nature Center. Inside the nature center, guests will see mounted and live animals, many of which are native to eastern North Carolina. The largest and perhaps most fascinating exhibit is Snakes of Eastern North Carolina. Snakes on display include a brown watersnake, a copperhead, a cottonmouth, a timber rattlesnake, an Eastern hognose snake, a rat snake, a corn snake, an Eastern diamondback rattlesnake, and an Eastern kingsnake. Non-native snakes include an albino California kingsnake, a red-tailed boa, and a ball python. Visitors will also see small mammals like a black-tailed prairie dog, a flying squirrel, and an African pygmy hedgehog, as well as an assortment of reptiles and insects such as a rose-haired tarantula, Madagascar hissing cockroaches, a veiled chameleon, a bearded dragon, a blue-tongued skink, a leopard gecko, and anoles. A good-sized saltwater touch pool allows guests to examine various marine creatures.

Two birds named Max and Oliver are the highlights of a visit to the nature center. Max is an African grey parrot that can imitate humans, other animals, and technological devices. Most visitors attempt to "converse" with Max or entice him to make particular sounds. Oliver is an umbrella cockatoo that craves attention, according to the educational text panel outside his habitat. The text also reveals that Oliver's favorite song is "Happy Birthday to You." It is most entertaining to observe people singing this song to him. Oliver appears to enjoy hearing it. When he squawks a few notes back, tourists are elated.

Upon exiting the back door of the nature center, visitors can relax on the deck

Visitors can see small mammals like a black-tailed prairie dog at Exchange Nature Center.

and enjoy a view of the Neuse River. Afterward, they can walk behind the center to view several large aviaries or enter the Underground Cave to explore additional animal exhibits. The aviaries, located between the deck and the river, hold rescued birds of prey including various species of hawks and owls. The Underground Cave exhibit, located beneath the nature center, features a fennec fox, turtles, a green iguana, a bullfrog, and several species of fish found in the Neuse River, including spot, croaker, crappie, flounder, redear and bluegill sunfish, channel catfish, largemouth bass, and longnose gar.

For travelers with children, Neuseway Nature Park is an enjoyable and free attraction worthy of a detour on the way to or from the coast.

Tip

- Nature-related events and programs are frequently offered at the park. If you know you are going to be in the area, visit the website for a list.

Outer Banks Wildlife Shelter

100 Wildlife Way
Newport, N.C. 28570
Phone: 252-240-1200
Website: www.owlsonline.org
E-mail: owls@owlsonline.org

Hours: Open year-round. "Behind-the-Scenes Tours" are available Tuesday, Thursday, and Saturday at 2 P.M. Self-guided tours are available Monday through Saturday from 10 A.M. to 4 P.M. and Sunday from 1 P.M. to 4 P.M.

Directions: From U.S. 70 East at Newport in Carteret County, turn right on Hibbs Road. Travel approximately 3 miles and turn left on Freedom Way (N.C. 24). Drive 0.5 mile and turn left on Wildlife Way, which dead-ends at the shelter.

"... visit with our resident owls, hawks, ducks, falcons, and vultures ..."
Outer Banks Wildlife Shelter brochure

Inside an unassuming brick house off N.C. 24 in Newport, countless injured, sick, and orphaned native wild animals are cared for on a daily basis. The Outer Banks Wildlife Shelter (OWLS) might escape the eyes of passing tourists if not for a business sign at the top of the driveway and lighted signs in the windows. Founded in 1988, OWLS has admitted close to twenty-three thousand patients since opening its doors. Dedicated staff and volunteers provide care for numerous species by supplying each animal medical treatment, an appropriate diet, and shelter.

OWLS is an exciting place to visit. Guests who take a "Behind-the-Scenes Tour" get a thorough look at wildlife rehabilitation and the work it entails. Upon entering the shelter, they are told the mission of OWLS and given guidelines for taking a tour. Afterward, they are led to the Education Room. The shelter uses its Education Room for in-house, outreach, and summer-camp programs. Staff and volunteers feel

Blanca, a leucistic rat snake, educates the public about snakes and their beneficial qualities.

OWLS cares for animals like this orphaned baby opossum on a daily basis.

strongly that they must educate the public about the impact of human activity on wildlife injuries or their work will be pointless.

Several "education ambassadors" are appropriately placed in the room. Blanca, a leucistic rat snake (a rat snake with reduced skin pigmentation), was found on a window sill. She is used to teach the public about snakes and their beneficial qualities. Blanca is a permanent resident at OWLS, as her white coloration prevents her from adequately hunting or hiding in the wild. Otis, another ambassador, is an Eastern box turtle that tears at the heartstrings of every visitor who meets him. Otis was hit by a Bush Hog, has major nerve damage in his back legs, and requires weekly physical therapy. A resilient little turtle, Otis educates people about North Carolina's official state reptile and its near-threatened status.

The next stop on the tour is the Baby Bird Nursery. This room is full of babies only during certain times of year—generally spring and summer. Upon opening the door—after making sure all residents are secured—visitors may be astounded to see what appear to be hundreds of baby birds. Playpens, used to contain the hopping baby birds, line the walls and fill every available space. Although it is not possible to predict what types of baby birds will be on view, songbirds are typical. Songbird or not, each baby bird knows how to chirp, which makes the room a bit boisterous. Staff and volunteers are kept extremely busy in the nursery, as they feed the baby birds every two hours until they are capable of self-feeding. After further growth and development, the birds are taken to a flight cage and are later released. The Baby Bird Nursery also contains eggs and an incubator with chicks.

Guests will ooh and aah upon entering the Baby Mammal Nursery. The overwhelming cuteness of the animals is guaranteed to hold their attention; most visitors will be reluctant to leave. Again, it cannot be stated what animals will be on view, but baby opossums and squirrels are frequent intakes during certain months of the year. As with the baby birds, the goal is to rehabilitate and release the baby mammals back into the wild. Native wild animals in the nursery and those that are "education ambassadors"—permanent residents—are the only animals that visitors can view. Animals that will soon be released into the wild do not interact with the public.

After viewing the nurseries, guests are shown the Exam Room if no animals are inside. Native wild animals brought to the shelter are placed in the Exam Room and left alone for approximately one hour to calm down and recover from stress. The staff emphasizes that stress can be detrimental to the health of injured or scared animals and gives instructions on how to properly transport an animal to a rehabilitation center or shelter. For example, if someone is transporting a baby bird in their car, they should not play the radio or talk loudly, as this can be frightening to the animal.

Some native wild animals come to the shelter with immediate physical problems—such as profuse bleeding—and are taken straight to the Intensive Care Room. Although this room is off-limits to tours, visitors will learn about injuries commonly seen on intakes. Other rooms on the tour include the lab, where blood work, surgeries, and x-rays are performed, and the kitchen, where daily meals and medications are prepared.

Upon completing the inside tour, visitors are taken outside to see more of the shelter's permanent residents, including Xena, a turkey vulture hit by a car; Zelda, a black vulture with wing damage; Phoenix, a peregrine falcon with major nerve damage; Chili and Pepper, two Eastern screech owls with eye injuries; and Dinah, a barred owl hit by a car. Dinah is a special resident. According to her biography, she serves as a foster mother for orphaned baby barred owls admitted to the shelter, which prevents them from imprinting on humans.

While touring the grounds, visitors will see large flight cages where rehabilitated birds prepare for release. They will also learn about the steps that can be taken to reduce animal injuries. For instance, the shelter stresses that seagulls, ducks, and geese should not be fed bread, French fries, or potato chips. When birds eat these types of food, they can become malnourished and eventually lose their strength to fly.

After the outside tour, visitors can explore a two-acre wooded hiking trail on their own, visit the gift shop, or feed fish and turtles in the pond, food for which can be purchased in the gift shop. Tourists who do not take a guided tour are welcome to walk the grounds, hike the trail, and visit the gift shop. A guide that documents plants along the trail is available inside the shelter. Educational text panels affixed to each habitat present interesting facts about the animals.

OWLS asks, "Whooo will help all the owls and other native wild animals in distress in Eastern North Carolina?" It responds with, "You, that's who!" When visiting Carteret County, make sure you stop at OWLS, where you will have a unique opportunity to see the daily operations of a wildlife shelter, meet an array of native wild animals, and learn, as the shelter puts it, "how to happily and peacefully coexist with wildlife."

Tips

● Try to schedule your visit during a guided tour, as you will see and learn so much more than on a self-guided tour.

● After touring the shelter, head to the North Carolina Aquarium at Pine Knoll Shores (see pages 224–28), located approximately sixteen miles away, to discover even more amazing wildlife.

● If you will be in the area a day or two, grab a seat on a water taxi—several depart from the waterfront in nearby Beaufort—and coast over to Shackleford Banks, where you can view a unique herd of wild horses (see pages 228–31).

North Carolina Aquarium at Pine Knoll Shores

1 Roosevelt Boulevard
Pine Knoll Shores, N.C. 28512
Phone: 800-832-3474, ext. 3, or 252-247-4003
Website: www.ncaquariums.com
E-mail: pksmail@ncaquariums.com

Hours: Open daily year-round from 9 A.M. to 5 P.M. Closed Thanksgiving, Christmas, and New Year's.

Directions: From U.S. 70 East at Morehead City in Carteret County, bear right on the Atlantic Beach Causeway. Follow the causeway for approximately 2 miles, turn right on N.C. 58, drive about 5 miles, and turn right on Pine Knoll Boulevard. In less than 0.5 mile, turn left on Roosevelt Boulevard, which dead-ends at the aquarium.

"Touch a stingray."
North Carolina Aquariums website

*A sand tiger shark in the
Living Shipwreck exhibit*
PHOTOGRAPH BY CRAIG DAVIES

The theme of the North Carolina Aquarium at Pine Knoll Shores is "North Carolina's Aquatic Life from the Mountains to the Sea." The North Carolina Aquariums' website states the theme eloquently: "Thousands of aquatic animals take [visitors] on a journey from the state's grand peaks to the open Atlantic, much as a raindrop makes its way to the ocean." Indeed, guests will encounter only species found in North Carolina.

Visitors begin their exploration in the Mountain Gallery, where a cool mist from a mountain waterfall greets them. Among the several species of freshwater fish in this gallery are trout, minnows, and muskellunge, or muskies. The muskellunge is an ancient species that has lived in North Carolina waters for more than ten thousand years. In the early to mid-1900s, pollution devastated the population in the western region of the state. Today, the water is cleaner, and muskellunge have been successfully reintroduced.

The next stop is the Piedmont Gallery, the site of the liveliest exhibit. Three male river otters—appropriately named Neuse, Pungo, and Eno after North Carolina rivers—entertain guests with their swimming, diving, and wrestling. "Otter Enrichment Programs" offered at special times during the week draw considerable interest, as aquarium staff use food treats and other stimulants to encourage the otters to explore, hunt, and swim within their enclosure. The Piedmont Gallery also displays a variety of animals found in freshwater habitats. In the Fairway Pond exhibit, guests can examine a grass carp, a spiny softshell turtle, and other species, while the Man-Made Lakes exhibit features blue catfish, common carp, pumpkinseed, and many other fish.

Before heading into the next gallery, guests should step outside and take a stroll along the Marsh Boardwalk. Two overlooks offer views of Bogue Sound and a variety of native wildlife, particularly birds and crabs. The boardwalk is also the location of

Pungo, Neuse, and Eno, a trio of river otters, amuse themselves and visitors in the Piedmont Gallery. PHOTOGRAPH BY CLAIRE AUBEL, COURTESY OF NC AQUARIUMS

the Snakes: Hidden Inhabitants of the Maritime Forest exhibit.

Returning to the aquarium, visitors will enter the Coastal Plain Gallery, where the main attractions include American alligators, a variety of turtles, and longnose gar. The small Roadside Wonders exhibit in this gallery is one of the most intriguing in the aquarium. Roadside Wonders illustrates how ditches are important ecosystems that provide habitats for frogs, fish, watersnakes, crayfish, and mosquitoes. In most cases, people take ditches for granted, but this exhibit demonstrates how they are essential to the environment and should be kept clean.

The Tidal Waters Gallery is quite popular, as its two touch pools offer hands-on encounters with whelks, crabs, skates, and stingrays. It is also a favorite for visitors who admire Blackbeard the pirate. Inside the gallery, the *Queen Anne's Revenge* exhibit re-creates the scene of what is believed to be the wreck of the pirate's flagship. Bonnethead sharks, sea turtles, cobia, and a variety of other fish swim around the "wreck." Visitors should ready their cameras for this gallery, as it offers a fun photographic opportunity. Guests can stand behind a reproduction of a megalodon shark jaw.

Just beyond the Tidal Waters Gallery is the Big Rock Theater. Daily programs offered in the theater include "Creature Feature" and "Winging It: Birds in Flight." During a "Creature Feature" presentation, guests learn about a particular animal. A highly recommended program is the one regarding venomous snakes, during which attendees are taught how to recognize venomous snakes even when they are in water. "Winging It: Birds in Flight" was introduced in the summer of 2010. The program, unique to the Pine Knoll Shores aquarium, allows visitors to learn about raptors and shorebirds on an up-close basis. Pelicans, hawks, owls, vultures, and other native birds perform aerial routines inside the theater while educators present fascinating facts about them. Depending on where you sit, a bird may fly directly over your head! "Winging It: Birds in Flight" is likely the only program in North Carolina where visitors can observe a pelican at such close range.

Next, guests will descend into the Ocean Gallery to discover the largest aquarium tank in North Carolina—the 306,000-gallon Living Shipwreck exhibit. This exhibit features a replica of the German submarine *U-352* and is populated by sand tiger, nurse, and sandbar sharks; various species of snapper; and a multitude of other fish species. The fearsome-looking jaws of the sand tiger sharks capture visitors' attention. Julie Powers, public-relations coordinator, notes that few people can dive to shipwrecks but that the aquarium makes it possible for everyone to view a realistic re-creation of a wreck and observe the marine communities it attracts. The aquarium's "Live Dive" program actually puts divers inside this exhibit and allows them to talk to and answer questions from visitors. This is achieved through the use of underwater microphones.

Upon exiting the Ocean Gallery, visitors can browse the gift shop or proceed outside for a frozen treat or a hot dog; a Dairy Queen® is located on-site. Those who enjoy spending time outdoors will be pleased to learn that the aquarium is surrounded by nearly 300 acres of the Theodore Roosevelt Natural Area, where several nature trails are available for exploration.

According to Powers, the North Carolina Aquarium at Pine Knoll Shores was designed to make learning about aquatic environments an intensely personal experience. Through exceptional exhibits, touch tanks, and interactive daily programs, it has achieved exactly that. The knowledgeable and friendly staff, over three thousand animals, and engaging educational programs combine to make this a unique and exciting destination.

Tips

* "Winging It: Birds in Flight" is offered only certain days and times. I highly recommend scheduling your visit on a day when you can partake of this excellent educational program.

* If you are staying in the area, check the aquarium's monthly calendar and sign up for a few of its special programs and activities. Off-site programs include canoeing, kayaking, exploring the beach in search of loggerhead turtle nests, surfing, and a host of other fun and educational events. Note that programs are often limited to a specific number of registrants and that they fill up fast. Don't forget to check the daily

events schedule when arriving at the aquarium or you could miss some fabulous activities.

⬤ If you have time, head over to the Outer Banks Wildlife Shelter (see pages 220–24), located approximately sixteen miles away, where you can view native wildlife being rehabilitated. You might also want to take a boat ride to Shackleford Banks to learn about the island's wild horses (see pages 228–31).

⬤ If you are a certified diver or would like to become one, several local dive centers offer training and dive excursions. To learn more, contact Discovery Diving (252-728-2265; www.discoverydiving.com), located at 414 Orange Street in Beaufort, or Olympus Dive Center (252-726-9432; www.olympusdiving.com), located at 713 Shepard Street in Morehead City.

Wild Horses of Shackleford Banks

Foundation for Shackleford Horses, Inc.
306 Golden Farm Road
Beaufort, N.C. 28516
Phone: 252-728-6308
Website: www.shacklefordhorses.org
E-mail: info@shacklefordhorses.org

Hours: Not applicable

Directions: From U.S. 70 East at Beaufort in Carteret County, turn right on Pollock Street. In less than 0.5 mile, turn left or right on Front Street. Note that these directions do not lead to Golden Farm Road; the foundation's address is for contact purposes only. The horses are located on an island; visitors must take a boat to get there. The directions lead to Front Street, where several water taxis and ferries provide this service.

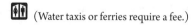 (Water taxis or ferries require a fee.)

Wild horses of Shackleford Banks wade near Cape Lookout Lighthouse.
PHOTOGRAPH COURTESY OF CAROLYN MASON FOR F.S.H.

"The Shackleford Banks wild horses are a
unique historic and cultural legacy."
Foundation for Shackleford Horses website

On a daily basis, Atlantic Beach, Morehead City, and Beaufort deliver beautiful beaches, first-class fishing and diving opportunities, historic attractions, nature excursions, and a variety of other activities. The area has such a rich history—pirates, wars, shipwrecks, etc.—that many visitors come in search of buried treasure. Yet Carteret County has priceless jewels that anyone can behold but few are aware of.

Shackleford Banks is one of the barrier islands that comprise Cape Lookout National Seashore. No one knows for certain how, why, or when, but at some point in time, wild horses came to live here. It is known, however, "that these wild horses descended from a core group of Spanish horses from 400 years ago," according to the *Wild Horses of Shackleford Banks* brochure published by the Foundation for Shackleford Horses. Today, the horses are a direct connection to North Carolina's past and living historical treasures.

Oral histories and traditions support the idea that the horses were originally aboard ships bound for the English colonies. As numerous shipwrecks occurred along the coastline, it is plausible that the horses swam to the island from a sinking ship. They are able to survive because the island is rich in vegetation and has springs that provide fresh water. When the horses are not near the springs, they simply dig for water. According to Carolyn Mason, president and chairman of the Foundation for Shackleford Horses, a freshwater "lens" can be found under every barrier island, which explains how the horses can find water through this means.

Although the horses on Shackleford Banks live in the same manner as their ancestors, there are a few slight differences. Today, the National Park Service and the Foundation for Shackleford Horses cooperatively manage the herd. They observe

Dueling stallions are a sight to behold.
PHOTOGRAPH COURTESY OF
CAROLYN MASON FOR F.S.H.

the horses, watching particularly for health issues and injuries; maintain a registry; conduct genetics testing; share information with the public; and work with other organizations to ensure that the horses are protected and preserved.

Touring Shackleford Banks is free. The island is not accessible by car, nor are vehicles allowed on it. Visitors must be transported by boat. Several water taxis and ferries, particularly on Front Street in Beaufort, provide this service for a fee. The island does not have an operating schedule; it is open all day, every day. However, transportation to the island is limited during the cold months.

When visitors arrive, they should be respectful of the horses. The herd is covered by the Shackleford Banks Wild Horse Protection Act, a federal law that protects the horses from being fed, chased, or harassed. Tourists should maintain a distance of fifty feet. Typically, 110 to 130 horses are on the island at any given time. When the herd exceeds a certain number—based on recommendations set forth by equine experts—some horses are removed from the island and adopted. Horses selected for adoption are chosen according to certain genetic standards. An adoption farm is located in Bettie, North Carolina, where the horses learn to be touched, to walk on a lead, and to eat commercial horse feed. In most instances, Shackleford Banks horses are adopted as pets. In some cases, they are ridden. It is not recommended, however, that they be ridden by anyone over 185 pounds.

In the future, the foundation hopes to create an exhibit on the wild horses of Shackleford Banks and display it in a local museum to educate people about their significance. Tourists should not pass up an opportunity to visit the island and see these unique and beautiful horses. If they do, they will miss a chance to stand in the presence of "living legends" and to create memories that will last a lifetime.

Tips

* Plan your trip in advance, as many water taxis and ferries require reservations. Trips are usually full during summer. Note that most water taxis and ferries simply drop off visitors and return several hours later to pick them up, so it is imperative you be aware that amenities are not available on the island (except for a primitive bathroom near the ferry landing). It is wise to bring water, sunscreen, a camera, and perhaps a snack. If you visit in May or June, insects—particularly biting flies—can ruin your day. *Always* take insect repellent when visiting Shackleford Banks.

* To see the horses, you will likely have to walk toward the interior of the island. If you don't plan to do much walking or exploring, pack a beach umbrella, especially during summer.

* Shackleford Banks is also known for its wonderful shells, so bring a collecting bag!

The Walter L. Stasavich Science and Nature Center at River Park North

1000 Mumford Road
Greenville, N.C. 27858
Phone: 252-329-4560
Website: www.riverparknorth.org

Hours: Open year-round Tuesday through Saturday from 9:30 A.M. to 5 P.M. and Sunday from 1 P.M. to 5 P.M. Closed New Year's, Easter, and two days each for Thanksgiving and Christmas. The park follows the same schedule except that its hours change seasonally.

Directions: From U.S. 264 East at Greenville, take Stantonsburg Road. Travel approximately 2.5 miles and bear left on South Memorial Drive (U.S. 13). After 2 miles, turn right on Airport Road. After about 0.5 mile, the name changes to Mumford Road. Travel approximately 1 mile. The park is on the right.

The Turtle Touch Tank allows visitors to get an up-close look at turtle species native to North Carolina.

"Come see the 70-seat theater, 10,000 gallon freshwater aquarium, live turtles and snakes . . ."

Greenville Recreation and Parks Department brochure

In September 1983, a one-room, fifteen-hundred-square-foot nature center maintained by the Greenville Recreation and Parks Department opened in the city. It contained wildlife dioramas and a few live animals. In 1988, a modern, six-thousand-square-foot *science* and nature center emerged. In 1994, the new center was officially named in honor of Walter L. Stasavich, a former city superintendent of parks. According to Howard Vainright, parks coordinator of River Park North, "Walter was the driving force in turning an ugly trash dump into a beautiful 324-acre natural area called River Park North."

The newly expanded center offered a variety of wildlife dioramas that showcased animals from around the world, numerous live animal exhibits, and hands-on activities that encouraged children to explore science, health, nutrition, and safety. In 1999, however, tragedy struck the center when Hurricane Floyd brought extreme flooding to eastern North Carolina. Four feet of water filled the building and destroyed it. After all that had been accomplished, the center had to be rebuilt. Nearly six years later, the current center was completed. It opened on May 25, 2005.

When visitors arrive at the center today, the first thing they will likely notice is the compelling marker outside the entrance that documents the high-water mark from the disastrous September 1999 flood. Inside, they can browse the gift shop, attend a program (if one is scheduled) in the seventy-seat theater, visit a small display area that features several hands-on activities, and explore the exhibit hall; a small fee is charged to tour the hall.

In the exhibit hall, visitors will find various displays including wildlife dioramas that showcase mammals of North America and waterfowl of the Atlantic, a large case with unusual and colorful shells, and a computerized interactive frog identification

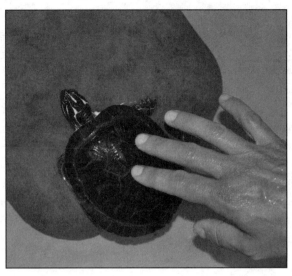

A visitor touches the shell of a yellowbelly slider.

game. Other displays feature live North Carolina wildlife.

One exhibit, Venomous Snakes of North Carolina, features an Eastern diamond-back rattlesnake, a timber rattlesnake, a copperhead, and an Eastern cottonmouth. Large educational text panels accompanying the displays provide intriguing information about each snake. One, for example, reveals that "the Copperhead is responsible for over 90 percent of our venomous snakebites."

Another exhibit, Reptiles of North Carolina, presents an Eastern kingsnake, a species "especially fond of eating other snakes including pit vipers (copperheads, cottonmouths, and rattlesnakes)," and a common snapping turtle, "North Carolina's largest freshwater turtle."

In the center of the hall, visitors can peer into a ten-thousand-gallon freshwater aquarium. This exhibit, Amazing Fish in Our Waters, introduces an assortment of North Carolina fish including common carp, bowfin, bluegill sunfish, channel catfish, yellow perch, chain pickerel, largemouth bass, black crappie, white crappie, and longnose gar. The text panels reveal the typical weight of each fish, as well as the state record. For example, an average largemouth bass weighs one to six pounds, while the state-record fish weighed fifteen pounds, fourteen ounces.

The last of the live wildlife exhibits, and a highlight of the self-guided exhibit-hall tour, is the Turtle Touch Tank. Although many aquariums and science and nature centers have marine touch tanks, this may be the only one in the state with turtles. Visitors have the opportunity to meet several species including Eastern painted turtles, yellowbelly sliders, common musk turtles, and Eastern mud turtles. The most intriguing is the common musk turtle, also known as the stinkpot and the Eastern musk turtle. Although it measures only from three to five and a half inches, this little turtle has the power to secrete a large musky odor. Fortunately, it releases the smell only when threatened. Because the public is permitted only to touch the turtles and not to lift them from the water or turn them upside down, it is unlikely anyone will ever partake of the stinkpot's fragrant odor. For those who participate in this activity, hand sanitizers and paper towels are readily available.

After touring the exhibit hall, visitors should head outside to explore River Park North, which offers an abundance of recreational options such as picnic facilities, pedal and fishing boats, three hiking trails, five ponds, two fishing piers, a volleyball court, and a fossil pit. Guests may want to bring fishing equipment, as the park participates in the North Carolina Wildlife Resources Commission's Community Fishing Program. Its largest pond is stocked with eight hundred channel catfish each month from April through September. For those who don't have fishing gear, rods and reels are available for loan, as the park also participates in the commission's Fishing Tackle Loaner Program.

River Park North is a remarkable place. An area that was once a trash dump now offers over 250 acres of bottom-land forest, over 20 acres of grassland, 50 acres of small lakes, and an impressive science and nature center.

Tips

• When visiting the nature center, be sure to allow time to explore River Park North, where numerous trails provide an opportunity to see North Carolina wildlife. If it's a warm day, watch where you step; during my visit, I had an encounter with a friendly, nonvenomous banded water-snake. For an added adventure, pick up a wildlife species checklist, available inside the center, before heading out on a trail. It is like a treasure hunt to see how many mammals, birds, reptiles, and amphibians you can spot in one day!

• If you plan to camp or use a pedal boat, call in advance, as reservations are required.

An alpaca at Livermon Park & Mini-Zoo

Livermon Park & Mini-Zoo

102 North York Street
Windsor, N.C. 27983
Phone: 252-794-4277
Website: www.windsorbertiechamber.com
E-mail: windsorbertiechamber@gmail.com

Hours: Open daily year-round. From March through October, the hours are 8 A.M. to 8 P.M. Monday through Friday and 9 A.M. to 8 P.M. Saturday and Sunday. From November through February, the hours are 9 A.M. to 5 P.M. daily.

Directions: From U.S. 17 North at Windsor in Bertie County, turn left on South King Street (N.C. 308). Travel about 0.5 mile and turn right on Dundee Street. Bear left on South York Street. The park entrance is on the left.

"Come enjoy a fun filled day at Livermon Park & Mini-Zoo!"
Livermon Park & Mini-Zoo brochure

Within walking distance of downtown Windsor, visitors will discover Livermon Park & Mini-Zoo. Calling this zoo "mini" seems inaccurate, as nearly thirty different

Guests can see native plants and wildlife along the Cashie Wetlands Walk.

species are featured at the twelve-acre attraction. Owned and operated by the town of Windsor, the facility opened in 1991. It was named in honor of L. T. Livermon, Jr., a former town mayor.

Across the street and located on the park grounds is the Windsor/Bertie County Chamber of Commerce. There, tourists can pick up travel material, acquire information about the park and mini-zoo, and browse the gift shop. Although drinks and snacks are not available in the park, snow cones are sometimes for sale on the chamber's front porch in summer. A concession stand will eventually be built in the park.

No fee is charged to enter Livermon Park & Mini-Zoo. Visitors may be so surprised at this that they spend their first few minutes around the entrance gate trying to locate someone to pay. Upon entering, they will see a large playground, restrooms, and picnic tables. One item in the playground, an authentic red fire truck, has a magnet-like effect on children.

Next to the playground is the mini-zoo. A large barn-like building holds several species of birds including turkeys, pheasants, chickens, peacocks, pigeons, doves, guineafowl, and lovebirds. One of the most interesting is the royal palm turkey, which exhibits a striking black-and-white color pattern. A small breed of turkey, it is mainly an exhibition bird. Royal palm turkeys are currently on the watch list of the American Livestock Breeds Conservancy, the only organization in the United States that works to conserve rare breeds and genetic diversity in livestock.

Beyond the bird display, several freestanding animal shelters with perimeter fencing house animals such as donkeys, miniature horses, llamas, sheep, goats, and geese. Between the fences and along the pathways are numerous chickens. Past the goats and toward a large open area, guests will encounter a family of bison. The bison, like other animals at the mini-zoo, will approach the fence. Visitors should be aware, however, that animals here may not be fed or petted.

Across the street and beside the chamber of commerce building, more animals await discovery. Visitors will encounter emus, ostriches, and alpacas. A few steps down from the alpacas is the entrance to the Cashie Wetlands Walk. A free reference map and informational brochure is available at the chamber of commerce. The walk, which follows an elevated boardwalk, lets visitors experience the natural beauty of a wetland up close. Trees and plants bear identification, and educational text panels discuss why wetlands are important to the environment. Visitors who wish to explore the area by canoe should check in at the rental booth at the park entrance or inquire at the chamber; canoe rentals are also free. Those who try a canoe have a good chance of seeing a variety of native wildlife including cavity-nesting birds, white-tailed deer, and a number of small mammals.

Livermon Park & Mini-Zoo offers an array of recreational activities that will suit the interests of any age group. This clean, easily accessible park is a relaxing place to observe animals, enjoy a picnic, and embark on an educational journey through a wetland. And as the chamber of commerce's website notes, "The best part? It's all free!"

Tips

- If you visit during summer, bring water, as refreshments are not always available on-site.

- Make sure you pick up a reference map and informational brochure for the Cashie Wetlands Walk before heading out, as it includes interesting facts that will make your walk or canoe trip more enjoyable.

- After exploring the park and mini-zoo, make time to visit the Roanoke/ Cashie River Center. Located approximately a mile away, this Partnership for the Sounds educational center interprets the Roanoke River system. It has exhibits and a gift shop inside and a boardwalk outside. A highlight of the center is a free boat ride on the Cashie River every Saturday morning; preregistration is required. The center is located at 112 West Water Street in Windsor. To learn more, call 252-794-2001 or visit www.partnershipforthesounds.org.

Visitors can see fish species native to eastern North Carolina in the hatchery's aquarium.
PHOTOGRAPH COURTESY OF
U.S. FISH & WILDLIFE SERVICE

Edenton National Fish Hatchery

1102 West Queen Street
Edenton, N.C. 27932
Phone: 252-482-4118
Website: www.fws.gov/edenton
E-mail: stephen_jackson@fws.gov

Hours: Open daily from 7 A.M. to 3:30 P.M., including most holidays.
Closed on weekends and holidays from December 20 through March.

Directions: From U.S. 17 North near Edenton in Chowan County, take
Exit 224 (the Edenton/Fairgrounds exit). In less than 0.5 mile, turn right
on West Queen Street (U.S. 17 Business) and drive about 2 miles. The
hatchery is on the left.

> "... plan a trip to learn more about our programs ..."
> **Edenton National Fish Hatchery website**

Established in 1898, Edenton National Fish Hatchery produces fish for public
use and restoration programs. Operated by the U.S. Fish & Wildlife Service, it is the
only federal hatchery in North Carolina; two others did exist but were closed due to

budget cuts. According to the hatchery's informational brochure, "Fish raised on Federal hatcheries are stocked in public waters to support Federal fishery responsibilities mandated by law. Those include fish for restoration where, for example, man-made dams have altered a stream's natural reproductive capability; to recover threatened or endangered populations; to restore interjurisdictional fish populations; or to support depleted recreational fish populations in Federal and state waters."

Edenton National Fish Hatchery is a warm-water hatchery, meaning it is intended for fish that do best in water temperatures above sixty-five degrees. It mainly raises Atlantic striped bass and American shad. However, according to Stephen Jackson, supervisory fishery biologist, it occasionally raises other species such as largemouth bass to assist the state in recovering impacted populations. Generally speaking, state hatcheries focus on recreational fish like largemouth bass, catfish, and trout, while federal hatcheries concentrate on interjurisdictional and imperiled species like salmon, Atlantic striped bass, and sturgeon.

Just as at state-operated hatcheries, fry (newly hatched fish) can be seen at federal hatcheries only during certain months. At Edenton National Fish Hatchery, American shad can be seen in April and Atlantic striped bass during June. Because the work inside the holding and hatching building can be sensitive in nature, it may not always be open to the public. Visitors who wish to tour the building, especially during April or June, should schedule a reservation.

Those who arrive outside April and June will still find a visit to the hatchery a pleasurable experience. The main entrance features a seven-hundred-gallon aquarium and three smaller tanks. The aquarium highlights aquatic species typical of eastern North Carolina; it most recently showcased blenny, gambusia, banded killifish, redfin pickerel, Atlantic striped bass, white bass, largemouth bass, blue catfish, white catfish, channel catfish, yellow bullhead, white perch, yellow perch, bluegill sunfish, redbreast sunfish, bluespotted sunfish, pumpkinseed, black crappie, American shad, gizzard shad, Atlantic croaker, spot, red drum, sheepshead, tautog, summer flounder, longnose gar, American eel, and an American alligator.

The entrance to Edenton National Fish Hatchery & Aquarium

Behind the aquarium building are a number of rearing ponds. Guests are welcome to walk around the ponds; between harvests and during winter, however, the ponds are dry. In summer, most of the ponds are filled with water and contain fish. As with most hatchery ponds, guests will probably not see the fish unless they are being fed or are swimming near the surface. Behind the ponds, visitors can explore a nature trail that leads along a raised boardwalk through a natural wetland to Pembroke Creek; the hatchery is a stop on the Charles Kuralt Nature Trail and the North Carolina Birding Trail.

Tourists who decide to make Edenton National Fish Hatchery one of their Chowan County destinations will gain an appreciation for the serious conservation work done here. For example, it is successfully restoring interjurisdictional Atlantic striped bass and interjurisdictional American shad, the goal being "to stock three million fry per year into the Roanoke River," according to hatchery's brochure. When disasters occur, either man-made or natural, the hatchery stands ready to restore fish to devastated waters by providing "fishery management assistance to National Wildlife Refuges in the Carolinas and Virginia."

Hatcheries offer so much more than meets the eye. Visitors will be surprised to learn the role they play in conserving, protecting, and enhancing our nation's aquatic resources.

Tips

- To guarantee seeing hatchery operations and newly hatched fish, schedule a reservation or call the hatchery manager to determine the best time to visit.

- At the aquarium, you can pick up the free brochure *U.S. Fish & Wildlife Service, North Carolina National Wildlife Refuges and National Fish Hatcheries*, which contains a listing of locations to observe native wildlife in natural habitats. Should the aquarium be closed, brochures are available outside in the information kiosk.

- Make sure your plans include exploring Edenton's charming waterfront historic district. You'll find historic sites, shops, restaurants, and various recreational and cultural activities in North Carolina's first colonial capital. If you need a light meal or refreshments, stop in at The Soda Shoppe at 301 South Broad Street. It offers a great variety of sandwiches and the best milkshakes in town.

Red Wolf Howling Safaris

Red Wolf Coalition
P.O. Box 96
Columbia, N.C. 27925
Phone: 252-796-5600
Website: www.redwolves.com
E-mail: redwolf@redwolves.com

Hours: Howling Safaris are offered for a fee on Wednesday evenings throughout the summer, typically at 7:30 P.M. Howl-O-Days are free howlings offered in the fall and winter; check the website for dates and times. Groups must register in advance, and individuals are encouraged to do so as well. Registration can be completed online or over the phone.

The howls of red wolves can be heard in northeastern North Carolina.
PHOTOGRAPH COURTESY OF KIM WHEELER

Directions: The Red Wolf Coalition's office is *not* the location for Howling Safaris and Howl-O-Days; the above address is for contact purposes only. Events take place at Alligator River National Wildlife Refuge, located at East Lake in Dare County approximately fifteen minutes from Manteo. Participants meet at the Creef Cut Wildlife Trail. To get there, follow U.S. 64 West from Manteo and turn left on Milltail Road. Parking is on the right.

> "Learn about endangered red wolves, found only in the wilds
> of northeastern North Carolina, and get the chance of a lifetime
> to hear their harmonious howls."
> **Red Wolf Coalition website**

Northeastern North Carolina is home to a rare but recovering population of red wolves. By 1980, red wolves—once top predators in the southeastern United

The red wolf is one of the most endangered animals in the world.
PHOTOGRAPH COURTESY OF
KIM WHEELER

States—had been officially declared extinct in the wild. Only a few remained in captivity. From that captive population of seventeen red wolves, fourteen were selected for a breeding program. In 1987, four captive-bred red wolves were released into Alligator River National Wildlife Refuge, and the Red Wolf Recovery Program began. Today, over one hundred red wolves survive in northeastern North Carolina. Indeed, the region is "the only wild red wolf mainland population site in the world," according to *Endangered Red Wolves*, an informational brochure from the U.S. Fish & Wildlife Service.

Because of the red wolf's status in the wild, it is easy to understand why tourists are eager to participate in Howling Safaris. Thousands of visitors attend the events, presented each year by the Red Wolf Coalition in cooperation with the U.S. Fish & Wildlife Service. In fact, there is so much interest that reservations are essential. Guests can see the schedule for Howling Safaris on the Red Wolf Coalition's website and make reservations online or over the phone.

Those attending a Howling Safari are instructed to meet at the Creef Cut Wildlife Trail in Alligator River National Wildlife Refuge, located at East Lake. The refuge is a 154,000-acre wetland habitat that is home to a variety of species including red wolves, American alligators, and red-cockaded woodpeckers.

When the Howling Safari begins, visitors will be greeted by a Red Wolf Coalition staff member—likely Kim Wheeler, executive director—and given a short presentation about red wolves and the Red Wolf Recovery Program. They will learn why red wolves became extinct in the wild, how they were reintroduced into the refuge, how captive-breeding programs are helping to ensure red wolves' survival, and what obstacles hinder their continued existence.

At the conclusion of the presentation, participants head out to the "howling site" to wait anxiously for a sound they likely have never heard before—at least not in the wild. As Wheeler puts it, "I hear them [red wolf howls] a lot, and I still am amazed." Wheeler or another Red Wolf Coalition staff member will howl in an attempt to entice a response. Although there are no guarantees, Wheeler said they are generally successful. Once the howling starts, guests join in the fun and see if any red wolves will answer.

Some visitors may be disappointed that they will not *see* a red wolf during a Howling Safari. Red wolves are wary animals and do not typically come near people. The goal of a Howling Safari is to get the red wolves to howl, not to get visitors close to them. The program is an opportunity for the public to learn about these extremely rare mammals. Hearing melodious howls coming from unknown locations within a dark forest offers an intriguing and mysterious appeal that sparks the imagination.

Eventually, the Red Wolf Coalition and the U.S. Fish & Wildlife Service plan to open a red wolf education center inside Pocosin Lakes National Wildlife Refuge, located just south of the town of Columbia. The center will feature a health-care facility, indoor exhibits, outdoor informational kiosks, and an enclosure for red wolves. "Two significant benefits are expected from the construction of this enclosure," according to the coalition's website. "The first will be increased public commitment to the long-term survival of wild red wolves and to the importance of becoming stewards of our national wildlife refuge. The second will be the value to the local community of making the region's visitors more aware of the beauty and allure of red wolf country."

"There is always hope for an endangered species," Kim Wheeler says. "The red wolf program has succeeded because there were and are people that care about the survival of the red wolf." When visiting Dare County, tourists should consider attending a Howling Safari to help ensure the future of a rare and remarkable animal.

Tips

• Allow time to explore Alligator River National Wildlife Refuge before embarking on your Howling Safari, as a plethora of wildlife is waiting to be seen. According to the U.S. Fish & Wildlife Service's website, the refuge is "likely one of the few spots on the east coast where you can predictably see a black bear in the wild." Speaking of bears, the refuge offers its "Bear Necessities at Alligator River" program on Wednesdays during summer. Visitors listen to a presentation about bears and take a tram ride to look for them. The trip returns in time for the Howling Safari. If you hike on the Sandy Ridge Wildlife Trail or take a guided canoe trip, you may see bears, alligators, or other interesting wildlife and are guaranteed to have a memorable experience.

● If you visit in summer, remember that you are in a wetland habitat. Take precautions against bugs and poisonous snakes by wearing repellent and appropriate shoes. Howling Safaris last approximately two hours, so being prepared for these conditions could make your trip more enjoyable.

● If you have time, visit the nearby North Carolina Aquarium on Roanoke Island (see pages 244–47), where marine life and other interesting creatures await.

● Although you will not see red wolves during your Howling Safari, you can view them in captivity at the North Carolina Zoo in Asheboro (see pages 126–31), the Western North Carolina Nature Center in Asheville (see pages 25–29), the Museum of Life and Science in Durham (see pages 149–54), and Dan Nicholas Park in Salisbury (see pages 97–100).

North Carolina Aquarium on Roanoke Island

374 Airport Road
Manteo, N.C. 27954
Phone: 800-832-3474, ext. 4, or 252-473-3494
Website: www.ncaquariums.com
E-mail: rimail@ncaquariums.com

Hours: Open daily year-round from 9 A.M. to 5 P.M. Closed Thanksgiving, Christmas, and New Year's.

Directions: From U.S. 64 East heading toward Manteo across the Manns Harbor bridge, turn right on Airport Road and drive 1.5 miles. The aquarium is on the right.

A sand tiger shark in the Graveyard of the Atlantic exhibit
PHOTOGRAPH BY RAY MATTHEWS, NAGS HEAD
COURTESY OF NC AQUARIUM ON ROANOKE ISLAND

". . . touch a bamboo shark in the Close Encounters exhibit."
North Carolina Aquariums website

The theme of the North Carolina Aquarium on Roanoke Island is "Waters of the Outer Banks." Visitors can explore the region's coastal and inland waters and view over two thousand animals.

They will first examine the Coastal Freshwater Gallery, where they can study fish that inhabit creeks and rivers, as well as other animals such as frogs and venomous snakes. Next is the Wetlands on the Edge Gallery, which showcases American alligators, river otters, various species of turtles, and fish found in brackish water. Several times a week, visitors can attend a "Wetland Feedings" presentation and watch aquarium staff feed American alligators.

In the summer of 2010, a new exhibit called Sharks! opened at the aquarium. It features several interactive displays, a ten-thousand-gallon aquarium with small species of sharks, and graphic panels that educate visitors about these oft-misunderstood creatures. A simulated shark cage backed by a wall painted with swimming sharks makes the perfect setting for a photograph. As visitors continue through the aquarium, they will soon discover other shark-related exhibits.

In the Marine Communities Gallery are fish that make their home in grass flats, like summer flounder and spottail pinfish, and ones that reside among offshore wrecks, like balloonfish, striped burrfish, squirrelfish, and Caribbean spiny lobsters.

A Close Encounters Touch Tank allows visitors to get hands-on with stingrays and horseshoe crabs.
Ray Matthews Photography, Nags Head
courtesy of NC Aquarium on Roanoke Island

Visitors enjoy viewing the fish along the corridor of this gallery, as they are quite unique and colorful.

As at the other North Carolina Aquariums, the popular touch tanks feature stingrays, horseshoe crabs, hermit crabs, etc. However, one of the tanks here contains a species not present at the other two aquariums. Guests are sure to notice the bamboo sharks swimming about and will be excited to have a chance to touch this small species of shark.

Arriving in the Open Oceans Gallery, visitors have a chance to view *larger* sharks in the waters of the Graveyard of the Atlantic exhibit. This 285,000-gallon aquarium tank features a replica of the USS *Monitor*—the famed Civil War ironclad—and a number of sharks including sand tiger, sandbar, and nurse sharks. Among the numerous species of fish that constantly pass in front of visitors in the exhibit are red drum, Atlantic tripletail, hogfish, sheepshead, queen triggerfish, blue runner, permit, red grouper, and many more. The "Dialog with a Diver" program, presented twice daily, allows visitors to ask questions about the wreck and the animals swimming around it.

Once they have examined the galleries, visitors may browse the gift shop or grab a bite to eat at Good Life Gourmet Express. Afterward, they can dig for fossils underneath a massive sculpture of a megalodon shark tooth. Children race out of the area with treasures that predate dinosaurs. Their excitement, says public-relations coordinator Bruce Nunemaker, "is electric!"

Nunemaker says visitors will encounter something new on each visit to the North Carolina Aquarium on Roanoke Island. The Sharks! exhibit, he says, will continue to grow as new sharks and other animals are added. The website of the North Carolina Aquariums states that the Roanoke Island facility is a place of "unforgettable events." Take their word for it. When in Dare County, be sure to visit the North Carolina Aquarium on Roanoke Island.

Tips

- Don't forget to look at the daily and monthly event calendars, as you don't want to miss any of the aquarium's offerings.

- After visiting the aquarium, drive a couple miles down the road to Island Farm, a living-history site that interprets life on Roanoke Island during the mid-1800s. At the farmstead, you'll see and learn about several types of farm animals including sheep, chickens, a horse, and a cow. It is located on U.S. 64 north of Manteo. To learn more, visit www.theislandfarm.com.

Wild Horses of Corolla

Corolla Wild Horse Fund
1126 Old Schoolhouse Lane
Corolla, N.C. 27927
Phone: 252-453-8002
Website: www.corollawildhorses.org
E-mail: info@corollawildhorses.com

Hours: Not applicable

Directions: From N.C. 12 North at Corolla at the far northern end of the Outer Banks, bear right on North Beach Access Road. Note that these directions do not lead to the office of, or the museum operated by, the Corolla Wild Horse Fund. They lead to the location where those with four-wheel-drive vehicles can access the beach and search for horses on their own.

Visitors have the opportunity to pet and ride rescued horses on special-event days.
PHOTOGRAPH COURTESY OF
COROLLA WILD HORSE FUND

~~~~~~~~~~~~~~~~~~~~~~~~~~~

**"Nowhere else can you see wild Mustangs walking along
the beach and grazing among beach homes."**
Corolla Wild Horse Fund website

A long and narrow road leads to Corolla. Driving up the beach, visitors might wonder, much like children, if they will ever arrive. Those who make the trip to see the wild horses but who have vehicles without four-wheel drive will likely be disappointed when they arrive. If they have not made reservations for a wild horse tour, they will probably be disheartened. Many people think they can simply drive to Corolla, walk out on the beach, and see wild horses, but that is simply not the case.

Because wild horses were being killed and injured by cars on N.C. 12, "the Corolla Wild Horse Fund worked with Currituck County, U.S. Fish & Wildlife, and the N.C. Estuarine Research Reserve to have 7,544 acres of the northern-most beaches defined as a horse sanctuary," according to the horse fund's website. "By 1996, the remaining horses were relocated behind two sound-to-sea fences." The location can be accessed only by four-wheel-drive vehicles.

Just as with the wild horses of Shackleford Banks, no one is certain of the Corolla horses' origins. However, it is believed Spanish settlers established the original herd in the 1500s. In February 2007, the "Horse of the Americas Registry as well as the American Indian Horse Registry inspected the herd . . . and found them to be Colonial Spanish Mustangs, eligible for registration," as stated in *The Wild Horses of the Currituck Outer Banks*, an informational brochure by the Corolla Wild Horse Fund. "Skeletal evidence as well as DNA studies have strengthened these findings." Accordingly, the "Colonial Spanish Mustang is on the Critical Breed list of the American Livestock Conservancy and on the Critical list of the Equus Survival Trust." Because of the Spanish mustang's rare and historic stature, the general assembly adopted it as the official horse of the state of North Carolina in June 2010.

Eighty-six horses are presently in the Corolla herd. According to Karen McCalpin, executive director of the Corolla Wild Horse Fund, staff members count the horses from a helicopter once a year and track them daily. Besides the eighty-six horses, there are ten foals; foals are not counted until they have lived at least six months. The horse fund is currently working, through legislation, to have the minimum herd size increased. Doing so would maintain the herd's genetic health. McCalpin is a recognized expert on her subject. She recently published a book on the Corolla and Shackleford Banks herds entitled, *Saving the Horses of Kings*. The book tells the history of these amazing horses and their struggle for survival and also addresses the issues they face today and the role humans can take in protecting and preserving them.

A wild horse near the surf

Tourists who wish to see the wild horses and learn their fascinating history may schedule a "Trip of a Lifetime" tour—a "*National Geographic*–like experience," in the words of McCalpin. This tour is the only one offered by the horse fund. It is available with the purchase of a Mustang Defender ($250) or Charter ($500) membership. A membership at one of these levels affords visitors—and a certain number of guests—a rare chance to accompany the herd manager, who is solely responsible for the health, safety, and well-being of the herd. Participants can assist with daily documentation or sit back and enjoy this one-of-a-kind educational experience. The tour generally lasts four hours. The proceeds support the horse fund's mission of protection and preservation.

Those who do not have sufficient time or who would rather have a more general tour can schedule one with a commercial tour company. Guests have at least seven to choose from; all charge a fee.

The horse fund operates the Corolla Wild Horse Museum, located in the Old Corolla Schoolhouse in historic Corolla village. Here, visitors can view interactive displays, learn about the horses as well as local history, enjoy hands-on activities, and visit the gift shop. Although the museum sells water, restrooms and other amenities are not available.

The museum presents special programs throughout the year, some of which allow visitors to meet a colonial Spanish mustang face to face. From May to September, the museum typically has a horse that can be petted on-site one day a week. It plans to add horse rides one day a week as well. One of its big events is "Wild Horse Days," held during three days in July. Visitors can pet or ride a mustang, view wild horse training demonstrations, see a dressage demonstration, listen to music, eat food, and participate in various other entertainments. The horses used during these programs are rescues and have been socialized to humans. The horse fund's purposes in its events are to educate people about the horses, to raise funds for their care, and to engage the public in becoming an active part of the efforts to save them. "These horses," says McCalpin, "are direct descendants of the best horses that the royal Spanish breeding farms had to offer and have survived nearly five centuries of hurricanes and nor'easters."

People can read about and view photographs of wild horses, but that does not compare to seeing them in their natural element. To truly appreciate these animals, they must come to Currituck County and observe them. Seeing the horses come over the top of a sand dune and stand with their long manes blowing in the breeze is an unforgettable scene. It is at such moments that visitors will comprehend the historic and cultural importance of these horses and understand why they must forever remain wild and free.

Tips

● You will not see wild horses simply by driving to Corolla. The best ways are by scheduling a "Trip of a Lifetime" with the Corolla Wild Horse Fund or a commercial tour. If you want to use a commercial tour company, visit the Currituck County Department of Travel and Tourism's website (www.visitcurrituck.com) for a list. If you have a four-wheel-drive vehicle, you can access the beach and try to locate the horses yourself. However, your best chance lies in scheduling a tour. In doing so, you will not only see the horses but also learn fascinating facts about them. No matter what your choice, be sure to follow the wild-horse ordinances; feeding a horse or getting closer than fifty feet is an arrestable offense.

● While in the area, visit the Outer Banks Center for Wildlife Education, operated by the North Carolina Wildlife Resources Commission. Here, you can explore exhibits of native fish and decoys, watch a documentary film, take part in nature programs, and browse the NC Wild Store. The center is located at 1160 Village Lane in Corolla. To learn more, call 252-453-0221 or visit www.ncwildlife.org.

Acknowledgments

One of my greatest experiences in creating this travel guide was meeting people whose professions put them in contact with animals on a daily basis. From animal curators to farmers and everyone in between, they provided insightful knowledge regarding their facilities. For that, I am extremely grateful. I appreciate each facility for allowing me to use facts from their websites, brochures, etc., that may prove of importance to readers. Because this guide could not have been completed without their assistance, I would like to extend a special thank-you to the following people.

In the mountains: Rob Scheiwiller of Hawkesdene House; Alex and Nicole Denison of Otter Creek Trout Farm; Julie L. Clark of Santa's Land Fun Park & Zoo; Lucy Lowe of English Mountain Llama Treks; Mark English of Llamacaddy; Emilie R. Johnson of Pisgah Center for Wildlife Education; Janene Donovan of Carl Sandburg Home National Historic Site; Sarah Oram and the staff of Western North Carolina Nature Center; Linda Seligman and David Holt of Round Mountain Creamery; Nancy Brown and Sarah Hallback of Full Moon Farm Wolfdog Rescue & Sanctuary; Elizabeth "Liz" Mahaffey of The Wolf Sanctum; James Fisher of the James Fisher Gallery; Catherine Morton of Grandfather Mountain; Teresa Zinck of Avery County Chamber of Commerce; Leslie Hayhurst and James True of Genesis Wildlife Sanctuary; and Cathy Robbins of Tweetsie Railroad.

In the Piedmont: Johnny White, Kristi Coggins, and Chris Cook of Harvest-Works Inc.; Mary Katherine Creel of Catawba Science Center; Calvin and Judy Sell of Baa Moo Farm; Scottie Brown, Shellem Cline, and Mattie Jeffery of Zootastic Park; Mike Todd and Pat Roberts of BirdBrain Ostrich Ranch; Sarah Beth Rogers of Lazy 5 Ranch; Amber Rosintoski, Natalie Childers, and Daniel Bumgarner of Carolina Raptor Center; Logan Stewart of Discovery Place; Natividad Lewis and Lisa Hoffman of Charlotte Nature Museum; Joanie Benson of Horse Protection Society of North Carolina; Bob Pendergrass of Dan Nicholas Park; Lea Jaunakais and Mike McBride of Tiger World; Karen Miller of Southeast Old Threshers' Reunion; Mark and Sharon Berry of Bloomtown Acres; Michael and Patricia West of Divine Llama Vineyards; Debbie Cesta of SciWorks; Nora Cammer of all-a-flutter Butterfly Farm; Roxanna Burkhart of Natural Science Center of Greensboro; Teresa Johnson and Ann Poole of Caraway Alpacas; Rod Haring of the North Carolina Zoo; Ann Terry of Sunny Slopes Farm; Doug Evans and Julia Matson of Conservators' Center; Joe Thompson of Thompson's Prawn Farm; Dennis DeLong of the Department of Biological and Agricultural Engineering at North Carolina State University; Allison Nichols, Susan Nichols, and Paul Sexton of Maple View Agricultural Center; Keith Morris and David Haring of Duke Lemur Center; Taneka Bennett of the Museum of Life and Science; Jonathan Pishney of the North Carolina Museum of Natural Sciences; Bill and Pam Banks of Banks Miniature Horse Farm; Loretta Byrd of the Benson Area Chamber of Commerce; Deborah Davis, for the Benson Mule Days™ photographs; Dora Turner and Carie Page of Noah's Landing; Bo McLamb of Duffie's Exotic Bird Ranch; James Bass of Jambbas Ranch; Tag Leon of Talamore Golf Resort; S. Lee Crutchfield of Aloha Safari Zoo; Jaime Osborne of San-Lee Park Nature Center; Scott Miller of Carolina Tiger Rescue; Brit Pfann of Celebrity Dairy; Sherry and Bill Boncek of Wildwood Learning Farm; Brent Lubbock and Katie Gipple of Sylvan Heights Waterfowl Park; and Tony Teague, who facilitated the tours at Carolina Tiger Rescue and Conservators' Center. Thank you also, Tony, for the little extras that made both days special.

At the coast: Pat and Herlar Faircloth of Little Man's Zoo; Barry Midgette and Jeff Evans of Watha State Fish Hatchery; Scott McKenzie of Cape Fear Serpentarium; Amy Kilgore of the North Carolina Aquarium at Fort Fisher; Jean Beasley and Lisa Brossia of The Karen Beasley Sea Turtle Rescue and Rehabilitation Center; Gary Evans of Lynnwood Park Zoo; Bill Ellis of Exchange Nature Center at Neuseway Nature Park; Trish Slape and Herta Henderson of Outer Banks Wildlife Shelter; Julie Powers of the North Carolina Aquarium at Pine Knoll Shores; Craig Davies, for the sand tiger shark photograph; Carolyn Mason of Foundation for Shackleford Horses, Inc.; Howard Vainright of The Walter L. Stasavich Science and Nature Center at River Park North; Stacie Dunlow of Windsor/Bertie County Chamber of Commerce; Stephen Jackson of Edenton National Fish Hatchery; Kim Wheeler of Red Wolf Coalition; Buster Nunemaker of the North Carolina Aquarium on Roanoke Island; and Karen McCalpin of Corolla Wild Horse Fund.

Special thanks also go to the talented staff of John F. Blair, Publisher, particularly Carolyn Sakowski, Steve Kirk, and Debbie Hampton. Thank you for your invaluable assistance.

Finally, to my husband, Larry: I do not have the words to express my gratitude for your support of this project. You have been my travel companion, photographer, proofreader, sounding board, and more than anyone could ask for. Thank you for everything.

Appendix
Creating Your Own
Animal Adventure

In addition to the locations listed in this guide, other places in North Carolina provide opportunities to observe and learn about animals. Below are some ideas that may help you create an animal adventure all your own.

Before heading out in any direction, check out www.visitnc.com, the website of the North Carolina Department of Commerce, Division of Tourism, Film and Sports Development. Here, you can search events; order free brochures, maps, and travel guides; check ferry schedules; find places to stay; and get up-to-date information on attractions.

Agritourism farms provide opportunities to interact with and learn about barnyard animals. Particularly during the fall, many farms—some not generally open to the public—welcome visitors to partake of hayrides, petting zoos, pumpkin patches, and other attractions. To learn more, check out www.VisitNCFarms.com, the website of the North Carolina Department of Agriculture and Consumer Services.

The Got to Be NC Festival, held at the state fairgrounds in Raleigh during three days in May, celebrates the state's agriculture, music, and food. Spectators can view horsepower demonstrations, enjoy petting zoos, and more. For more information, visit www.ncagfest.com.

Many working farms are open to the public only during specialized educational tours that support the efforts of the Carolina Farm Stewardship Association. For the price of a ticket, you can visit numerous farms to learn about sustainable agriculture and enjoy the fruits of each farmer's labor. To learn more, visit www.carolinafarmstewards.org.

If you would like to spend a night on a working farm, visit www.farmstayus.com. Whether you prefer to collect eggs, assist with farm chores, milk goats, pick berries, gather produce, make cheese, or simply relax and view the scenery, this website will lead you to the perfect accommodation.

Alpaca lovers will be interested to learn about National Alpaca Farms Day, when farms not typically open to the public welcome visitors. During the event, sponsored by the Alpaca Owners and Breeders Association, you can learn about these unique animals and meet the people who raise them. To see a list of participating farms and the date of the next event, visit www.nationalalpacafarmdays.com.

Nature centers can be found in most North Carolina counties. Some display numerous animals, others a few, and some none at all. However, all of them offer nature programs or outings during which visitors can explore the outdoor world and native species. To find a nature center near you or at a location you will be visiting, check out http://en.wikipedia.org/wiki/List_of_nature_centers_in_the_United_States.

When native animals are found with injuries or illnesses, they are taken to a wildlife rescue or rehabilitation center. If you would like to volunteer at one of these centers and assist in the critical work, the website www.ncwildliferehab.org can help you locate a nearby center and find out what its needs are.

North Carolina's state parks provide hiking trails, ranger programs, and wildlife viewing opportunities. For example, the largest concentration of bald eagles in the eastern United States may be found at Jordan Lake State Recreation Area in Apex. To locate the parks and view their event calendars, visit www.ncparks.gov.

North Carolina has ten national wildlife refuges. The refuges provide an incredible opportunity to observe wildlife in natural environments. Acres upon acres are available for hiking, paddling, and driving. These are some of the best wildlife viewing locations in the state. To learn more, visit the website of the U.S. Fish & Wildlife Service at www.fws.gov.

The Nature Conservancy manages sixty-four preserves in North Carolina and protects nearly seven hundred thousand acres of the state's land. Its preserves, or projects, provide a chance to explore some of the best natural areas in the state. To locate a site, visit the Nature Conservancy's website at www.nature.org. Click on "Where We Work," then choose "North Carolina" from the drop-down box; once on the North Carolina home page, click "Places We Protect." You might also purchase *North Carolina Afield: A Guide to Nature Conservancy Projects in North Carolina*. Written by Ida Phillips, Maria Sadowski, and Maura High, the book gives a history and description of each preserve and information on how to get there.

If you are interested in birds and bird watching, visit www.ncbirdingtrail.org, the website of the North Carolina Birding Trail, which will help you locate trails based on the types of birds you hope to see.

If you would like to experience wildlife at home, visit the National Wildlife Federation's website at www.nwf.org. Here, you can learn how to create a certified wildlife habitat in your own backyard. Whether you have a deck or a hundred acres, the federation can show you how to attract wildlife and help restore natural habitats in the areas closest to you.

Index

mL

4/1